THE OTHER CANDIDATES

THE OTHER CANDIDATES

Third Parties in Presidential Elections

FRANK SMALLWOOD

Published for Dartmouth College
by University Press of New England
Hanover and London, 1983

University Press of New England
Brandeis University
Brown University
Clark University
Dartmouth College
University of New Hampshire
University of Rhode Island
Tufts University
University of Vermont

Copyright © 1983 by Trustees of Dartmouth College

Printed in the United States of America

LIBRARY OF CONGRESS CATALOGING IN PUBLICATION DATA

Smallwood, Frank.
  The other candidates.

  Bibliography: p.
  Includes index.
    1. Presidents—United States—Election—1980.
  2. Third parties (United States politics)   I. Title.
JK526 1980D   324.973'0926   82-40478
ISBN 0-87451-256-5
ISBN 0-87451-257-3 (pbk.)

To

Virginia Close and Robert Jaccaud,

Reference Librarians,

Dartmouth College,

for their help on many research projects

CONTENTS

PREFACE

The popular myth that anyone can grow up to become president of the United States is such a basic part of the American dream that it seems simple. Yet the realities of practical politics dictate otherwise. Over the course of almost two centuries there have been many presidential aspirants, but very few were chosen to serve in the White House. The odds against one of the two major-party challengers being elected are fifty-fifty under the best of conditions. The odds against independent and third-party candidates are astronomically higher.

The magnitude of the obstacles facing this latter group of candidates came into focus for me in June of 1980 when I was unexpectedly asked to run as John Anderson's stand-in vice-presidential nominee during his Vermont write-in petition drive. Under the United States Constitution, "Each State shall appoint [presidential electors] . . . in such Manner as the Legislature thereof may direct,"[1] which means that each state has the authority to adopt quite different laws to regulate who appears on the ballot. Large states like California require over 100,000 petition signatures to qualify for a ballot position, while small states like Vermont require only 1,000 signatures. Yet there can be additional wrinkles in many state laws, as there are in Vermont, which does not permit candidates to petition to run for president unless they have designated a vice-presidential nominee. As of June 1980, Anderson had not yet announced his vice-presidential running mate. Since I was a relatively visible local supporter, I agreed to fill in as Anderson's temporary vice-presidential candidate in Vermont during the petition drive until he named former Wisconsin governor Patrick Lucey as his official national nominee.

Although all the Anderson campaigners in Vermont realized that his candidacy was a very, very long shot, we spent a mas-

sive amount of time soliciting funds, giving speeches, appearing on local radio talk shows, distributing literature, and
performing the host of other chores that are involved in any
grass-roots political effort. In November 1980, Anderson received 14 percent of the total Vermont popular vote for president, a respectable showing, but hardly enough to gain him
any electoral college votes.

When I reflect on the Anderson campaign, I cannot help
wondering why anyone becomes involved in third-party politics. Over the course of American history, third-party candidates have appeared under a wide variety of labels—the
Anti-Masons, Free-Soilers, Know-Nothings, Greenbacks, Prohibitionists, Populists, Socialists, Communists, Socialist Workers, States' Righters, and Libertarians, to name but a few. Yet,
despite this almost continuous outpouring of third-party aspirants, the Republicans were the last successful group to challenge the two dominant parties, a feat they accomplished with
Abraham Lincoln's victory in 1860. Since that time, over 200
third-party and independent candidates have tried to duplicate
this achievement, yet only 8 have managed to capture more
than one million popular votes:[2]

1892	James B. Weaver, Populist	1,041,028
1912	Theodore Roosevelt, Bull Moose	4,119,538
1924	Robert LaFollette, Progressive	4,822,856
1948	J. Strom Thurmond, Dixiecrat	1,176,125
	Henry A. Wallace, Progressive	1,157,326
1968	George C. Wallace, American Independent	9,906,473
1972	John G. Schmitz, American	1,099,482
1980	John B. Anderson, Independent	5,720,060

Despite these results, many third-party candidates have
demonstrated dogged persistence in their pursuit of the White
House. Socialist Norman Thomas ran for the presidency six
times between 1928 and 1948, while another Socialist, Eugene
Debs, ran five times between 1900 and 1920. Both Socialist Labor Party candidate Eric Hass and Socialist Workers Party can-

didate Farrell Dobbs ran four times, while communist candidates William Z. Foster and Gus Hall each ran three times. As evidence of third-party durability, the Prohibition Party has run candidates in twenty-eight consecutive elections since 1872. However, their most successful nominee of all, John Bidwell, received only 271,000 popular votes back in 1892.[3]

The more I learned about third-party candidates, the more I wondered what forces motivate these individuals to press forward in their quest for the presidency. Because I first entered this arena during John Anderson's 1980 presidential campaign, I decided to return to the 1980 race to find out how many other candidates ran. At the top of the list were the two major-party nominees, Ronald Reagan and Jimmy Carter. Next came the independent candidate, John Anderson. In addition, I was surprised to discover no fewer than ten other third-party candidates who ran for the presidency in 1980 in at least two or more states. The complete cast (with ages and occupations shown as of November 1980) is shown on Table 1. These third-party nominees represent a rich cross-section of contemporary America—male and female, wealthy and poor, young and old, black and white, liberal and conservative, northern and southern, eastern and western. Yet, though these other candidates were contestants in the nation's largest election they were virtually ignored by the major television networks and other national media and enjoyed little opportunity to present their views to the voting public. Thus a host of questions remain unanswered: Who are these people? What do they believe? How do they view the 1980 campaign? What are their hopes and fears for the future?

This book attempts to answer these questions through a series of interviews with each of the third-party nominees who ran in two or more states in 1980, as well as with independent candidate John B. Anderson. At the outset, it is important to emphasize what the book does not attempt to do. No effort has been made to analyze or to censor the candidates' comments. Instead, the third-party nominees were encouraged to

TABLE 1. Popular Votes for President: 1980 Election

Candidate	State	Affiliation	Age	Occupation	Popular Vote	Percentage
Ronald Reagan	(Calif.)	Republican	69	Ex-Governor	43,904,153	50.75
Jimmy Carter	(Ga.)	Democrat	56	President	35,483,883	41.02
INDEPENDENT						
John Anderson	(Ill.)	National Unity	58	Congressman	5,720,060	6.61
THIRD PARTIES						
Edward Clark	(Calif.)	Libertarian	50	Attorney	921,299	1.06
Barry Commoner	(N.Y.)	Citizens	63	Professor	234,294	0.27
Andrew Pulley	(Ill.)	Socialist Workers	29	Steelworker	49,038	0.05
(plus DeBerry and Richard Congress)						(Combined Total)
Gus Hall	(N.Y.)	Communist	70	Party Official	45,023	0.05
John Rarick	(La.)	American Independent	56	Ex-Congressman	41,268	0.05
Ellen McCormack	(N.Y.)	Right To Life	54	Homemaker	32,327	0.04
Deirdre Griswold	(N.J.)	Workers World	44	Editor	13,300	0.02
Benjamin Bubar	(Me.)	Prohibition (National Statesman)	63	Baptist Minister	7,212	0.01
David McReynolds	(N.Y.)	Socialist	50	Antiwar Activist	6,898	0.01
Percy Greaves	(N.Y.)	American	74	Economist	6,647	0.01
Write-Ins and Miscellaneous*					43,223	0.05

*Margaret Smith received 18,116 votes as the Peace and Freedom Party candidate in California but she ran only in one state.
Other miscellaneous and write-in votes were cast for: Kurt Lynen, middle-class candidate (3,694); Bill Gahres, Down With Lawyers (1,718); Frank Shelton, American (1,555); Martin Wendalken, Independent (923); Harley McLain, National Peoples League (296); and write-ins (16,921).
Source: Richard M. Scammon and Alice V. McGillivray, eds., *America Votes 14* (Washington, D.C.: Congressional Quarterly, 1981), p. 18.

tell their own stories in their own words with the expectation that the reading public would make its own evaluation of their differing viewpoints. A note on the methodology that was employed in the interviews appears at the end of the book. A number of common themes emerged during the course of the interviews with the different third-party candidates. Among these are the institutional obstacles the candidates faced—including such problems as ballot access, campaign finances, and media exposure—resulting from the dominance of our two-party political system. These institutional barriers are subjected to fairly intensive scrutiny in chapters 1 and 7 because they pose fundamental questions about democratic theory in our supposedly open political system. In addition, chapters 2 and 8 examine the historical impact of third parties on our past presidential elections and speculate on the role of such parties in future elections.

The heart of the book, however, consists of the interviews with the various third-party candidates. These interviews are designed to shed light on a group of political aspirants who most voters never had an opportunity to meet, see, or hear during the 1980 presidential campaign. Since many of the ideas these candidates expressed will undoubtedly be advanced once again in 1984 and in subsequent presidential elections, it is hoped that this book will serve as a useful guide for those interested in looking beyond the two major parties for alternative approaches to the political issues that the nation faces.

ACKNOWLEDGMENTS

A large number of people provided assistance in the preparation of this book. I am indebted to all of the third-party and independent candidates who granted me interviews and to the many candidates who also took time to review their interview transcripts for accuracy before returning them to me.

A number of colleagues provided helpful comments on different parts of the manuscript, including Philip Williams and L. J. Sharpe of Nuffield College, Oxford University; Professor Gerald Pomper of Rutgers University; Associate Professor Daniel A. Mazmanian of Pomona College; and Professors Raymond Hall, Robert Nakamura, Vincent Starzinger, Richard F. Winters, and James Wright of Dartmouth College.

Five individuals rendered valuable research assistance. Rhodes Cook of the *Congressional Quarterly* staff helped me locate the different third-party candidates, and he also provided up-to-date information on various financial aspects of the 1980 campaign. Donald J. Rendall, Jr., and Susan L. Smallwood performed legal research on the ballot access issue. Vermont Secretary of State James Douglas assisted in the collection of information on voter registration in the different states, and Dartmouth College research librarian Robert Jaccaud was extremely helpful in all aspects of documentary research.

Typing assistance was provided by three members of the Dartmouth staff: Nancy McGee, Deborah Hodges, and Kathy Schonberger. I am also grateful to the Public Affairs Center and the Faculty Research Committee at Dartmouth for providing financial support to help cover travel costs incurred in interviewing the candidates.

Finally, as always, I owe a special debt of thanks to my wife, Ann, who patiently read the entire manuscript and provided many suggestions designed to improve its clarity.

I appreciate the interest and encouragement I received from all of the above, with the full understanding that I bear final responsibility for all facts and judgments presented in the book.

Hanover, New Hampshire   F.S.
September 1982

I HISTORICAL BACKGROUND

1 THE TWO-PARTY MONOPOLY

After completing six unsuccessful campaigns for the White House, Socialist Party candidate Norman Thomas reached the rueful conclusion that "no third party has ever grown like an oak from an acorn."[1] Third parties in this country have had to struggle to even survive. A brief overview of the historic roots of our two-party system will highlight the political challenges that the third-party candidates faced in the 1980 presidential election.

The two major parties have maintained a tenacious stranglehold over the presidency since 1860, when the Republicans emerged to successfully challenge the Democrats as the nation's second major party. Since then, Americans have lived under what the late Clinton Rossiter described as "a persistent, obdurate, one might almost say tyrannical, two-party system. We have Republicans and we have Democrats, and we have almost no one else."[2]

Rossiter's terse observation does not describe accurately the 1980 presidential election in which voters could actually choose from among a Republican, a Democrat, and no less than eleven third-party and independent candidates. His central point about the strength of our two-party system, however, is clearly illustrated in Figure 1, which compares the lifespans of third parties with those of the two major parties. Why have the two major political parties been able to exercise such complete control over presidential elections for such an extended period of time? Our two-party monopoly is the result of a complex mixture of influences—historical, cultural, geographical, social, and political—two of which have been critically important. As political scientist Daniel Mazmanian observed in an earlier study of third parties, "the American two-party system stems from the nation's cultural values and electoral institutions."[3]

A variety of cultural values have perpetuated the two-party

Figure 1. Political Parties in Presidential Elections

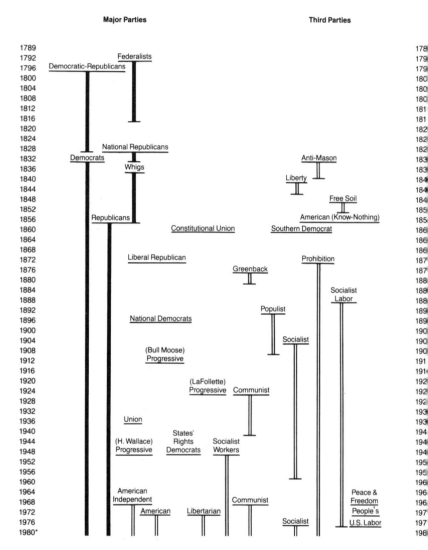

*New third parties which contested the 1980 presidential election included Citizens, Workers World, and Right-to-Life parties.

SOURCE: Adapted from Congressional Quarterly, *Guide to U.S. Elections* (1975), p. 176.

system. At the most deep-seated level, one group of scholars has argued, America's underlying political culture is clustered around a common set of egalitarian beliefs that have been described as the liberal tradition.[4] Among these scholars is Louis Hartz, whose central thesis is that, since America never experienced a feudal social structure, we avoided the types of deeply divisive class and religious antagonisms that characterized the political life of many older European societies. Instead, we developed a more moderate middle ground of political values that tended to minimize extreme class conflicts. According to this line of reasoning, the two major parties have preempted this middle ground and thus blocked the emergence of more radical third parties.

A second group of scholars has advanced the more pragmatic argument that the major parties have occupied the middle ground as a matter of political expediency in order to minimize controversy and gain the allegiance of as many voters as possible. According to analysts such as Rossiter, the Republican and Democratic Parties have deliberately blurred their outer edges to become "vast, gaudy, friendly umbrellas under which all Americans . . . are invited to stand for the sake of being counted in the next election."[5] As a result, the two major parties have consciously adopted a strategy of avoiding major controversies whenever possible. On those rare occasions when they have broken away from the middle ground to adopt more extremist positions—as was the case under Republican Barry Goldwater in 1964 and Democrat George McGovern in 1972—the major parties have suffered significant losses at the polls.

Whichever argument is correct, there is little doubt that the American political tradition has been characterized by a moderate, egalitarian, middle-ground approach. A variety of historical and geographical influences have insured its continuation. One of the most powerful of these influences was the American frontier.

In his famous paper on "The Significance of the Frontier in

American History" (1892), Frederick Jackson Turner advanced the hypothesis that both "the growth of nationalism and the evolution of American political institutions were dependent on the advance of the frontier . . . but the most important effect of the frontier was its promotion of democracy."[6] According to Turner, "the primitive organization of society on the frontier encouraged self-reliance and independence [and] . . . this frontier individualism has from the beginning promoted democracy."[7]

Although some of Turner's ideas were later criticized by historians for being too vague and even contradictory, there is still considerable support for his basic concept that our vast, underdeveloped frontier made it possible for many farmers and working-class men to achieve positions of social, economic, and political status. Although minority groups within American society did not obtain such status, the concept of equality promoted by the frontier did have a profound impact in shaping our general political values and beliefs. As the late historian Ray Allen Billington explains:

Basically, frontier individualism stemmed from the belief that all men were equal . . . and that all should have a chance to prove their personal capabilities without restraint from society. This seemed fair in a land of plenty, where superabundant opportunity allowed each to rise or fall to his proper level. . . . Faith in the equality of men was the great common creed of the West.[8]

Frontier egalitarianism played a key role in the election of Andrew Jackson to the presidency in 1828, and in the subsequent establishment of Jacksonian Democracy. The Jacksonians renamed themselves the Democratic Party, and formed the historic base for the present-day Democrats. They were initially opposed by the Whig Party. Following the Civil War, the Whigs were succeeded by the Republicans. Hence, by the 1860s, both the Democrats and the Republicans had emerged as the nation's two major parties.

Other historical habits and attitudes have tended to

strengthen the two-party tradition in American politics. In his classic study, *Politics, Parties and Pressure Groups*, V. O. Key has asserted that one such influence is the "persistence of initial form." According to Key:

Human institutions have an impressive capacity to perpetuate themselves or at least to preserve their form. The circumstances that happened to mold the American party system into a dual form at its inception must bear a degree of responsibility for its present existence. They included the confrontation of the country with a great issue that could divide it only into the ayes and the nays: the debate over the adoption of the Constitution. As party life began to emerge under the Constitution, again the issue split the country into two camps.[9]

Thus the issue that initially divided the country—and also led to the rise of our earliest political parties—involved the interpretation of the Constitution. The Federalists, spurred by Alexander Hamilton, took a "broad constructionist" view of the Constitution and favored a strong national government. They were opposed by the Jeffersonian Republicans, led by Thomas Jefferson, who took the "strict constructionist" view that the Constitution limited the power of the national government in favor of individual liberties.

The origins of these earliest parties is still a matter of dispute. As Professor Richard McCormick explains:

How these early parties emerged and what they represented remain subjects of controversy. My own view would be that a cleavage first developed within the administration. . . . In due course, a comparable cleavage manifested itself in the Congress. . . . The formation of these Congressional factions encouraged the building of parties in the states. In 1796 a new factor was introduced with the contest for the Presidency between Adams and Jefferson. . . . Whereas in 1790, parties had not been found in any state, by 1800, in most of the states, politics was conducted on a party basis.[10]

The clear-cut dualism involved in the initial controversy over the Constitution surfaced again in American politics during the 1820s and 1830s when the more egalitarian Jacksonian Democrats succeeded the Jeffersonian Republicans, and the more aristocratic Whigs replaced the Hamilton Federalists. Over the course of the next century, American political life was dominated by other major political issues that repeatedly split the nation into two camps. Prior to the Civil War, regional antagonisms pitted the proslavery South against the antislavery North and led to the development of the Republican Party as the successor to the Whigs. Following the Civil War, midwestern agrarian populists and Democrats vied with Republican eastern commercial interests over issues in which debtor groups favored cheap money while creditors pushed for a strong national currency. Hence, there was an ongoing tendency in American life to divide the nation into distinct political groups along the lines described by Key, and, in the process, to strengthen the two-party tradition.

Another ideological factor that has reinforced the two-party system is our process of political socialization—the process through which people acquire their political ideas and opinions. As Michael A. Krasner and his colleagues have explained,

The earliest political learning occurs in the family. . . . Children pick up knowledge and beliefs from their parents. . . . Children also tend to acquire their parents' party allegiance, especially if the mother and father agree. It used to be that nearly 75 percent adopted the same party as their parents, but more recent studies indicate that only 60 percent do.[11]

Despite this recent drop, the fact that so many children adopted their parents' party allegiance played a significant role in strengthening the two major parties. Once the Republicans and the Democrats became the predominant political parties, parents transmitted their allegiance for one or the other of these two parties to their children who, in turn, tended to pass along the same political allegiance to their own children. This self-fulfilling, self-perpetuating process gained momentum over time and enabled the two parties to maintain—and even expand—their respective positions.

A final, and very practical, ideological concern that has tended to benefit the two major parties is the fear of the "wasted vote." Public opinion studies have indicated that a sizable number of Americans who prefer a third-party candidate actually cast their presidential ballots for one of the two major parties because they are afraid of wasting their votes and enabling the other major-party candidate to win the election. Both of the major parties have used this "wasted vote" fear to their advantage for a great many years. In analyzing the 1924 election, Norman Thomas argues that Robert LaFollette, that year's Progressive and Socialist Party candidate, lost "hundreds of thousands of votes" when the major parties used this strategy to attack him.[12] In recalling his own presidential campaigns as the Socialist Party nominee, Thomas concludes that

the average American voter . . . may prefer a minor party candidate, but will cast his vote for one of the major party candidates. . . . Almost up to election day, he may think he will vote for his real preference, a minor-party candidate who managed to get on the ballot in his state, but then he will decide that he can't take a chance lest that [other] so-and-so get in. How often I have been told just that![13]

Thus a combination of cultural and ideological influences, which originally nurtured the two-party monopoly, have strengthened and reinforced this monopoly over time. As a result, the ultimate irony within our system of political beliefs is the widespread conviction that it is somehow un-American or subversive to even become involved in third-party politics. As Key explains, "whatever its origins, once the two-party system became established, [it] possessed great durability and . . . exerted great influence in conditioning behavior."[14]

The institutional arrangements that have helped to sustain the two-party monopoly are even more obvious than the cultural influences. One of the most important institutional factors that benefits the two major parties is our method of conducting elections. Our use of a single-member district/plurality system produces "winner-take-all" results in both congressional and state legislative contests. The same "winner-take-all" approach is used in presidential elections where all of the electoral college votes in each state go to the candidate who receives the highest number of popular votes in that state. These electoral mechanisms mean certain death for third-party candidates who may receive a sizable portion of the popular vote: they fail to gain any political rewards because they do not receive the highest number of total votes. Under a different system, such as proportional representation, for example, a party that wins 20 or 30 percent of the popular vote might end up controlling 20 or 30 percent of the offices decided in that election. Under a single-member district/plurality or electoral college system, however, such a party will win nothing at all if one of the major parties receives a higher total of the popular vote. Our method of electing public officials is heavily biased in favor of the two major parties, since they are better equipped to command plurality and majority support in elections.

A second institutional barrier against third parties is found in the restrictive ballot access laws that many states have adopted. Throughout most of the nineteenth century, the po-litical parties—rather than the states—prepared and distrib-uted election ballots. This practice changed with the adoption of the secret Australian ballot during the 1890s. "Under this reform each state now prepared an 'official' ballot that listed all parties' candidates. . . . By 1900, nearly 90 percent of the bal-lots cast had restrictions on which candidates could appear." [15]

The ostensible purpose of these restrictions was to conduct fair and orderly elections and to minimize the confusion that could result if large numbers of frivolous candidates were al-lowed to flood each election contest. In reality, however, the major parties have often manipulated these restrictive state laws to their own advantage by making it extremely difficult for minor-party and independent candidates to appear on the ballot. Some states, for example, have required early filing deadlines for such candidates, while other states require ex-tremely large numbers of petition signatures in order to qual-ify for a position on the ballot. These restrictive laws place a heavy burden on third-party candidates.

A third institutional constraint on third parties grows out of their own meager resource base. Many of these parties are so small that they have not been able to develop strong "grass roots" organizations at either the state or the local levels. In addition, these parties are usually underfunded, often as a result of their small size and lack of past success. As a result, they do not have the financial resources to purchase enough media advertising (especially television) to compete effectively with the major parties. Their lack of resources leads to a lack of electoral success which, in turn, makes it more difficult to raise future resources. In this manner, the third parties can be caught in a vicious spiral. While the major parties have been the beneficiaries of the self-fulfilling and self-reinforcing influences described earlier, the third parties are often paralyzed by self-denying and counterproductive downward pressures.

The final institutional hurdle that is especially difficult for third parties to surmount is our national system of presidential elections. Occasionally it has been possible for minor parties to gain a strong foothold in specific states, or groups of states, as in the case of the Progressive Party in Wisconsin, or the Populists in the midwestern and Great Plains states. It is much more difficult, however, to translate these state and even regional loyalties into national pluralities because of the legal, financial, and media costs involved in conducting national campaigns.

Under the circumstances, it would seem difficult for the third-party candidates to enjoy any significant success. Yet, as the next chapter indicates, there have been a number of presidential elections in which the third parties have actually managed to play an influential role.

2 THE HISTORICAL IMPACT OF THIRD PARTIES

Although no third-party candidate has come close to winning a presidential election in the past 120 years, the overall performance of third parties has been stronger than might be expected in light of the cultural and institutional influences that have helped to reinforce the two-party monopoly. According to a recent study by Steven Rosenstone and his colleagues at Yale University:

In one of three elections since 1840, they [third-party candidates] have captured over 5 percent of the presidential popular vote; in one of five, over 10 percent. Because of third parties, 40 percent of the Presidents since 1840 have entered the White House without winning a popular vote majority. In 13 of the 36 elections, third parties have controlled enough votes in the right states to have theoretically changed the Electoral College results.[1]

This same study also points out certain trends, or clusters, that have characterized third-party support in past elections:

Historically, good years for third parties tend to occur together, as do bad years. In the two periods 1848 to 1860 and 1904 to 1924, third parties only once received less than 5 percent of the presidential vote; the median was 8.1 percent. In other years, such as 1864 to 1872, third parties never received as much as 1.0 percent of the vote cast. In the five elections immediately following World War II, third parties barely averaged 1 percent.[2]

In an effort to explain these divergent voting patterns, different studies of past third-party performances have revealed three factors that can increase the extent of third-party support: conditions of political crisis; levels of voter dissatisfaction with the major parties; and the prominence and visibility of the third-party presidential candidates.

These three factors can have a cumulative impact. For example, if a political crisis exists, and if there is a high degree of dissatisfaction with the major parties, a less prominent candidate may triumph, as was the case in 1860 when Abraham Lincoln, a one-term congressman from Illinois, led the Republicans to victory over the Whigs during the tumultuous controversy concerning the extension of slavery prior to the Civil War. In turn, if there is a high degree of dissatisfaction with the major parties, and a visible third-party candidate runs, this candidate is likely to do well at the polls, as was the case with George C. Wallace, the controversial and strident governor of Alabama, who exploited a climate of racial unrest and dissatisfaction over the stalemate in Vietnam to receive almost ten million votes in the 1968 election.

The first of the three factors—conditions of political crisis—has influenced a variety of presidential elections. In his study, *Third Parties in Presidential Elections*, Daniel Mazmanian cites a number of "episodes of intense conflict" that have led to the emergence of third parties.[3] Many of these episodes fit quite neatly into a three-fold "agenda of politics" that another political scientist, Everett C. Ladd, claims has shaped our political parties over time. According to Ladd's analysis, our first political agenda, from 1790 to 1860, focused on the issue of egalitarianism in American society. As our earlier rural-agricultural society was transformed into an urban-industrial society following the Civil War, a second major agenda developed around issues of rapid industrial growth and economic development. Since the Great Depression and the New Deal of the 1930s, the agenda has shifted to a third major area—the role of the managerial state in minimizing the economic dislocations of industrial growth through governmental intervention in society.[4]

Ladd's scheme provides a useful way of classifying the types of conflicts that have led to major spurts of third-party activism. The first real third party in American politics, the Anti-Masons, appeared during the late 1820s in response to concern over the issue of egalitarianism. The major objective of the Anti-Masons was to challenge the concepts of elitism and privilege in American society by opposing the ritualistic order of the Masons and other secret societies. The new party flashed across the political scene quite rapidly. In September 1831 over 100 Anti-Mason delegates from twelve states gathered at our first national political party convention in Baltimore to nominate William Wirt of Maryland, a former attorney general of the United States, as their presidential candidate. Although Wirt polled more than 100,000 votes, or 8 percent of the total cast in the 1832 election, he was only able to capture seven electoral college votes, all from the state of Vermont. As a result, the party declined after the election, and the Anti-Masons became part of the political coalition that organized the Whig Party in 1834.

Subsequent events made it clear, however, that political conflicts over the issue of egalitarianism did not disappear with the demise of the Anti-Masons. Despite attempts to defuse the issue, the explosive crisis that surrounded the question of slavery led to the next outburst of third-party activism. The Liberty Party, which appeared in 1840, was the nation's first explicitly antislavery party. It was succeeded in 1848 by the Free-Soil Party, which advocated a program of "free soil, free speech, free labor, and free men"—an expression of opposition against the extension of slavery into the western territories that was coupled with a desire for cheap western land.

Just as the slavery controversy was heating up, a curious third party emerged that took an entirely different position on the issue of egalitarianism. The American, or "Know-Nothing," Party appeared in the early 1850s as a nativist Protestant-oriented political coalition that attempted to restrict the number of immigrants then entering the United States, particularly the Irish Catholics. The party was organized around two groups: the Supreme Order of the Star Spangled Banner and the National Council of the United States of North America. When asked about these organizations, members replied that they didn't know anything about them; hence, they were promptly dubbed the Know-Nothings.

The American Know-Nothing Party became particularly strong in the northeastern states where Irish and Catholic immigration was the highest, and by the mid-1850s, Know-Nothing candidates had been elected as governors in Massachusetts, Connecticut, Rhode Island, and New Hampshire. Even the Know-Nothings, however, could not escape the divisive issue of slavery. When the party gathered for its first, and only, national convention in 1856, a large and very vocal contingent of southern delegates showed up in Philadelphia. They successfully blocked an attempt by the northern delegates to nominate a candidate who opposed the extension of slavery into the new territories, and they also pushed through a proslavery platform. The northern delegates fled the convention, and the remaining southern delegates nominated the former Whig president, Millard Fillmore, as the American Party candidate. In the 1856 election Fillmore received 875,000 votes, or 21 percent of the total cast, but he was only able to capture eight electoral college votes, all from the state of Maryland. The North-South split at the convention marked the collapse of the party, for it was never able to resolve the issues of sectionalism and slavery.

The 1856 election signaled a critical turning point in American politics because both of the two major parties—the Whigs and the Democrats—proved unable to cope with the slavery issue. The Whigs, who split into the antislavery "Conscience Whigs" and the proslavery "Cotton Whigs" disappeared as a party after 1856, though one of their former candidates, John Bell, ran as a Constitutional Union candidate in the 1860 election. The Democrats, who were also torn apart by the slavery issue, ended up nominating two candidates in 1860—Stephen A. Douglas (a northern Democrat) and John C. Breckinridge (a southern Democrat). The political coalition that was able to capitalize on this situation was the Republican Party, which was organized in Ripon, Wisconsin, in 1854. Only two years later, the party's first presidential nominee, John C. Fremont, received one-third of the popular vote and carried eleven states in the 1856 election. In 1860 the Republicans completed the re-alignment of our political party system when Abraham Lincoln captured the White House. The following year the nation was plunged into civil war. After the North won, the Republicans permanently replaced the Whigs as our second major party and proceeded to dominate the American presidency for the next three-quarters of a century.[5]

Once the slavery question was resolved by the Civil War, egalitarianism was less of an issue in third-party politics throughout the remainder of the nineteenth century. A few small groups, such as the women's suffrage Equal Rights Party, nominated candidates in the 1884 and 1888 elections, but by this time the major political issues had shifted to questions of rapid industrial growth and economic development that accompanied the shift from a rural-agrarian to an urban-industrial society. The conflict that grew out of this shift spurred the development of a new set of third parties that appeared during the latter part of the nineteenth century.

As the emerging corporate industrial monopolies began to exert growing political influence following the Civil War, a variety of protest and reform groups appeared to counteract these trends, especially in the agrarian regions of the Midwest. These political groups, which grew out of such farm organizations as the Granges of the Patrons of Husbandry, opposed large land grants to the private corporations and demanded reforms to regulate railroad rates and to modify banking laws. An immediate cause of concern was the conflict over the money supply. Creditors favored hard money that was pegged to some fixed external standard, such as gold, to protect the value of their investments and loans. Debtors advocated cheaper inflationary paper currency that would reduce the burden of their obligations.

After the Civil War, the Panic of 1873 culminated in a major economic depression that was particularly hard on farmers because it resulted in declining agricultural prices. This led to the formation of a third party in the 1870s that was known as the Greenbacks since it opposed the gold standard and called for the retention of the inflationary paper money (known as greenbacks) that had been issued as emergency currency to help finance the Civil War. The Greenback Party polled over one million votes in the 1878 congressional races and won fourteen seats in the House of Representatives. As economic conditions began to improve, however, the fortunes of the Greenback Party declined, and their 1880 presidential candidate, Representative James B. Weaver of Iowa, received only 300,000 popular votes.

The disappearance of the Greenbacks did not signify an end of the conflict over the course of the nation's economic development. A second, considerably larger, agrarian reform movement resulted in the establishment of the People's Party in the early 1890s. The People's Party, commonly called the Populists, was formally organized in Cincinnati, Ohio, in 1891, and the movement quickly spread into the farm states in the Midwest, the Far West, and even the South. The party was still heavily concerned with the currency issue and favored the free coinage of silver. It also advocated other economic and political reforms, including government ownership and operation of the railroads; postal savings banks; a graduated income tax; direct election of United States senators; and the use of the initiative, the referendum, and secret ballots in elections.

The People's Party selected former Greenback Party candidate James Weaver as its nominee in the 1892 presidential election, and he received over one million votes, plus twenty-two electoral college votes from states in the Great Plains and the Far West. The party continued to grow in strength when, in the 1894 races, its congressional candidates polled nearly 1.5 million votes, and the Populists elected six senators and seven representatives. If ever it appeared that a third party was about to cut into the two-party dominance of the Republicans and the Democrats, this was the occasion. Then, in one single stroke, the Democrats preempted the Populists by nominating William Jennings Bryan as their 1896 presidential candidate on a free silver platform following Bryan's famous "Cross of Gold" speech. As one political observer has noted:

Of all the scores of minor parties that have skipped fitfully across our political landscape, only one, the Populists, seems in retrospect to have mounted a serious challenge to the hegemony of the two major parties. . . . Yet the nomination of Bryan by the Democrats in 1896 smashed their dreams with one blow of the hammer, and the Populists proved how complete the wreckage was by hastening to nominate Bryan themselves. . . . One of the persistent qualities of the American two-party system is the way in which one of the major parties moves almost instinctively to absorb (and thus be somewhat reshaped by) the most challenging third party of the time.[6]

At the same time that the Democrats were capturing the Populist Party, a shift was taking place in the basic nature of the third-party movement in the United States. Whereas the Greenbacks and the Populists had been parties of economic protest that drew upon an indigenous regional base of popular support, a new group of third parties began to emerge at the turn of the century that V. O. Key has called "doctrinal parties," since they were designed to propagate a particular set of economic and ideological doctrines.[7] A number of short-lived workingmen's parties had previously been organized during the 1820s, beginning in Philadelphia, where "the first labor party in America was formed in 1828."[8] This movement spread to New York, where a workingmen's party was briefly active during the 1830s. These early labor parties had strictly local origins, however, and they were designed to deal with specific grievances involving working conditions and educational reforms.

The first efforts to organize the so-called doctrinal parties began after the Civil War, when many of the immigrants who were pouring into the country, particularly those from Germany, were influenced by socialism and Marxism. Attempts were made to promote a Marxist-oriented party in the early 1870s, and unity within the movement was formally achieved in July 1876 when delegates from the First International met in Philadelphia to organize the Working Men's Party of the United States, which was renamed the Socialist Labor Party in 1877. In 1892 the Socialist Labor Party nominated its first presidential candidate, Simon Wing, who received slightly more than 20,000 votes. During the 1890s, the party became increasingly militant when it was taken over by Daniel DeLeon, a former Columbia University law lecturer who was a doctrinaire Marxian revolutionary.

As a result, the more moderate Socialist Party, a splinter group that broke away from the Socialist Labor Party in 1901 under the leadership of Eugene Debs, Morris Hillquit, and others, was established. The Socialist Party grew quite rapidly. By 1912, "on the eve of World War I, a total of 667 Socialist Party officials held public office" at the state and local levels.[9] The party also did quite well in national elections, as its earliest presidential candidate, Eugene Debs (who ran in five different elections), received over 900,000 votes in both the 1912 and the 1920 campaigns. However, the Socialists were hurt when many Americans rejected their pacifist views during the First World War, and in 1919 the Communists split away from the Socialists to organize their own new political party.

Two other sizable third-party efforts were launched during this period. The first of these was led by ex-president Teddy Roosevelt, who organized the "Bull Moose" Progressives in 1912, and the second by Senator Robert LaFollette, Sr., of Wisconsin, who ran as a National Progressive Party candidate in 1924.

Both Roosevelt and LaFollette represented the more liberal reform wing of the Republican Party, and both became involved in third-party progressive politics after breaking away from the Republicans. The "Bull Moose" Progressives were created when Roosevelt, after failing to win the Republican Party nomination, announced that he would run for president as a progressive candidate in the 1912 election. Roosevelt's platform called for a "new nationalism" program of reform that included stricter regulation of corporations, downward revision of tariffs, popular election of United States senators, women's suffrage, and support for the referendum, initiative, and recall.* Roosevelt managed to capture over four million popular votes and eighty-eight electoral college votes, thus throwing the 1912 election to Woodrow Wilson, who was only the second Democrat to occupy the White House since the Civil War. However, Roosevelt never intended to establish a totally new third political party, and once he withdrew from the political scene, the "Bull Moose" Progressives disappeared.

The LaFollette Progressive Party of 1924 grew out of its members' disillusionment with both the Republican and the Democratic Party's probusiness platforms. Spearheaded by the Conference for Progressive Political Action, LaFollette's 1924 program called for public ownership of the nation's water power, strict control and conservation of all natural resources, farmers' cooperatives, legislation to make credit available to farmers and small businessmen, and a constitutional amendment to provide for the direct election of federal judges for terms of not more than ten years. LaFollette, who received the endorsement of the American Federation of Labor and the Socialist Party, polled 4.8 million popular votes, but he received only thirteen electoral college votes, all from his home state of Wisconsin.

The LaFollette campaign of 1924 signified the culmination of third-party activity that was stimulated by rapid industrial growth and economic development.[10] With the advent of Franklin D. Roosevelt's New Deal in the 1930s, the political agenda shifted to the third issue cited by Ladd—governmental intervention aimed at minimizing the economic dislocations of the Great Depression. Roosevelt charted a new course of federal

*The referendum, initiative, and recall were reform measures passed to increase citizen participation in government by allowing the public to vote upon or initiate policies and to recall public officials prior to completion of their term of office.

activism that was destined to characterize American political life until the 1980 election. During the past half century since Roosevelt initiated the New Deal, significant third-party initiatives have been intermittent. The doctrinal parties—the Socialists, Communists, and some later Trotskyite groups such as the Socialist Workers—have continued to nominate numerous presidential candidates, but they have received a relatively low level of public recognition and support. Former vice-president Henry A. Wallace launched his Progressive Party (American Labor) campaign in 1948, but he failed to win any electoral college votes, despite receiving over one million popular votes. The two third-party movements that have had the most impact on presidential elections during the past fifty years have been protest groups that campaigned against excessive governmental intervention in social affairs, particularly in the areas of civil rights and race relations.

In 1948, the States' Rights Democratic Party—popularly known as the Dixiecrats—appeared in opposition to President Truman's civil rights proposals that called for congressional legislation abolishing poll taxes and making lynching a federal offense. When the Democratic Party endorsed a strong civil rights plank in its 1948 platform, the States' Rights Party nominated J. Strom Thurmond, the democratic governor of South Carolina, as its presidential nominee. Thurmond received over 1.1 million popular votes, and he won thirty-eight electoral college votes from five southern states. Although the Dixiecrats disbanded after the 1948 election, their emergence as a political movement signified a growing split between conservatives and liberals within the Democratic Party that was to become more pronounced in later years when Thurmond and other prominent southern Democrats shifted their allegiance to the Republican Party.

In 1968, the American Independent Party was established as a vehicle for the presidential ambitions of Alabama Governor George C. Wallace, who opposed President Lyndon Johnson's "Great Society" civil rights activism of the 1960s. The growing tensions surrounding race relations during the period were heightened by frustrations over the Vietnam War. Wallace capitalized on these tensions by conducting a hard-line "law and order" campaign that made major inroads among disgruntled middle-class white voters, as well as among blue-collar workers. As a result, he was able to win forty-six electoral college votes and 9,906,473 popular votes—the largest popular vote total ever received by a third-party candidate in the nation's history.

Thus conflicts over the appropriate role of governmental intervention in society did produce two important third-party efforts during the past fifty years. After Wallace was paralyzed by an assassination attempt in 1972, the American Independent Party and its offshoot, the American Party, continued to nominate presidential candidates, but neither of these parties was able to approach Wallace's 1968 level of support. There were other indications, however, that the immediate crisis over Vietnam and the more long-range political controversy over the issue of governmental intervention in social affairs were continuing to activate new third parties. In the 1972 election, the People's Party nominated Dr. Benjamin Spock on an antiwar platform, and another new group, the Libertarian Party, was organized to oppose governmental intrusion into private affairs. Thus while voter support for third parties was not widespread during the post-New Deal era (with the exception of the Thurmond and the two Wallace campaigns), there was a continual flurry of third-party activism during this period.[11]

The second factor that can influence third-party turnouts—voter disillusionment with the major parties—has been described in the preceding discussion. Voter dissatisfaction with the major parties was very evident during the 1850s conflict over the slavery issue, and it led directly to the rise of the Republican Party and the victory of Abraham Lincoln. The same was true in the 1912 election when charismatic Teddy Roosevelt and Socialist Eugene Debs received 34 percent of the total popular vote as third-party candidates, thus enabling Woodrow Wilson, a Democrat, to be elected as a plurality president with only 42.5 percent of the popular votes cast. A third example was the 1968 campaign of Governor George Wallace. The crux of the Wallace argument was his famous quote, "there ain't a dime's worth of difference between the Democratic and Republican Parties."[12] By arguing that both of the major parties were too soft on American blacks and the Viet Cong, Wallace managed to capture almost ten million popular votes, or 13.5 percent of the total votes cast.

The third factor that has influenced the level of third-party support is the prominence and visibility of the third-party candidates. When well-known national leaders, for example, have headed third-party tickets, their support has been quite high. Thus the former Whig president, Millard Fillmore, received 21 percent of the popular vote as the American "Know-Nothing" Party candidate in 1856, and ex-president Teddy Roosevelt received 28 percent of the popular vote as a "Bull Moose" Progressive in the 1912 election.

These examples support the thesis that prominent candidates are more apt to run as third-party nominees during times that the public perceives a political crisis, or when there is widespread public dissatisfaction with the major parties. These three factors can feed into each other to produce a cumulative impact, a point that the Rosenstone study stresses:

Support for third parties will be high when prominent elites think that major parties are vulnerable (and thus run), and when citizens . . . have weak allegiance to the two dominant parties. . . . One of the most important factors that affects a third party vote is a prestigious, well-known candidate at the head of its ticket.[13]

Hence, though both the cultural and institutional barriers against third-party candidates are formidable, there are certain key factors—or, more important, combinations of factors—that can increase the level of voter support for third parties. The fact remains, however, that no third-party or independent candidate has been able to generate enough support to capture the presidency in well over a century.

Under the circumstances, many Americans might question whether these parties have played any positive role in our political history at all, or whether their primary purpose has been to discharge a negative "nuisance function" by threatening to send close election contests to the House of Representatives for final resolution. Evidence from studies by political historians and social scientists suggests that third parties have actually made a number of distinctive contributions to the political process.

First, some of these parties have served as outlets for frustrated minorities unable to find relief within either of the major parties. Because the major parties have often tended to ignore or minimize controversial social issues in their efforts to occupy the safe middle ground of American politics, pressures have built up within disaffected groups to organize their own third parties in an effort to promote their goals. These protest parties have provided minorities with access to the political arena, thus enabling them to work legitimately within the confines of the American political system.

This type of protest politics can become especially important when the major parties are unable to deal effectively with important issues such as the slavery controversy of the 1840s and 1850s. There is little doubt that the agitation provided by such groups as the Liberty and the Free-Soil Parties helped to force the slavery question onto the nation's political agenda. These third parties harnessed the frustrations of the antislavery forces, and over time they brought about a realignment of the major parties. There are numerous other examples where third parties have helped to reorder our national priorities to accommodate issues ignored by the major parties. As Mazmanian has noted, "third parties crystallize issues that might otherwise go unheeded or receive little attention during a campaign."[14] Although the conflict over slavery resulted in a complete realignment of our party system, the more common practice has been for the major parties to respond to these issues by incorporating solutions proposed by third parties into their own programs. According to political historian William B. Hesseltine:

Third parties have performed the function of calling attention to serious problems and sometimes pointing a way to their solution. They have stimulated—sometimes by frightening them—the lethargic or timid politicians of the major parties. They have advocated reforms which the older parties have adopted and enacted into law.[15]

Consequently, many of the practices and policies that we take for granted today in American politics have appeared as a result of third-party initiatives.

Procedural reforms have also been effected by third parties. The first political party to hold a national nominating convention and to adopt a national political platform was the Anti-Mason Party in 1832. Third parties were also the first to advocate women's suffrage and a wide variety of election reforms, as mentioned earlier; they also were the first to call for stricter regulation of corporations, more aggressive programs to conserve our natural resources, tougher child labor laws, aid to small businessmen, postal savings banks, civil-service reform, and old-age pensions.

Another major function of third parties has been to propose and explain new ideas and policies to the public. As mentioned, these parties have often been successful in advancing initiatives that have later been incorporated into our political life. Even on those occasions where their ideas have been rejected, third parties have acted as a sounding board by providing a forum for discussion and debate.

Finally, third parties serve as a check on the effectiveness of the two major parties. Many Americans have found this to be the most threatening, and potentially dangerous, aspect of third-party politics because they fear that the presence of these parties might deadlock or stalemate elections so that the nation could end up without a clear-cut majority president. In essence, the third parties represent competition, always waiting in the wings to possibly capitalize on major-party weaknesses or mistakes. As a result, they could have a potentially destabilizing effect on our political system, insofar as they could weaken the majority support that the two major parties have relied upon to govern the nation.

Paradoxically, however, the fact that the third parties pose this threat has served in the past to stimulate the major parties to be more responsive to genuine public concerns. Consequently, the major parties have been able to preempt and capture third-party support, and no third party has been able to mount a consistent challenge against the major parties over a sustained period. Such a situation might occur in the future, but only if the major parties prove incapable of dealing effectively with political issues of public concern. In short, the American public constitutes the ultimate jury on this question.

Yet, while the major parties have access to a wide variety of mass media to express their views, information on third parties is scarce. The primary purpose of this study is to redress this imbalance by clarifying the role of the third parties in the 1980 presidential election.

The interviews in Part 2 of the book provide background information on each of the third-party candidates and help clarify what positions they advocated; how they viewed the various institutional barriers they faced; what they felt they accomplished during the campaign; and whether they are optimistic or pessimistic about the future of their own parties and the current trends in American politics. Part 3 of the book analyzes the current status of the two-party monopoly and evaluates the potential impact of the third parties in future presidential elections.

II THE CANDIDATES SPEAK

3 A VOICE FROM THE PAST

PROHIBITION PARTY

Until recently only two of our nineteenth-century third parties still remained active in presidential politics. The Socialist Labor Party nominated candidates in every election from 1892 to 1976 when they finally dropped out of presidential politics. The Prohibition Party, which nominated its first presidential candidate in the 1872 election, continued to remain active in the 1980 presidential race. Thus, the Prohibitionists qualify as the oldest and the most persistent third party in American history.

The Prohibition Party was formally organized in Chicago in 1869. During the long course of their involvement in presidential politics, the Prohibitionists claim to be the first political party to:

grant women equal status as convention delegates (1869);

advocate universal women's suffrage, civil service reform, and direct popular election of United States senators (1872);

promote inheritance and income tax legislation (1890), legislation prohibiting child labor (1908), and old-age pensions (1916).

Despite this wide range of concerns, the basic goal of the party throughout its history has been the enactment of laws prohibiting the manufacture and sale of liquor. The late historian Roger C. Storms has pointed out that the party's historical evolution was marked by divisions between the "narrow-gauge" Prohibitionists, who regarded this as a single-issue cause, and the "broad-gauge" Prohibitionists, who felt the party needed a wider range of issues in order to gain major public support.[1]

Storms describes three distinct periods in the development of the party. The "Prophetic Period" (1869–1896) was dominated by the broad-gauge approach when the party's first leaders adopted an evangelistic political style similar to that of the Old Testament prophets. These leaders had originally helped to organize the Republican Party. After the Civil War, they felt betrayed when the Republicans were captured by the big business corporate interests. As a result, they advocated a wide variety of social reforms, noted above, that were designed to transform American society.

The "Pragmatic Period" (1896–1932) was marked by the more narrow-gauge approach. During this period, the party's leaders no longer envisioned replacing one of the major parties. Instead, their chief objective was to persuade the major parties to support their position on prohibition. The "Fundamental Period" (1932 to the present) has been marked by an alienation from modern American society, and a call for a return to the fundamental moral values of an earlier social order.[2]

Although the party's first nominee, James Black, received only 5,600 popular votes in the 1872 presidential election, the Prohibitionists grew in strength to a point where their 1892 candidate, John Bidwell of California, attracted over 270,000 votes. The party maintained its voting strength at this level until 1920, when it began to lose support after the Eighteenth Amendment (Prohibition) to the U.S. Constitution was ratified in 1919. Its popular-vote total dropped sharply from 195,000 in 1920 to 16,000 in 1976. Following the 1976 presidential election, the party adopted a new name, National Statesman, in an effort to indicate that its programs extended beyond the issue of prohibition alone. However, the National Statesman label tended to confuse its hard-core supporters, and the party has decided to return to its previous name after it got on the ballot in only eight states, and its vote fell to only 7,200 in the 1980 presidential election.

Benjamin C. Bubar, who ran as the party's candidate in both the 1976 and the 1980 presidential elections, has been active in the Prohibition Party since the early 1950s. At age sixty-four, he serves as the executive director of the Christian Civic League in Waterville, Maine, and he lives in the nearby community

China Lake, Maine. I interviewed Mr. Bubar in his league headquarters office in Waterville in mid-July 1981.

Benjamin C. Bubar

We're not a one-issue party. We've always had more than one string in our fiddle. We've been around for a long time.

PERSONAL BACKGROUND

Smallwood: Tell me a little about your background. When did you get started in politics?

Bubar: Oh, I'm what you'd call an old-timer now because I first got into politics many years ago. I ran for the Maine state legislature when I wasn't even old enough to vote for myself in the primary. My twentieth birthday came three days after the primary.

When was this?

Let's see. It was back in 1938. I was living in the northern part of the state. They tell me I talk like a New Brunswick Yankee because I grew up in the little town of Mars Hill way up in Aroostook County. There are a lot of Bubars up and down the line all through that area. We live on both sides of the border, so half are Canadians and the other half Americans, but I think we were all pretty well shook out of the same tree.

I ran for the legislature as a Republican. It was during the depression. Almost everybody up there was Republican in those days, since Maine and Vermont were the only two states that supported Alf Landon against Roosevelt in the '36 election. I was working part-time cutting pulpwood and part-time in a grocery store for twenty-five cents an hour, very proud of my big wages.

Why did you decide to run for the state legislature?

We had a lot of good men in the legislature out of that area, but some of the young folk were dissatisfied, no different than they are today. When I look back on it, the only thing I can find wrong with the guy I ran against was that he was sixty years old. We thought he was over the hill and it was time to ditch him.

Four of us were discussing it at a soda fountain one night. The question was what were we going to do. You can stand outside, throw spitballs, and criticize. We said, well, why don't one of us run for the legislature and put that fellow away? Then the question was who was going to run. We drew straws. I got the short one, so I was the one who ran, even though I was only nineteen at the time and not even old enough to vote for myself in the primary.

What kind of campaign did you run?

Well, it took three months for folks to take us serious. When we put in our nomination petition to go up and file, the folks laughed about it. It was a big joke in the area. The fellow I worked for in the grocery store came along one day and asked me if I was just kidding around about wanting to go to the legislature. I said, "No, I'm serious. I'm going to run, and these fellows are going to campaign for me." It was an extremely rural area, like nothing you've come through this morning. It was right back in the boondocks. We campaigned. I spoke to my dad about it, and he thought it was great. I wasn't able to go to college—couldn't afford it. He thought this would be a good education for me. He told me that if I ran half a dozen times, someday I'd make it, because Abe Lincoln ran many times before he made it. The sad part of it was, I got elected the first time.

How long did you serve in the state legislature?

I was elected in 1938, so I was in the House in 1939. I served for six years, until 1945. I'm still the youngest person ever to have served in the Maine legislature.

Your entry into politics sounds almost accidental. Was your family interested in political matters?

My father certainly was interested. He was a clergyman for sixty years, but every two years, when a campaign came around, he'd have to go out and stump for somebody. It was just in his blood. He felt it was part of his Christian witness to get involved, to see that decent men and women were elected to public office. He was in the state legislature back in '34–'35. Some of my other family members have been in the House and the Senate.

What happened after you got out of the state legislature in 1945?

I had started taking courses at Ricker College in Houlton part time when I was still in the legislature. I was also serving as chairman of the Board of Selectmen in my little town, and I was supplying three small churches in the area. It all dovetailed. After I finished up in the legislature, I had a chance to come down here to Colby College in Waterville. There were a couple of little Baptist churches down here that needed someone to fill in. They couldn't afford a regular pastor. I came down as lay pastor, and I went to Colby.

Did you ever get back to northern Maine again?

Oh, yes. There was a family problem—sickness in the family—so I had to go back up to Aroostook County. I started a weekly newspaper in Mars Hill. After a few years, I sold it. I got out by the skin of my teeth. I never worked so hard in my life, lost so much money, or had so much fun.

I went from there to a little church in Allagash, way, way up in northern Maine. It was the dead end of the line, thirty-five miles northwest of Fort Kent. You sing in church, you know, "When I Get to the End of the Way." Well, this was it. About 600 people back in there, Scotch and Irish. They didn't mix much with the French. They were lumbermen. I was there for five years. Then this job opened up here in Waterville. The work was kind of on the bottom, so I came with the Christian Civic League in 1952. I've been with them ever since; it's thirty years now.

What does the league do?

A lot of our work involves education. We're interested in public issues, but mainly on the state level. We're concerned about honesty and integrity on the part of public officials. If we find they're not living up to what they should be doing, we go to court with them. We're opposed to gambling, drugs, and alcohol. We think liquor and drugs are corrupting influences; we've successfully sponsored legislation which requires a special state liquor tax to cover some of the costs of alcohol rehabilitation and treatment centers. We're basically involved in different social and political issues which are of concern to our church members.

Is the Christian Civic League related to the Prohibition Party?

No. They're two separate organizations, although they're pretty much in agreement on a number of issues. But the league is my job. I'm the superintendent, a paid executive. This is how I make my living. I could never make a living from the Prohibition Party!

You ran for the state legislature as a Republican. When did you get involved with the Prohibition Party?

I've been interested in the Prohibition Party indirectly for as long as I can remember. You see, the Maine law back in 1856 was the first state law, and Maine was a prohibition state until 1933. My dad and my grandfather were both members of the party. My dad cast his first vote for a Prohibitionist when they used to run a full slate of officers in the state. So I've been interested in the party for a long time, although I didn't get actively involved until the 1950s.

POLITICAL IDEOLOGY

The Prohibition Party has been around for more than a century. Where do you stand today? Are you a single-issue group, or are your concerns broader than the prohibition of alcohol?

No, we're not a single-issue party. We've always had more than one string in our fiddle. We've been around a long time. Over the years we've initiated many major reforms. Way back in 1872, we were the first party to call for universal suffrage for all groups, including women's suffrage. We were the first to advocate civil service reforms and the direct election of senators. Although I hate to admit it, we were also the first to call for an income tax way back in 1896, but we're vehemently opposed to the rip-off we've got on our hands at the present time.

If you look at our 1980 platform, it was very comprehensive. For example, take economic issues. We favor a return to the gold standard, a constitutional amendment for a balanced budget, the end of excessive government regulation, and a systematic reduction in the national debt. We think our current money system is a real mess; it's getting us into bankruptcy. We don't have money in this country any more, just some credit slips in our pockets that say Federal Reserve. All we're doing is handing out a lot of paper that can't be redeemed for anything. We got into the mess gradually, and we can gradually go back to hard money. The Federal Reserve buys this stuff we carry around in our pockets from the U.S. printers just like you and I buy stationery at the local store.

A lot of parties are concerned about our economic problems. What issues besides prohibition separate you from these other parties?

We're at loggerheads with the Republicans and Democrats on many issues. The Republican and Democratic Parties have ignored the Constitution. They've allowed the Supreme Court to do the legislating for them. We believe in separation of church and state, but we think they have misinterpreted both freedom of speech and freedom of religion. The founding fathers never intended it to be freedom from religion, but freedom of religion. The big problem historically was to avoid state-sanctioned churches. This is what the founding fathers were afraid of. There's a big difference between freedom from religious coercion and freedom to practice religion. The courts have gone too far in this area.

We broke away from the Republican Party after the Civil War, and they have tried for many years to hold themselves up as the party of morality, which is an awful sham. The only difference between the Republican Party and the Democrats in the state of Maine is that, when they have conventions, the Republicans drink whiskey and vodka and the Democrats drink beer. They go to a hotel and have their convention, and it costs more to clean up after the Republicans than the Democrats. The Democrats make more noise, but the Republicans leave more of a mess.

How about issues of foreign policy? What are your positions in this area?

We believe we should promote American liberty and freedom throughout the world, but only by helping those nations who are friendly to the U.S. and who share our devotion to freedom. We condemn the giveaway of the Panama Canal and the sellout of nationalist China in contradiction to our treaty commitments.

When it comes to loaning money, we've wrecked ourselves by giving away money. We've demeaned the third-world nations. We've embarrassed the life out of them by being Santa Claus, instead of allowing them a little dignity to pay it back. Finland is the only country that had the dignity to pay us back. We built the Russian navy, and we've pretty well built the Russian air force. See what we're doing now for China. They have no intention of paying us back. Why should they? Our party believes we should help those nations that need it. We should loan them money at the going rate of interest. Then we should allow them the dignity to at least make some attempt at paying it back. If we did this, Fort Knox wouldn't be empty.

In the area of social issues, your party has advocated many very progressive reforms over the years. How would you characterize your own position on social issues today? As a progressive or a conservative?

Well, personally I think we're a conservative Christian-oriented party. Of course, it all depends on how the pendulum swings. When I was in the state legislature, I was accused of being a left-wing radical because I supported things like social security—not the hodgepodge we've got today, but a sound, actuarial program. My philosophy hasn't changed much, but now I'm probably accused of being a right-wing radical.

Take the issue of women's rights. We were the first American political party to support equal rights for women, but we don't support the so-called ERA. This would grant women no new rights, and it would strip them of many of the privileges they now enjoy. Or look at the abortion issue. We abhor the use of public funds for abortion on demand, but I don't think a constitutional amendment is necessary on this. It's a private decision, but it shouldn't be subsidized by the federal government or the state government either.

So I'm opposed to both of these constitutional amendments. Is this progressive or conservative? It all depends on where you stand. One thing for certain, we're a strong states' rights party, and we always have been. We believe you can't have an orderly society without good strong government, but it shouldn't be dictatorial. We believe in the right of states and localities to make their own decisions on many social issues, such as voluntary prayer in the schools. These matters shouldn't be dictated from Washington.

One social issue that your party has always focused on is prohibition. Why has this always been so central to you?

Actually, we support a state-by-state approach to this issue. We think the problem of drinking, which is the major drug problem in this nation, is way out of hand. Here in Maine, we have over 70,000 alcoholics, which is more than the population of our three smallest counties. We're not as bad on a per capita basis as some of the other states, but for the little state of Maine, with only one million people, this is pretty rough.

Since this issue has been so important to your party, I'd like to clarify your position. If you believe in individual freedom, why do you think you have the right to tell people whether or not they can drink alcohol?

This is a public issue. It affects the public welfare and safety, which are legitimate government concerns. Why not repeal the rape laws or the robbery laws? As far as I'm concerned, you can drink, but you have no right to go out on the road and jeopardize me, because it's just as dangerous to point a high-powered automobile at me as a high-powered rifle.

The facts speak for themselves. Nationally, by very conservative estimates, 24 million Americans are now alcoholics or problem drinkers, and an estimated 500,000 Americans die each year because of highway deaths, homicides, and health problems which can be traced directly to alcoholic beverages.

When I was in the Vermont legislature, one of my very conservative colleagues opposed a mandatory motorcycle helmet law because he said this was a matter of individual choice. Why is alcohol so different that it shouldn't be a matter of personal choice?

Well, I agree that it should be optional whether or not anyone wears a motorcycle helmet. However, whether they drive with their headlights on at night shouldn't be optional. If they want to bat their brains out against a tree or rock or something, that's their tough luck. I can't do anything about it if they don't want to wear a helmet unless it's one of my own children.

However, the headlights on the motorcycle, that's totally different. This affects other people. The public good is the issue. One of the duties of government is to protect people against themselves and against other people. This is not a socialist philosophy. Alcohol is the most addictive drug around today. If you become addicted to opium or morphine, you can take the cure. If you become addicted to alcohol, the brain damage that is done is never overcome. It never regenerates. The devastation to your nervous system and to your body is never regenerated.

As a practical matter, we've already tried national prohibition with the Eighteenth Amendment. By all the accounts I've read, it wasn't successful. Why do you think it will work today?

You know, it's interesting, but the Eighteenth Amendment wasn't really pushed very hard by the Prohibition Party. We favor a state-by-state approach. It was primarily the product of old Bishop Cannon, the "Dry Messiah," the "Methodist Bishop," a real kingmaker. He really built a powerful political machine, the Anti-Saloon League. It was probably a mistake to try national prohibition. When the Eighteenth Amendment went into effect in 1919, there were already thirty-one states that were dry. I think we've got to go back to a state-by-state approach in order to control the problem.

It's been argued that once the Eighteenth Amendment was adopted, this led to the decline and virtual demise of the Prohibition Party because your mission was completed. Is this one of the reasons you've experimented with new names, like the National Statesman Party, in an effort to resurrect your fortunes?

I was one of the fellows who was pushing to change the name because I felt with a comprehensive platform like ours, prohibition was just one part of it. But it took several funerals before we were able to get it through. Some of the old-timers in the party wouldn't listen to it. There was only one plank in the platform as far as some of the old-timers were concerned. I started agitating for a name change back in the 1950s. In 1976, we finally decided to try it for three or four years to see what would happen.

Why did you choose the name National Statesman?

I felt this was a term that spoke well for the platform. There were real strong feelings on the matter. As I said, it took several funerals over a period of years before the old-timers would let go.

Do you think the name will be changed back again to the Prohibition Party?

Yes. I think that's probably in the cards. In states like Alabama, Colorado, and Kansas, people were asking, "New Statesman Party—what's that?" But you'd say the old Prohibition Party, and they knew just exactly what you were talking about. So I think we'll go back to the old name. The drinking problem is getting out of hand, so I think we've got to do it.

THE PRESIDENTIAL CAMPAIGNS

You indicated that you became active in the Prohibition Party in the 1950s. How did you end up as the party's presidential nominee in 1976 and 1980?

Well, I attended a couple of national party conventions. They'd been after me to try to help. They wanted a younger fellow, but I had more than I could handle right here with this work. Then, I finally agreed to go as a candidate for president in 1976.

What were the 1976 and 1980 campaigns like? Did you go out and visit a lot of different states?

Yes, we traveled quite a bit in 1976. We were on the ballot in fourteen states, and we visited every one of those states. In 1980, however, we were only on the ballot in eight states, and I didn't campaign much. We didn't have the money.

Was it difficult for you to get on the state ballots?

You said it! The Democratic and Republican Parties are fighting hard to keep the third parties off the ballot. They say they both support the free-enterprise system, but they sure don't want any competition in their own backyard. Massachusetts is a pretty good example. They now require about 60,000 names to be on the ballot down there. We didn't even make it on the ballot here in my home state. We listened to the Democratic attorney general and the Republican secretary of state, or just the reverse, and they botched everything up so we couldn't even run in Maine. Otherwise, we would have been on the ballot.

How did you actually campaign in 1976? Did you give a lot of speeches and hold public rallies?

Usually we held a news interview. We'd meet with a group of church people and have a small rally. It was pretty low-budget, low-key. To give you one example, we spent three days in Colorado. The American Broadcasting people sent out a crew of four people to cover us. They flew into Denver and hired a car. Then they went with us to Fort Collins and some of the surrounding towns. ABC spent more money on those four people than we did on our entire national campaign budget.

How much did the party spend on the 1976 campaign?

I would say it was probably around $15,000. It was mainly for travel and a few brochures we had printed up.

You mentioned the ABC crew. What about general media coverage? Did the press pay much attention to you?

It was exceptionally good. I had been warned, "Ben, you have a thick hide, so don't let it bother you, but you're going to take an awful razzing." I didn't find this at all. The press would ask me if I really planned to go to the White House. I looked back at them and replied, "Do I look that stupid?" Then they'd ask me why I was running. I told them we've got some issues that need to be discussed. It gave us a springboard. We have a political message that we think America needs. We're not going to the White House, and we may not win, but we're having an impact. If you don't believe that the Prohibition Party has had an impact, just go and look at all the programs we've initiated over the years. So we got some good coverage in areas we visited—Denver, Topeka, Wichita, Knoxville, Chattanooga. They gave us front-page coverage.

Political campaigns are getting more and more expensive. You indicated you didn't have enough money to campaign in 1980. How does the party plan to deal with this in the future?

Well, I hope we're going to be a little bit more practical and go after more money, like Jerry Falwell does, for instance. It's out there. The problem is lack of communication. I attended the party's executive committee meeting in June out in Coldwater, Michigan, which, incidentally, was a good place for them to meet. There were a few bruises that came out of the session, because I rode herd on them. I thought we should put the brass knuckles on and get across to the general public; get the message out to the American people; hire a commercial firm to raise money and spread the word; hire somebody who knows what they're doing.

What was their reaction to this suggestion?

They felt it was a little un-Christian to use these tactics, but I think we're coming to it.

PERSONAL IMPRESSIONS

You just mentioned Rev. Jerry Falwell in connection with fund raising. Many people are expressing concern that fundamentalist religious groups are becoming more active in politics. Are you associated with the Moral Majority movement?

We agree with them on a number of issues, but we're not officially tied in with them. We're independent. We have a much broader range of concerns than the Moral Majority. The thing that really separates us off, I'll grant, is the stand we've taken on alcohol and drugs. Jerry Falwell is steering away from that. He's taken no stand at all. I've met him a few times, but I'm not intimately acquainted with him. You read their material. They absolutely will not get involved with the drug trade.

How do you feel about groups like the Moral Majority getting actively involved in politics? Do you think there is a danger that they will try to impose their own brand of morality on everyone else?

As I told you, we support the separation of church and state, although we think the courts have gone too far in prohibiting free exercise of religion. The Moral Majority may be a little carried away in some of their tactics; I'm really not close enough to them to know.

We're definitely against religious discrimination of any kind. We've pledged to end this kind of activity in our platform. You may be a Jehovah's Witness; I may be a rabid Baptist. I don't agree with a lot of your philosophy, but you have just as much right to stand up and propound your philosophy as long as you don't interfere with me. I'll stand on one street corner and shout, and you can stand on the other corner and shout even louder because you're younger than me. That's American liberty. We have a platform on religious liberty. We believe in the freedom of individuals to worship, evangelize, and educate in accordance with their beliefs.

Are you optimistic about the future of the country and the party?

Yes. Maybe I shouldn't be, but I'm optimistic. There are a lot of signs that people are beginning to wake up. For instance, tax revolt groups are growing. People are tired of having the government throw away their money. We spend millions of dollars telling people not to smoke, but then we spend millions more subsidizing the tobacco industry. It doesn't make any sense at all. I think people are becoming concerned enough about the decline in the value of our currency and the decline in the quality of our public life to demand changes.

Let me conclude with a question about personal motivation. What drives someone like you to run for president of the United States in the light of such overwhelming odds? Is it personal satisfaction? Some set of political ideals? A sense of duty to the party?

My wife says I have a very perverted sense of humor, or I wouldn't stay involved. But actually we've got a message we think America needs to hear. We believe in a representative republic, but what we've got right now is a socialist democracy bordering on anarchy. This is bad. Everybody is doing his own thing. When America was growing, becoming great and having worldwide respect, we were a representative republic.

So we have a message we think America needs. We've lost our first love, which was honesty and integrity in government. We've lost pride in serving as public officials. Men of integrity don't want to run. There's no national pride in public office. It's even difficult to get people right here in Waterville to run for local office. Why? Because the public has contempt for government.

If we don't turn this around, we are going to fall like Rome fell. We're rotting from within. Our public officials lack integrity. We raise their salaries, and the more they get, the poorer the quality of men and women who are willing to serve in public office. I think we have to turn this around. This is what keeps me going.

What about the future? Do you plan to stay active in the party?

Yes, it has been worth it to help get the message across, but I won't be a candidate for president again. I've already climbed up that mountain twice, and I didn't get very far. It's time for some of the younger people to take over. Political parties have been coming and going ever since this country was organized. This is the oldest third party. If we get some fresh, new, young leadership, we'll be around for a long time to come.

4 VOICES FROM THE LEFT

The four oldest third parties, after the Prohibitionists, that ran candidates in the 1980 presidential election were the Socialists (organized in 1901), the Communists (1919), the Socialist Workers Party (1938), and the Workers World Party (1959). All four of these groups fall under the heading "doctrinal parties," a phrase coined by V. O. Key, and all are commonly classified as leftist.

Although the terms *left* and *right* are now used widely, and often quite loosely, to characterize many facets of American political life, they did not originate in the United States. "*Left* and *Right* were first used as political terms in France during the Revolution of 1789, but the precise circumstances of the origin of this usage are obscure. . . . What is certain is that within a very short time, the more revolutionary deputies were sitting on the left of the National Assembly and the more conservative on the right."[1]

The terms *left* and *right* gradually spread to other countries, including the United States, where they have been used to characterize political movements according to their underlying ideologies. As a general rule, parties on the left have been viewed as more liberal in that they advocate political change and believe that the state is primarily responsible for economic and social welfare, while parties on the right are viewed as more conservative in that they are skeptical about change and emphasize individual freedom rather than state intervention.

The various socialist- and communist-oriented parties in America have been marked by the same types of divisions, splits, mergers, and realignments that have characterized these groups on the international scene. To appreciate the distinctions between the different American parties, it is helpful to gain an understanding of the ideological roots of the socialist and communist movements that emerged in Europe during the nineteenth century.

Despite their broad, everyday usage, the words socialism and communism are often surrounded by considerable confusion and ambiguity. In its most general sense, socialism describes any economic doctrine that advocates the collective public ownership of productive property and natural resources as a means of promoting the common welfare.[2]

The concept itself is very old, and throughout history it has taken quite varied forms—guild socialism, utopian socialism, evolutionary socialism, syndicalism, and even anarchism, to name but a few. The modern origins of the socialist political movement, as we know it today, first appeared in Europe in the late eighteenth and early nineteenth centuries, when a number of visionaries began to advocate idealized communal settlements that were designed to achieve spontaneous social harmony. These were the original "utopian Socialists" who believed that such communities could be realized peacefully through the altruistic cooperation of the privileged classes. Saint-Simon (1760–1825), Robert Owen (1771–1858), and Charles Fourier (1772–1837) were among those who were quite successful in spreading utopian concepts. "By 1840, the term socialism was commonly used throughout Europe to connote the doctrine that the ownership and control of the means of production—capital, land, or property—should be held by the community as a whole and administered in the interests of all."[3]

The modern doctrine of communism grew out of a reformulation of these utopian socialist concepts. Communism advocates a social and economic system in which there is no private property. Instead, capital and consumers' goods are held in common by all workers.[4] The movement literally exploded onto the world scene with the publication of *The Communist Manifesto* in 1848 by two German revolutionary theorists, Karl Marx (1818–83) and Friedrich Engels (1820–95), who advanced a new theory of history that is often called "scientific socialism."

Marx believed that the utopian Socialists were naive and

even simple minded in their belief that the privileged classes could ever develop a socialist society through altruistic, cooperative means. Instead, he held that a new social order—namely, communism—would result only from class conflict and class struggle.

In *The Communist Manifesto* Marx and Engels argued that this struggle would occur between two groups—the proletariat (the industrial working class, or "wage slaves") and the bourgeoisie (the capitalist "owners of the means of social production and employers of wage labor").[5] They contended that the inherent contradictions in capitalism made it inevitable that the proletariat would eventually destroy the bourgeoisie. In a later work, entitled *Socialism: Utopian and Scientific* (1880), Engels predicted that once the proletariat had triumphed, the state would become unnecessary since its only purpose was to protect the propertied classes, and would die out naturally.[6] The result would be pure communism, a classless society.

Because Marx and Engels were convinced that they had uncovered a universal theory of history, they advocated internationalism from the very beginning. In the words of *The Communist Manifesto*, "the proleterians have nothing to lose but their chains; they have the world to win. Workingmen of all countries, unite!"[7] Marx helped to lead the First International, which was held in London in 1864, in an attempt to unify small political and trade union groups to carry out the aims of *The Manifesto*. The First International, which was a failure as a result of internal ideological conflicts, was followed by the Second, or Socialist, International, organized by Engels after Marx's death and held in Paris in 1889.

The failure of the First International foreshadowed future splits between various socialist and communist factions. Once Marxism began to spread throughout Europe, bitter ideological disagreements arose as to what strategies were most appropriate to bring about the economic and political transformations of society that Marx had predicted.

The more moderate socialist parties, such as the Fabians in

England and the Social Democrats under Eduard Bernstein in Germany, called for a gradual form of evolutionary, or democratic socialism that would work through the machinery of the existing state.[8] They advocated mass democratic political parties that would nationalize the basic means of industrial production through a system of public ownership.

A second, more militant approach, which was advanced by other factions, argued that revolutionary means should be used to overthrow the existing state machinery in order to hasten the arrival of the new society. This second approach found two of its most influential advocates in Russia—Vladimir Ilyich Lenin (1870–1924) and Leon Trotsky (1879–1940).

Although Marx had predicted that the breakdown in capitalism would first occur in the most advanced industrial nations, it was the decay of backward agrarian Russia that paved the way for the emergence of the modern Communist Party. In 1898, a group of Russian revolutionaries secretly organized the Russian Workers Social-Democratic Party. The party soon split over questions of strategy between the Bolsheviks (the "majority" or *bolsheviki*), led by Lenin, and the Mensheviks (the "minority" or *mensheviki*), led by Plekhanov. Whereas the Mensheviks argued for a gradual revolutionary approach, the Bolsheviks argued for a more direct and immediate revolutionary overthrow of the existing regime.

In a paper published in 1902, entitled *What Is To Be Done?*, Lenin argued that the workers, left to themselves, would never be able to achieve a Marxist state because they would develop "trade union consciousness" and be bought off by concessions from the bourgeois class. Hence, it was necessary to organize an elite vanguard party, led by a highly centralized and disciplined organization of professional revolutionaries,[9] to act on behalf of the workers in order to bring about the revolutionary changes necessary to transform the existing state.* In a later

* It is important to recognize that the concept of the elite vanguard party remains operative in the Soviet Union today. Although many Americans be-

work, entitled *State and Revolution* (1917), Lenin expanded his theory by arguing that, while a communist society was eventually inevitable, as Marx had predicted, it was desirable to give history a push to speed up this process. In Lenin's words: "The replacement of the bourgeois by the proletarian state is impossible without a violent revolution."[10] Leon Trotsky also formulated a doctrine of revolutionary strategy in 1905 that became known as "the theory of permanent revolution." According to Trotsky, the proletariat must take the lead in enlisting the peasantry in revolutionary activity, and this must be done on a worldwide, rather than a country-by-country, basis. Trotsky held that the only way to guarantee the success of the revolution inside Russia was by fostering genuine revolutions in other "overripe" capitalist countries outside Russia.[11]

Hence, it can be said that, while Marx and Engels were the theoreticians of the "ends" of scientific socialism (namely, pure communism, the death of the state, a classless society), Lenin and Trotsky advocated the "means" that should be used to bring about a communist society (that is, a vanguard elite party that would organize the revolution). Many of the other socialist parties did not accept these means. While some still called themselves Marxist, they did not accept the more revolutionary Marxist-Leninist strategies that were advocated by Lenin or Trotsky.

The story now leaves the realm of theory for the realm of history. By 1917, Russia was suffering severely as a result of staggering losses in World War I. The Germans, sensing a chance to further weaken the Russians, arranged to ship Lenin back to Russia from Switzerland (where he was in exile) in a sealed railway car. In April 1917, Lenin arrived at Finland Station in Petrograd (now Leningrad), where he immediately plunged into bolshevik activity. The result was the October Revolution of 1917, which led to the bolshevik take-over of

---

lieve that all Russians are members of the Communist Party, it is actually an elite organization and less than 10 percent of the population qualifies to join.

Russia. In 1918, the Workers Social Democratic Party renamed itself the Communist Party, and it renamed Russia the Union of Soviet Socialist Republics. In 1919, the Third, or Communist, International (known as the Comintern) was organized in Moscow to replace the Second Socialist International, which had broken up in 1914 as a result of the First World War.

Once he assumed power, Lenin installed Trotsky as the people's commissar for foreign affairs, and later as commissar for war. Trotsky was charged with the monumental task of organizing the Red Army in the civil war that followed the revolution. When Lenin died in 1924, a bitter power struggle broke out between the followers of Trotsky and the followers of Joseph Stalin, who was serving as general secretary of the Communist Party. Stalin succeeded in solidifying his power, and Trotsky was eventually expelled from the Soviet Union in 1929.

While in exile, Trotsky launched increasingly bitter attacks on the excesses of the Stalin dictatorship, which he saw as a betrayal of the communist ideal. Up until 1934–35, Trotsky advocated reforms within the Soviet Union. He broke with Stalin completely after Stalin executed many of the old Bolsheviks in the Moscow purge trials of 1936–38. Finally, in 1938, Trotsky called for the formation of a new Fourth International to overthrow the bureaucratic dictatorship of Stalin's personal rule by means of worldwide revolution.

The political parties on the left in the United States have been deeply influenced by the ideological divisions and historic events described above. The first leftist party in American politics, the Socialist Labor Party, was organized in 1876–77 as an outgrowth of the First International. In 1901, dissident members of the Socialist Labor Party split off to form the more moderate Socialist Party that resembled the English Fabian Society and the German Social Democrats. In 1919, more radical elements within the Socialist Party defected in response to the Third International (Comintern) and established the Communist Labor Party and the Communist Party of America; this latter party eventually merged into the Communist Party of the United States. In 1938, dissidents within the Communist Party USA broke away in response to Trotsky's call for a Fourth International to organize the Socialist Workers Party. Finally, in 1959, a splinter group within the Socialist Workers Party established the Workers World Party. A brief description of the Socialist, Communist, Socialist Workers, and Workers World Parties precedes the interviews with each of their 1980 presidential nominees.

THE SOCIALIST PARTY

The Socialist Party was officially organized in July 1901 at a unity convention held in Indianapolis, Indiana, that joined together dissident elements from the Socialist Labor Party with the Social Democratic Party of America that Eugene Debs had helped form in 1898.

The Socialist Labor Party was the first major socialist party in the United States, having been established by members of the First International in 1876. During the 1890s, the Socialist Labor Party was taken over by the autocratic Daniel DeLeon, a militant syndicalist, who ran the party with an iron hand. More moderate members of the party, led by Morris Hillquit, broke away from the Socialist Labor Party in 1901 to help form the new Socialist Party.

Eugene Victor Debs, the other major founder of the Socialist Party, was a labor activist who had served as president of the American Railway Union. An ardent pacifist, Debs was one of the leading figures in American socialism. Once he helped organize the new party, Debs totally committed himself to the socialist cause, running as the party's nominee for president in five different elections.

The Socialist Party made considerable headway in American politics at the turn of the century. In the presidential election of 1912, Debs received over 900,000 votes, and the Socialists elected many candidates to local offices, including thirty-four mayors. However, the party was badly damaged during World War I when many of its pacifist supporters, who refused to back the war effort, were accused of being sympathetic to German socialist ideals. As an offshoot of the anticommunist fears which began to sweep America after the Russian Revolution of 1917, other critics sneeringly criticized the socialist movement as "bolshevism with a shave."

Debs himself was caught up in the hysteria of the times. In 1918, he was convicted of violating the Espionage Act as the result of a speech he had given in Canton, Ohio, when he opposed the country's entry into the war. He was sentenced to ten years in prison. This led to the dramatic election of 1920, when Debs ran as the Socialist Party's candidate for president of the United States as convict number 9653 from Atlanta Federal Penitentiary and received 919,799 votes! President Harding pardoned Debs in 1921. Debs spent the last five years of his life in ill health, still speaking out for socialist causes, before he died in 1926. The Socialist Party had reached its all-time high vote in the 1920 election, though one of its most prominent members, Victor Berger, continued to be elected to Congress from Wisconsin from 1922 through 1929.

Following Debs's death, the leadership of the Socialist Party passed to Norman Thomas, a Presbyterian minister and social worker. Thomas ran as the party's presidential candidate in six successive elections from 1928 to 1948. A pacifist and an advocate of evolutionary socialism, Thomas had helped form the American Civil Liberties Union, and he advocated many innovative social ideas that were incorporated into Democràtic Party programs.[12] He received his greatest number of popular votes, 881,951, in the 1932 election, but thereafter his total declined steadily, though he did manage to capture 139,572 votes in the 1948 election.

When Thomas declined to run again for president in 1952, the Socialist Party named Darlington Hoopes as its candidate, and he also ran in 1956. The party's support dropped drastically, and Hoopes received only a little over 2,000 votes in the 1956 election. After 1956, the party suffered from such serious internal divisions that it did not run a candidate for the next twenty years. Finally, in 1976, the Socialists were reactivated, and they named Frank Zeidler, the former socialist mayor of Milwaukee, as their presidential nominee. Zeidler received just over 6,000 votes.

In the 1980 election, the Socialist Party designated David McReynolds, an antiwar activist, as its presidential candidate. McReynolds, age fifty, worked for the War Resisters' League in New York City. The party's vice-presidential nominee was

Sister Diane Drufenbrock, a fifty-one-year-old nun and school-teacher from Milwaukee. The Socialist Party candidates were on the ballot in ten states. They received a total of 6,898 votes in the 1980 election.

I interviewed McReynolds in his small, crowded, corner office at the War Resisters' League, 339 Lafayette Street, New York City, in June 1981. A soft-spoken, reflective, and remarkably open man, he offered his own overview of the role of the leftist parties in American politics during the past three decades.

David McReynolds

I don't think you can separate means from ends because the means will dictate the ends you are going to have.

PERSONAL BACKGROUND

Smallwood: Let's start with your own personal background. When did you first get involved in politics?

McReynolds: Well, no one believes it any more, but my first involvement with politics was in the Prohibition Party. I grew up in Los Angeles where I was raised in the Baptist Church as a Fundamentalist, and I drifted into the Prohibition Party.

When was this?

It must have been back in 1946 or 1947. I was about sixteen years old at the time, still in high school. I was very young, very interested in politics, and I enjoyed public speaking. I was also a very devout Christian. Someone in my church was active in the Prohibition Party, so I simply got involved with them. I was the ideological leader of their youth section. I drafted all the policy statements. However, I was already becoming left wing in my views, so I resigned after a couple of years. At the same time I was in the process of resigning, the Prohibition Party expelled the entire youth section for being Communists. This didn't have a shred, not the slightest basis, of truth, but they perceived our politics as such because they couldn't see how we could be left wing without being Communists. In fact, I was somewhat pro-Soviet at the time. This was in the period when the cold war had just begun, so when I had a chance to go to Europe in 1949, I jumped at it.

Did you go to Europe to study?

No, I went to a pacifist youth conference. I had become a pacifist in 1949. It was a very turbulent time in my life. I realized I was a homosexual, I had left Christianity behind, and then I went on to become an alcoholic. I'm now a recovered alcoholic, but that was a very difficult and confusing time for me.

When did you join the Socialist Party?

I became a pacifist back in 1948–49, and I officially joined the Socialist Party in 1951.

Where were you living at that time?

I was still in Los Angeles where I went to college at UCLA. In 1953, during the Korean War, I refused induction into the armed forces because I was a pacifist. I was arrested, but the charges were dismissed because of technical errors in the government's case, so I finished my undergraduate work at UCLA in 1953.

Then I left Los Angeles for New York City where I've been ever since. I got a job as editorial secretary for *Liberation* magazine, the radical pacifist journal founded by Dave Dellinger and A. J. Muste. In 1954, I was elected to the National Committee of the Socialist Party, and that's where I worked closely with Norman Thomas and a lot of other socialist leaders.

When did you get involved with the War Resisters' League?

Let's see, it's been twenty years. However, I've also remained active in socialist politics during this period. The founders of the league were feminist women suffragettes who were members of the Socialist Party. They supported Eugene Debs and engaged in antiwar activities. Back in those days, if you were antiwar, you were usually involved with the Socialist Party. Today, I'm the only Socialist on the staff. Everyone else here is an anarchist, but the Socialist Party has had a long symbiotic relationship with the league, even though it's informal and unofficial.

Have you always been active only with the Socialist Party? Didn't you run for a congressional seat back in 1968 for the Peace and Freedom Party?

Yes, but I ran as a socialist candidate on the Peace and Freedom ticket. I was still a Socialist. It was a party decision for me to run. However, I was involved in a bitter struggle within the Socialist Party at the time, so I was halfway hoping they would expel me. It was a very difficult period, but that's a long story, and I'm not sure you want to go into that particular phase of our history.

HISTORICAL OBSERVATIONS

Quite frankly, I would like to get a little historical perspective from you. You've been involved with the American left for three decades, almost the entire post-World War II period. First, I'd like to know what happened to the Socialist Party. You didn't even run any presidential candidates between 1960 and 1976. Did the party self-destruct through internal dissension during this period?

No, not actually. Self-destruct is too strong a word. The party is in about the same position today as it was in 1956, except that our membership now is younger, which means we are stronger. I'd estimate we have about 700 to 800 members today, but that's all we had back in the mid-1950s.

You see, the Socialist Party did not really exist after 1948, but it thought it did. That was the year Norman Thomas ran in his last election, and he got well over 100,000 votes. The party thought it existed because, although the official membership was very small, actually tiny, hundreds of trade union leaders— shop stewards up to people like Victor and Walter Reuther— thought of themselves as Socialists. They weren't actually members of the party, but they thought of us as their party. If they didn't vote for us, they thought they would vote for us in the next election. If they didn't pay dues, they thought they would get around to it if we asked them to do so.

They had an emotional, psychological, historic attachment to the party. Yet, the reality was that we had a huge reservoir of sympathizers who thought of us as "their" party, but they didn't pay dues and they didn't actively support the party. It was obvious that we were in trouble, and that's when the internal dissension began.

How did that come about?

All during the 1950s, we considered different strategies. In the 1956 election, we got almost no votes. Darlington Hoopes, our presidential candidate, only got a couple of thousand votes, and that's the last time we ran candidates until 1976. We thought about running in 1960. We sent up a trial balloon. We saw some people in Congress. We thought about running Norman Thomas and Martin Luther King. That was the balloon we floated. We thought about it seriously, but it didn't go anywhere.

We also considered another strategy, which involved reaching out to other groups on the left in an effort to expand our base. This was when I made a big mistake, because I urged that we bring in Max Shachtman and Michael Harrington, the leaders of the Independent Socialist League, which was a Trotskyite splinter group. Shachtman, as you probably know, had helped to organize the Socialist Workers Party. I brought him into our party, not alone, but with the help of Norman Thomas.

However, Norman did not want Harrington in, but I persuaded him to yield on this. So both Shachtman and Harrington came into the Socialist Party in the late 1950s. It was a disastrous mistake, because the Shachtmanite group moved very far to the right. Eventually, they got control of the party, and dragged a lot of other people along with them.

Why did a Trotskyist splinter group favor a move to the right?

They argued that we should adopt a "realignment" strategy. They felt that what this country needed wasn't a third party, but a meaningful second party. So they attempted to align the Socialist Party more closely with the labor unions and with the Democratic Party, in order to gain more power within these groups.

However, in practice, this meant toning down all our positions. The realignment people were opposed to anything that separated us from labor or from Israel. So over time, they opposed the entire New Left movement because it irritated the AFL-CIO hierarchy, and eventually they ended up supporting the Vietnam War in order to appease the patriotism of labor leaders like George Meany. The Shachtman wing of the realignment caucus even opposed George McGovern in 1972, ostensibly because he was "soft" on communism! It was really devastating. They moved very far to the right, and many of them have stayed there. Now half of the hard-core Shachtmanites are over at the United Nations under Jeane Kirkpatrick, and the other half are down in Washington working for the CIA and serving as an unpaid lobby for the state of Israel.

Did the issue of Israel have a lot to do with the internal dissension?

Yes, it did, but in a very ambiguous way. Outside of New York, the Socialist Party has always had close relationships with the anti-Zionist International Jewish Labor Bund. The bund, or what's left of it since many of them were killed off by Hitler or Stalin, is made up of Jewish Socialists who did not support the creation of the state of Israel.

The reason for this is because Marx advocated international socialism. However, Zionism calls for the creation of a new national state, which is quite contrary to the Marxist international philosophy. So the Socialist Party's position was never strongly linked with Israel. We call for recognition of the PLO, for example, but under Max Shachtman, for reasons which are not clear to me, we began to compromise on Israel.

I've never quite understood what happened to Max Shachtman, the revolutionary, the Trotskyist. He was never my leader, but I thought it would be good to have him in the Socialist Party. However, he swung way over into supporting the Vietnam War, and he carried along Mike Harrington until 1971, when Mike finally broke with him. I've never understood what happened to Max. That's an interesting question.

How did the party ever resolve these internal conflicts?

It finally came to a head in the early 1970s. Actually, I had left the party temporarily in 1971 over the Vietnam issue, since I, as a pacifist, couldn't support the war. The whole thing was totally contrary to the principles of the Socialist Party as far as I was concerned, since historically we've been pacifists.

By 1972, the party was divided into a number of different factions. On the far right was the realignment caucus which consisted of the orthodox Shachtmanites who supported the Vietnam War and a lot of other reactionary causes. Second, there was the coalition caucus which was made up of the more moderate Shachtmanites who followed Mike Harrington after he split with Max. Then there was the Debs caucus, of which I had been a member. We advocated the more liberal policies of the old Socialist Party.

In the 1972 election, Shachtman's realignment group supported Henry Jackson for president, since he was the biggest hawk. Mike Harrington's coalition caucus supported McGovern. The Debs caucus backed Dr. Benjamin Spock, who was running on the Peoples Party ticket. After the election, Shachtman's realignment caucus, which still controlled the most power in the party, voted to change our name from the Socialist Party to Social Democrats USA.

That was their fatal mistake, thank God. Once they did this, the entire old party—the old Norman Thomas grouping you are familiar with—left overnight. It was amazing. They felt they could not leave until the name was changed, and you have to be an old party person to understand why that was so important. They had managed to put up with all the right-wing nonsense of the Shachmanites out of a sense of party loyalty.

However, once the name was changed, they felt they had permission to resign, and they left in droves because they no longer had this sense of historic allegiance to the old Socialist Party.

Within three months, this older group—Darlington Hoopes, Frank Zeidler, the Los Angeles local, and the rest—had reorganized as the Socialist Party again. So there was a three-month hiatus when the party did not actually have an existence. Then all the old members came back together to reorganize the historic party.

The Socialist Party today, of which I was a candidate in 1980, grew out of this reorganization. The former national secretary, the former national committee people, virtually all of the former candidates came back into the reorganized party, so we look at ourselves, without any question, as the legitimate heirs of the old Debs-Thomas party. In 1976, we nominated Frank Zeidler, who had served as socialist mayor of Milwaukee for twelve years until 1960, as our presidential candidate. Frank represents our claim to our historic legitimacy. He still serves as chairman of the reorganized party.

What about the Harrington group? Did they rejoin the party?

No. That was an interesting development. Immediately after the old party reorganized in 1972, Mike realized that he was vulnerable, he could be voted down by the Shachtmanites in the Social Democrats USA. Right wing as he was, he was much too far to the left of that reactionary group. So he pulled out and did a very effective job establishing the Democratic Socialist Organizing Committee, or DSOC. This is not a political party, nor are the Social Democrats USA a party any longer. Both groups function within the Democratic Party, and they both supported Jimmy Carter in 1976.

We have no interest in working with the Social Democrats USA, but we do maintain liaison with the DSOC group, and perhaps some day we may get together again. The final result of all this bickering is that the Socialist Party today is just about where it was in 1956. We have reorganized around the old socialist principles of the historic party. We lost almost twenty years between 1956 and 1976 due to internal conflicts, but we didn't disappear and we're now trying to rebuild our historic base again.

One of the oldest historic parties on the left actually does seem to have disappeared. The Socialist Labor Party ran candidates in every presidential election from 1892 to 1976, but suddenly in 1980, they didn't nominate anyone. Do you know what happened to them?

I really don't know. I was stunned when they didn't run. I think it may have been because Arnold Petersen died. He was their general secretary for years, and I'm told by people who know the party that he ran things with an iron hand. It's always been sort of a strange autocratic party. Daniel DeLeon, who was one of their original leaders at the turn of the century, was also a rigid disciplinarian who ran the party with an iron hand.

Actually, I think the party has been a dead organization for a long time. I'm not being at all bitter about this, and I'm not being vindictive. They were dead before I was born. They died sometime between 1910 and 1920. In all of my years in political life, I've never met anyone from the Socialist Labor Party at a peace demonstration, a trade union demonstration, a civil rights demonstration, any demonstration. The only time I ever saw any of them was on the street corner handing out flyers. It was sort of a "you come to us when you're ready" approach, because they certainly weren't very aggressive in going out to the people. So when Petersen died, I think that what little was left of the party began to reevaluate what it is, and it doesn't know any more. Petersen defined reality for it, but now they had to encounter actual reality, and there wasn't anything there.

The strangest thing of all is that I understand the party is very well funded. They have a half-million dollars in the bank, but the membership is down to a couple of hundred people, and their average age is sixty-five or seventy. The money came from estates that were bequeathed. It's honest money from the hardworking middle class, sort of skilled workers, second generation, third generation. They earned modest amounts of money and left some of it in their wills for the party. If you wait long enough, even modest amounts of money can build up over time, and now I understand it's something like a half-million dollars.

Politics can certainly take some strange twists and turns. They have the money, but they don't have any membership. Now the few of them who remain feel that everyone's after their bank account, so they are more withdrawn than ever. It's very strange.

POLITICAL IDEOLOGY

Tell me about your political philosophy. What positions do you advocate?

I consider myself to be a Marxist. The Socialist Party is not a Marxist organization, and many Socialists won't say they're Marxists because they think it's like believing in God where you have to have absolute faith. That's not true. I don't think that Marx was infallible, but I do think he was right when he analyzed economic class conflict as the basis of the other conflicts in society. So I favor the abolition of capitalism in favor of socialism.

Why are you opposed to capitalism?

Because it can never provide full employment. Capitalism, by its nature, cannot deal with the unemployment problem, nor can it provide for an equitable distribution of goods. In that sense, it's unworkable. It doesn't produce for human needs; its method of production must be for profit. You can't expect it to work on any other basis because it's based on a belief in the profit motive. Everything flows from that. In theory, it produces what you want. In reality, however, it produces things you may not want, but you are told you want, and it may not produce a lot of things you desperately need. For instance, it doesn't produce adequate health care, but it produces lots of cigarettes. It also produces the desire for these cigarettes. I'm saying this as a smoker. I'm not hostile to smokers. My desire to smoke was produced by advertising. I didn't grow up with the desire. It was advertised into me. This is only one example of the profit motive in action. We don't think that's how a society should be run.

Virtually all the parties on the left are opposed to capitalism. What distinguishes the Socialist Party from the rest of them?

There is one very major difference, one really huge distinction, that separates the Socialists from the Leninist or Trotskyist parties. The Leninist position holds that there must be a vanguard party which assumes the responsibility on behalf of the workers to bring about the socialist state. Lenin argued that this vanguard party should be made up of a small, highly disciplined party cadre who would theoretically represent, and act on behalf of, the working class. He also argued that liberation of the oppressed workers was impossible without revolution. Trotsky advocated these same basic concepts, and perhaps even went further than Lenin in calling for a permanent, worldwide revolution.

The Socialist Party never accepted these ideas. We think they may have made sense in Russia under the czar—that's an historic discussion one can have—but we do not accept the Leninist model for Western countries, and certainly not for this country. We don't think there has to be a vanguard party, and we don't advocate revolution because, as I've told you, many of us are pacifists. We don't view ourselves as a vanguard party. We assume there may be many different parties that all have validity, and we can conceive of working with many of them.

Basically, are your differences with these other parties over the means which should be used to bring about the ends of a socialist society?

Yes, that's correct. I don't think you can separate means from ends because the means will dictate the ends you are going to have. I think this is an error the Leninists have tended to make. History is not mechanical, it is not scientific, it's not even rational. However, I do think it is true that if you tend to lie, you'll tend to end up with a lying society. If you manipulate, you'll tend to end up with a manipulative society. You'd be well advised not to use these methods if you want a non-manipulative, honest, and decent society.

The Socialist Party is committed to peaceful means to achieve our goals. In terms of ends, we want a lot of the same things that Leninist and Trotskyist parties want, or at least they say they want. We favor social ownership of the basic means of production, with democratic controls and decentralization. We advocate an end to racism and sexism, including human rights and full equality for lesbians and gays. We strongly support affirmative action programs, better health-care programs, and the ratification of ERA. We call for the crash development of safe solar energy instead of nuclear power. We think the United States should unilaterally decommission its nuclear weapons. We favor disarmament for survival of the human race. In the Middle East, we support the right of the Palestinian people to their own state. We are opposed to the terrorism of both the PLO and the Israeli strikes into Lebanon. We believe peace cannot be achieved without a dialogue with the PLO.

We're willing to work within the system in an effort to achieve these ends. Personally, I believe strongly in the electoral part of the system. I also believe in strikes, demonstrations, and being arrested if necessary. However, I do believe in the chance of being able to validate your position in the polling place. I don't rule out the possibility of winning significant change in that way. So I'm thinking much more of Martin Luther King's mass movement approach than in some bizarre ultraleft terrorism. I'm thinking of the old American pattern of mass action, demonstrations, and elections.

Do you think it will ever be possible for the parties of the left to get together in light of the difference you've described? What about the Communists?

This may surprise you, but they're pretty predictable. They broke away from the Socialists in 1919. For years, they were simply a mouthpiece for the Kremlin, the only American political party that literally had direct ties with another country. They no longer have formal ties with the international communist movement, but they defend most Soviet actions so it's not hard to figure out where they're coming from on issues which involve the USSR.

Although we don't have much to do with them, in practice the Communists are pretty easy to work with, except on issues which directly involve the Soviet Union. The Trotskyists are really much more committed to the vanguard party theory than the Communists. The Communist Party is committed to it as a kind of eventuality, but they've been hit on the head so many times by reality—they've had to put up with the excesses of Stalin and all the rest—that many of them don't have true faith any more. When I was a kid, the Communists had true faith. They don't have this any more. They're plodding along. They're like Methodists as opposed to Fundamentalists. The party is their church, but they're not very excited about it any more. They're really a little dull and boring.

What about the other parties on the left, like the Socialist Workers and Workers World, that grew out of the Trotsky movement? Are they more complicated?

More complicated! Are you kidding? The Trotskyists will drive you nuts. At least they drive me nuts. You see, they went through a splitting process much different than the Communists. The Communist Party in its modern form was organized in response to a major historic event, the Russian Revolution. They felt no apologies at all when they split from the socialist parties. They didn't have to study or think too much. Russia was there to give them the answers. The Communists supported Lenin's twenty-one demands,* and we didn't, so they

*Lenin's twenty-one demands were imposed in 1920 as the ideological conditions required to join the Third, or Communist, International, which was organized in Moscow after the Russian Revolution.

left. That was it. They left. Period. We didn't ask them back in. There was some bitterness, but we went off in our different directions.

The Trotskyists emerged in the late 1930s because Leon Trotsky disagreed with Stalin. After Stalin gained control of the Communist Party, he expelled Trotsky from the Soviet Union, and Trotsky spent the rest of his life as an exile. However, the key point is that Trotsky split with Stalin for ideological reasons—not because of a revolution, but because of disagreements over ideology. As a result, the first thing the Trotskyists have to explain is why they broke away. Listen to them some time. They're more concerned with explaining what's wrong with the Soviet Union than what's right with their own political views.

So they start off from a defensive position, and I think this accounts for the neuroticism of the Trotskyist movement. It's a neurotic movement. Everyone in it has read a thousand books; they all carry on intense ideological discussions; and they've had endless splits. They are committed to endless, irreparable splits and splinters. Communists don't have splits that bad. Even Socialists don't have splits that bad, despite what I've just told you about our own party. But get together with Trotskyists, and you are dealing with people who have divisions and then more divisions, ad infinitum.

I have to trace this back to the fact that they originally grew out of an ideological split. All through their history, they have gone through the psychological process of explaining and justifying why they left. They spend their entire careers explaining what happened, what went wrong. They don't know what's going on in Russia today, but they do know every detail of what happened in Russia from the time Lenin crossed the border at Finland Station up to the time Trotsky was exiled. Maybe I'm exaggerating a bit. It's probably really not that bad. I find them easy to deal with as individuals, but very difficult to understand in any logical way.

Since you don't subscribe to the theory of the vanguard party, I assume that you don't accept the concept of democratic centralism. Is that correct?

Absolutely. I do not believe in democratic centralism. I emphatically don't. If you think about it, the whole concept is a contradiction in terms. In theory, the hierarchy of the party hands down the decisions—that's where the centralism comes in—and then the party workers at the local level are supposed to follow these decisions—that's where democracy is supposed to come in. However, this isn't democracy at all. It's exactly the form of rigid party discipline that Lenin advocated. I don't believe in that at all.

In describing your basic philosophy, you've advocated an evolutionary approach which is designed to achieve socialism through the existing system. How long are you prepared to wait for this?

It can't be done overnight, so that's an academic discussion. One of the problems I face in talking to the younger Socialists is to try to get them to focus on what we can do today, tomorrow, and next year, not to fight within the party over what level we're going to socialize business. If we had power tomorrow—which we're not going to have—it would take us ten years to absorb and deal with the oil companies, GM, U.S. Steel, and Rockefeller's interest in Chase Manhattan. It would take us ten years to cope with that. After that, we could worry about small businesses, shopkeepers, small factories. I think in the long run, way down the line, factories employing fewer than 500 workers may eventually become cooperatives. However, I don't want to fight about that now. I don't want to fight about it next year, or for the next twenty years, because it's a long way off.

One final question on political ideology. There's a theory that the key role of third parties is to feed innovative ideas into the political system. For example, many of the so-called radical ideas Norman Thomas advocated are now part of everyday American life. Do you think this is a valid theory?

It's a theory that is only a half-truth. It's true that creative thinking cannot be done by large bureaucratic institutions. That's a contradiction in terms. All creative thinking must be done by smaller, minority groups, by definition. A lot of this then gets picked up if it is acceptable to the majority. However, a lot which makes sense does not get picked up, because it is not acceptable to the majority.

Norman always used to argue that they had accepted many of his ideas that they found useful to maintain the structure— social security, unemployment compensation, and things like that. However, he also said that they missed the central thing. They still had an unworkable capitalist system. That's absolutely correct from our point of view. It's an unworkable system. From where I live, this is not a workable system. So maybe they pick up some of the ideas, often pretty important ideas. However, if they miss the really big things, the central concepts, it's pretty difficult to argue that we have had a profound impact on American politics.

THE 1980 CAMPAIGN

When were you actually designated by the Socialist Party to run for president?

It was in Milwaukee. It was at a special convention called by the national committee, partly because we were very distraught at the events that were going on at that time. The convention was called over the Christmas holidays in 1979. We had approached the newly emerging Citizens Party to seek some sense of unity with them, but we failed to get them to agree to anything other than that they were obviously going to nominate Barry Commoner.

The Iranians had just taken the hostages, which really unnerved many of us. It left us with the feeling that we better have a socialist campaign. We felt it was urgent to be sure there was a peace candidate. Once we decided to have a campaign, I was the only candidate, so I was nominated unanimously.

Did the same convention designate the vice-presidential nominee?

Yes. They nominated Sister Diane Drufenbrock, a Catholic nun. She had served as treasurer of the party for a number of years. I was very pleased with the choice, because I hoped a woman would run, and she is very strong. However, I couldn't designate my own choice. That's not how the Socialist Party operates. It's not automatically true that I'm the spokesperson of the party. The convention and the national committee make the decisions. If I want to have any input, I have to go to the conventions and lobby with the rank and file like anyone else.

I think you ended up on the ballot in about ten states. Was this a problem for you?

Any third-party candidate has difficulty getting on the ballot because the state laws are deliberately restrictive. It's very much a rigged system, very carefully rigged. The election laws are rigged by the major parties to make access by any new party very hard. They don't really care whether the party is left or right. I think the new parties on the right have as much trouble getting on the ballot as we do, unless they can get the Democrats to help them take away votes from the Republicans. The Libertarians ended up getting on the ballot in all fifty states, but they had a hell of a lot of money to spend, and even then it wasn't easy.

What kind of a campaign did you run? Did you actually visit many different states?

Oh yes. I campaigned very hard. So did the others in our party. The two of us, Diane and I, were in about twenty-five states. I've lost track, because I took off from work here at least three months, but I actually ended up campaigning full-time for closer to six months.

Was money a problem for you?

Well, it was a personal problem, because I was on the party payroll during the campaign at only half my regular salary, and my regular salary isn't very much. We relied mostly on small contributions. One or two people gave $1,000. We raised

$25,000 for the campaign relatively easily, so we paid off all our debts. It wasn't hard to raise the money, and it's certainly not hard to spend it.

However, you have to understand that the purpose of running the campaign was basically to win new members. It was never our intention to run a really big campaign. Our intent was only to publish some posters, a couple of buttons, a basic campaign flyer, some bumper stickers. I think we also took out a number of small ads in places like *The Nation*, classified-type ads. The main thing we were trying to do was to go out and meet a lot of people to establish the fact that the party existed, to define the political positions of the party, and to recruit new members for the party.

Do you think you were treated fairly? Were you harassed at all?

I expected I would be harassed, but I was not. I had thought I would be harassed by the right wing. I had assumed there would be some heckling, because you had a gay candidate running, which is very rare. You never had a gay running for president before.

You know, there's something very interesting that happens when you're running for president, which I hadn't been aware of before I got involved. I'd like to write about this because it's not a very healthy thing. There's a mantle of authority that descends on you when you run for president. People ask you totally inane questions, but you're supposed to have an answer. They would discuss questions about their dog, or the dogcatcher, or the landlord, and you're supposed to resolve these because you're running for president. So there is an enormous mystical authority about all of this. This is a country where, if you run for president, it's like being a pretender to the throne. You're a pretender, but who knows? Kings have died and been replaced by the pretender. Stranger things have happened. There is an odd psychology that I was totally unaware of until I stepped into that role. On one hand, it makes you a target for an assassin; but on the other hand, it acts as a protection and a shield.

How about the press and the mass media? Did they treat you fairly?

We got some good local coverage, really good coverage in the state of Washington and in some other places. In the larger cities, our coverage was terrible.

I am absolutely furious about the League of Women Voters' decision to block us out of any television debates. It makes a mockery out of democracy. If I run again—which I don't rule out—I would begin with a sit-in at the League of Women Voters. I wouldn't have any negotiations. I wouldn't have any dialogue with them. I would just march down and sit in at their office. I would do the same thing at the major television studios, where there was not one minute of public time given to any of the minor-party candidates. The way to remedy that is not to talk next time, but to move. I'm really angry at a very deep level about that.

The more I reflect on the arrogance of the mass media, the more I realize how biased and undemocratic the system is in this respect. Actually, next time I think I'd start with Bill Moyers, even before the League of Women Voters. I'd march into his office and start with that S.O.B., because his people covered me all day on one of my campaign trips, and he didn't run one second of it. Bill Moyers had a special obligation, since the Public Broadcasting television system did not allow access to any of the minor-party candidates. Therefore, Bill Moyers prepared a special "Journal" program for PBS on the third parties. It was a farce. He touched on Barry Commoner, and he touched on John Anderson, and then, careful and courageous man that he is, he ignored the left parties completely. So I'd start with Bill Moyers. The way to get media coverage is to go sit in at their offices and get arrested. Then you'll get coverage because you'll be "newsworthy." I'm perfectly prepared to do that.

One last question on the campaign. Did you run into any interference from the government itself? Did you feel free to go out and speak wherever you wanted to go?

I assume that the government spies on me. They did during the Vietnam War. I have a long FBI file up there on a shelf somewhere. They think I've got a bad record because I've been arrested in a lot of antiwar protests, and I work for the War Resisters' League, where we provide counseling for young people who are opposed to the draft. So I assume that the surveillance never stops. It doesn't do them much good. I think they're wasting a lot of money.

Take the Socialist Workers Party trial. The government has wasted an enormous amount of the taxpayers' money, your money and my money, spying on the Socialist Workers Party. Within the left movement, they are the most legal people, the most appallingly legal people. The Communist Party is a close runner-up for legality, precisely because they know they're always being spied on. Anyway, no, the government didn't put any restrictions on our campaign, aside from people spying on us, which we just take for granted.

PERSONAL IMPRESSIONS

What's your overall impression of the 1980 campaign? Are you satisfied with the Socialist Party's performance?

In one sense it was discouraging. I had no illusion of winning or of getting 50,000 to 100,000 votes. However, I had hoped we could double the 6,000 votes Frank Zeidler got in 1976. I felt that, if everything really went well, we might get as many as 15,000 or 20,000 votes. We only got about 6,500. However, it was encouraging that, in almost every state where we were on the ballot, we did better than four years ago, except for Wisconsin. Frank's name pulled the vote in Wisconsin, where he got about 4,000 in 1976. However, I wasn't as well known out there, and this time our vote dropped to around 800. If you discount this, we made progress in virtually all the other states, so I think we accomplished what we set out to do, which was to give some credibility to the Socialist Party name.

That was really our basic objective. Where we could talk, wherever we could get radio time or local press coverage in the small towns, we attempted to define socialism as a thinkable concept, as a human concept, as a peaceful concept, as a democratic concept. That's what we set out to do, and I don't think you can really do it any other way except by running for office.

What about the future? Are you optimistic about the Socialist Party?

Yes, in one very important sense, I am optimistic. We're still very small, tiny in fact, but we're beginning to attract a lot of young people. The convention we had in Iowa last month was primarily young people. Half of the national committee is under thirty-five. Nine of the fifteen posts are held by women, without any resolution or mandate requiring affirmative action. So I think the party is young, and it's purely working class.

I don't quite know why we're attracting young people, but we are. One thing I think is important to them is that the Socialist Party represents a kind of historic continuity, so when they touch it, when they feel it, the party is not totally new and alien to them. Also, it's the kind of left-wing movement that makes a lot of sense to them. It's not violent. It's not stupid. It's small, but it's human. So they can understand it. They can relate to it.

I think we're beginning to make some real progress. We have a local in Manhattan, which we didn't have before. Another local is starting in New Jersey. Los Angeles is stronger. We have a local organizing in San Francisco. We're still so small that you have to discuss it area by area. However, we're building a base for the future, so in this sense, I think the campaign was successful.

Do you think there is any possibility at all of forming a coalition with some of the other smaller political parties?

Yes, at least on some procedural issues. The Socialist Party's position is one of urging an alignment of the left. We began to move on that after the election. I called a meeting here to discuss the election-law problems, the problems of getting on the ballot. I haven't had time to follow through on that, but I got in touch with the Communist Party, the Socialist Workers Party, the Libertarians, the Citizens Party, and, as a courtesy, Anderson's office. Nothing much has happened yet, but we've had one meeting to discuss cooperation on that.

In other areas, it's more difficult because of the ideological differences between the parties. We would be very interested in exploring ways to work with the Citizens Party if they could accept the concept of joining on a federated basis. One of the problems stems from the fact that there seem to be two different Citizens Parties. One is a personality cult which is built around Barry Commoner, and the other consists of people who want to build a grass-roots network, but they can't seem to mesh with the Commoner people.

Also, we have a basic ideological difference with Commoner. He argues for social ownership or social control. We're very much in favor of the concept of social ownership. The Socialist Party has a genuine concern that the workers have a direct input into what is going on in their factories. We're not interested in having college graduates plan their production schedules just because they're economics majors. So we may run into a very basic split over this issue. We tried to talk with Commoner before the last election, but we got the cold shoulder. I'm not sure there's any real possibility of getting together in the future.

How do you feel about the current state of politics in America? Are you optimistic or pessimistic?

Well, it's very obvious that we're in a period of retrenchment, which is bad for the people, but good for the parties on the left. Reagan is really cutting back on social programs. As the level of suffering increases, I think more people are going to start to pay attention to what we are saying.

However, I'm most worried about Reagan's foreign policy. It's much more erratic and dangerous than I thought it would be. It's a very dangerous foreign policy. He's trying to provoke the invasion of Poland. He's trying to start the cold war all over again. It's one of the most dangerous policies I've ever seen.

I don't think he'll be able to destroy the American left. Actually, I think he's going to end up helping to strengthen the American left. Reagan is really a product of what capitalism is like when it's not working. There's high unemployment, a stagnated economy, and he said he was going to solve these problems. His method of solving them is high military spending, which may help the middle-income group, but he's alienating segments of the population that can become violent. Blacks and Puerto Ricans can become violent simply because they're desperate. It's not going to be fun and games. It's going to be police in the streets if we have high unemployment at the same time all the social aid programs are cut back. I worry a great deal about where we're going.

The final thing I want to touch on is the issue of personal motivation. You put a lot of effort and energy into running for president, with literally no chance of winning. What drives people like you to do this? Is it worth it? Did you get any personal satisfaction out of all of this?

Well, I think the campaign itself was very exhausting. I found it very tiring. I don't think it would be honest to say I enjoyed the campaign. There is a kind of poignancy which is difficult to explain. You're in a different place every day. You forget where you are. You're meeting people you may like, but you're never going to see them again. You may sit one night in Oklahoma with a Vietnam veteran who's in the Communist Party, or who thinks he's in the Communist Party. We had a wonderful long talk, and then I went down to a bar with him to pick up his wife who works as a bartender. I may never see him again. I hope he has since been recruited to our party. But he's only one person, and there are thousands like that you'll probably never see again. That's painful. You forget people's names, you really do forget what town you're in, and you're tired. So I don't think it would be accurate to say that I enjoyed the campaign.

Do I think it was worthwhile? Without any question. I was doing the job of explaining a political position that can't be done in any other way. The votes are not an important measurement if you are able to communicate the ideas. The votes would be charming, but if you're as far down as we are, you've won if you can simply get the ideas in circulation.

It's not the votes that are significant. It's the shifting of ideas and the winning of people. Look, Marxists take a very long-range view. Yes, we would like unity—we really would. No, I know I'm not going to see socialism in this country in my lifetime. But nothing is done without struggle. I don't think it's fun to campaign, but someone has to do it. What is the alternative? There's got to be an absolute commitment to it. Nothing is achieved without that.

THE COMMUNIST PARTY

The Communist Party was born in Chicago on September 1, 1919, though two different parties were actually created at that time—the Communist Party of America and the Communist Labor Party. The latter group was led by Benjamin Gitlow and John Reed, who has now probably received more posthumous publicity from the movie *Reds* than from his eyewitness account of the Russian Revolution, *Ten Days That Shook the World*.

Both of the early communist factions sought affiliation with the Third Communist International (Comintern) in Moscow, and they became subject to almost immediate government harassment as an outgrowth of the "red scare" that swept across the United States. As a result of raids by agents of United States Attorney General A. Mitchell Palmer, membership suffered a sharp drop and the movement was forced underground. In 1921, the Communists reorganized into the Workers Party of America, and they attempted to make inroads into the American labor movement. The party's position was strengthened when William Z. Foster, who had led the famous "big steel" strike of 1919, joined the movement in 1921. Foster ran for president as a candidate of the Workers (Communist) Party in both the 1924 and 1928 elections, and he ran for a third time in 1932 after the various factions within the party had finally merged into the Communist Party USA in 1929.[13] Foster was succeeded by Earl Browder, who ran as the party's nominee in both the 1936 and 1940 presidential elections. The party did not run any further candidates until it nominated Charlene Mitchell in 1968, originally because it supported Franklin Roosevelt's wartime coalition during World War II, and subsequently because it was subjected to severe governmental harassment in the form of McCarthyism, the McCarren Act, the Communist Control Act of 1954, and other cold war measures. As a result, its membership dropped from an all-time peak of about 55,000 in 1945 to an estimated 22,500 in 1955.[14]

Because it was originally affiliated with the Third International, or Comintern, during its earlier years the Communist Party USA was the subject of innumerable scholarly studies that attempted to determine its relationship with the international communist movement. There is little question that the party followed the Moscow line closely during this time, as it shifted its policies to accommodate shifts in Comintern policies. According to a study by Bernard and Jewell Bellush, during the New Deal years, "the Party embraced, without question, the centrality of Soviet policy in determining its own positions. Indeed, what was good for Mother Russia was good for American Communists."[15]

In 1943, however, the Soviet Union dissolved the Comintern in order to allay the misgivings of its allies, and in 1944, the Communist Party USA was disbanded as an official party to become the Communist Political Association. In 1948, the Communists supported the presidential candidacy of Henry A. Wallace on the Progressive Party ticket, but after the cold war turmoil of the 1950s, they did not become politically active again until 1966. As political analyst Harvey Klehr explains,

The McCarthy era saw the development of a national phobia about communist influence in all sectors of American life. In the 1960s attention turned elsewhere . . . [and] the issue of domestic communism faded from national attention and, seemingly, scholarly concern.[16]

Because the Communist Party USA has not been considered politically significant in the past two decades, it has been the focus of relatively few studies. As a result, it is difficult to determine the precise nature of the party's current relation to the Soviet Union.

Gus Hall, the general secretary of the party since 1959, ran as the communist candidate for president in the 1972, 1976, and 1980 presidential elections. Hall's 1980 vice-presidential running mate was Angela Davis of California. In the 1980 campaign, Hall appeared on the ballot in twenty-four states, and the District of Columbia; he received a total of 45,023 votes, with the largest numbers coming from Illinois (9,711), New York (7,414), and Pennsylvania (5,184).

I interviewed Simon Gerson, Hall's campaign manager, after I was unsuccessful in arranging a meeting with Hall himself. Gerson, who has been a member of the Communist Party for over fifty years, served as Hall's campaign manager in both the 1976 and the 1980 elections. He is a member of the central committee of the party, and he chairs the party's Political Action Department. We met at the Communist Party headquarters building in New York City in late December 1981.

Simon W. Gerson

I think we've got to recognize our individual differences in order to avoid a nuclear holocaust that could end up destroying the entire world.

PERSONAL BACKGROUND

Smallwood: I'm interested in getting some background information on Gus Hall, but since you were his campaign manager in the 1976 and 1980 presidential elections, why don't you first tell me a little about yourself?

Gerson: Well, you might say I'm a red-diaper baby. I was born in New York City on January 23, 1909. Both my parents were originally Socialists, although my mother became an early member of the Communist Party after it was organized in 1919. I grew up in an atmosphere of socialism and trade unionism. My father generally supported Norman Thomas, but my mother was for William Z. Foster, the first communist candidate who ran for president back in 1924, and again in 1928 and 1932.

When did you get involved with the party?

I joined the Young Communist League in 1926 when I first went to college. I was seventeen years old at the time, and I became active in what was known as the Social Problems Club. I became president of the club, and I was expelled from college for leading the antimilitarist fight there.

Where was this?

At CCNY—City College of New York. I was expelled in 1928.

What did you do after that?

Most of my life I've worked in journalism. I was a city hall reporter for the *Daily Worker*, and later I served as its executive editor, and in a similar capacity on its successor, the *Daily World*. During World War II, I served as an infantryman in the southwest Pacific, and I had some interesting experiences in New York City government during both the 1930s and 1940s.

What did you do in city government?

In 1938, during the second LaGuardia administration, I was named as an executive assistant to the Manhattan borough president, Stanley Isaacs, which made me the first openly avowed Communist to hold an appointive office in New York. I was very close to Peter Cacchione of Brooklyn, who was one of two Communists elected to the city council under the proportional representation [PR] voting system then in effect. After the war, in the November 1947 election, the PR system was abolished by referendum, and it literally broke Pete's heart. Two days later, he died of a heart attack. Under the provisions of the city charter, it was clear that the city council had to elect a new member from Brooklyn to replace Pete, and the Communist Party nominated me. However, the council refused to seat me. They just delayed the issue and never filled the vacancy—a tactic engineered by the dominant Tammany Hall group. I ran for the office in 1948, and did pretty well—about 18,000 Communist Party votes plus another 132,000 from the American Labor Party; under New York law you could run on two lines. However, I didn't win the election, so my career in active politics actually stopped before it ever got started.

How about Gus Hall? Tell me a little about his background.

Gus was born about twenty months after me, in 1910. He came from the iron ore range, the Mesabi Range, in Minnesota. He had a Finnish working-class background; his family were miners and steelworkers, and his father was a Communist.

According to his biography in Who's Who, *his original name was Arvo Halberg. Do you know why he changed his name?*

That's an interesting question. He never explained it to me. Maybe it's easier to fit Gus Hall into the headlines, but he wouldn't have known that as a kid when he changed his name. I really don't know.

Anyway, Gus never had too much formal education. He joined the Young Communist League in 1927, a year after I did, but I didn't know him until later. He was very active in union affairs, a member of the International Woodworkers, the Laborers International Union, the International Association of Bridge, Structural, and Ornamental Ironworkers. But basically he was a steelworker. He gained prominence as the leader of the 1937 strike against "little steel," which actually involved such giants as Republic, Bethlehem, and Weirton. It was a bitter, bloody confrontation. During World War II, Gus served with the navy in the Pacific theater. In 1959 he was named general secretary of the Communist Party. Of course, the 1950s were a very rough period for the party. The cold war had started, and we had to deal with the Smith Act, the Un-American Activities Committee, the FBI, the McCarren Act, McCarthyism, the whole works.

Has Gus Hall talked with you much about what it was like to be a Communist in those days?

He has talked about it, but he hasn't written much about it. He tells an interesting story—a couple of interesting stories. He was one of the Communist Party leaders who was convicted under the Smith Act, and he ended up spending eight years in jail, in Leavenworth Federal Penitentiary.

That was the famous Dennis *case in 1951, wasn't it?*

Yes. The Supreme Court upheld the Smith Act as being constitutional in a six-to-two vote. I remember it very well because I was indicted and tried under the Smith Act myself. It made it a crime to advocate the overthrow of the government by force or violence. Not to actually do anything, but to advocate it or teach it.

It was a First Amendment case—freedom of speech. We argued that the Constitution guaranteed the right to advocate controversial political ideas even if they may have been unpopular, but the majority of the Supreme Court upheld the act. I think it was Justices Black and Douglas who dissented. All twelve members of the party's political bureau were indicted under the act, but William Z. Foster, the chairman of the party, was dropped from the case because of illness. Eugene Dennis, the general secretary of the party, was one of the defendants, so they called it the *Dennis* case.

Eleven top leaders of the party, all except Foster, were convicted, and the sentences were severe. Gus Hall was given five years on the original sentence and an additional three years for contempt of court when he failed to show up for his sentencing. So he spent eight years in a federal prison while his wife and children—a son and a daughter—were on the outside. It was very rough.

Did he ever discuss how the Communists were treated in prison? Were they harassed by the other prisoners because of their political views?

I can only tell you about my own experience. I went to prison during the period of the trial until I could make bail. Eventually, I was acquitted, I assume because my work was patently public—in the legislative field. Incidentally, they called us the "second-string Communists." Only once when I was in prison did I hear some negative cracks during a movie that was shown to the prisoners. Somebody hollered "red bastards" or something like that, but most of the prisoners wondered what the Smith Act was. "What are you in here for?" "The Smith Act." "What the hell is that? Is it like the Mann Act? Were you transporting women across the state line?" I explained, "No. We're accused of advocating the overthrow of the government." They were astonished. "You mean they put you in jail for that? For something like that?" There was a lot of publicity surrounding the case. Our pictures were in the papers and on television; they saw substantial amounts of money being raised for our defense. One of them actually came up to me and said, "Jeez, you guys must have a good gang out there to back you up."

THE COMMUNIST PARTY

I want to ask you a number of questions about the 1980 election campaign, but let's start with a little information about the Communist Party. How many members do you have?

The actual card-carrying membership is probably between 15,000 to 20,000. In addition, we estimate there are over 100,000 other people in this country who regard themselves as Communists, but who aren't paying dues.

According to traditional communist ideology, the party is an elite vanguard group. Do you regard yourself as an elite organization?

Oh, no, no, no. Anybody can join, and we don't expect everybody who joins to be a full-fledged Marxist. We're seeking to become a mass party, rather than a cadre party. We want to represent all the elements in the working class. We're interested in spreading our message, and in building up our party base.

How is the party organized? Do you practice democratic centralism?

We hold party conventions where we debate issues and elect our central committee. There are about sixty-five of us on the central committee, and we designate party officers and candidates for elections, and edit and issue the draft platform. We practice a democratic centralist philosophy. A lot of information comes from the ranks, and a lot from the central committee itself. There's a pretty good interplay back and forth, and we hear from the districts and constituencies if they don't like the platform or they think something is wrong.

In terms of your platform, where do you stand today? What are your major political priorities?

Our chief objective today is to defeat Reaganism and Reaganomics. We feel that the people are thinking primarily in terms of the economic costs of this, and they're profoundly worried about the recession, about job security and unemployment. We have to join with the labor unions and other working-class groups to give Reagan a smashing rebuff. We're very concerned that Reagan's militarism, the big new arms buildup, will lead to nuclear confrontation, to war, and we're prepared to cooperate with other groups, working class or otherwise, to defeat this program.

How do you plan to do this? Do you view yourself as a revolutionary party?

In a fundamental sense, yes.

What does that mean?

It means in a long-range sense. We don't deny that we're for socialism. We're for basic social change through public ownership of the basic means of production in order to do away with capitalist exploitation of the working class. But we've never advocated violent overthrow of the government to achieve this goal, and we don't now. The degree of violence that may develop in the course of social change is not going to be determined by us, but by the level of resistance of the tiny minority who run things to accept social change. So we're not talking about barricades, or storming the Winter Palace, or stuff like that.

We have a different outlook. As long as the system affords

any possibility of democratic change, where the avenues of expression remain open, we're going to utilize them to the maximum. We still believe very strongly in the Bill of Rights, and we want to see it maintained and extended.

When the Communist Party was first organized here in the United States, you were accused of being a mouthpiece for the Soviet Union. What is your relationship with the Soviet Union today?

We're completely autonomous. We make our own independent decisions. We don't take an attitude of blanket endorsement of everything they do, nor do we fall into the trap of thumbing our nose at the Soviet Union or joining in Soviet-baiting. We think, by and large, the Soviets, particularly in respect to peace policy, have shown a brilliant example of socialist political morality. That's number one. Number two, their support of the national liberation movements is exemplary. I feel very strongly that they have made innumerable sacrifices for peoples of other countries, including Poland. So it's an object of admiration. Of course, there are things they don't have—the amenities we have, the standard of living we have. However, they have other things like national health insurance, free hospitalization, and free education.

Gus Hall has been critical of some of their attitudes with respect to art and in some other areas. But we regard them as part—in fact, the leading element—of the socialist family, and we're not going to join in any unwarranted onslaughts against them. We're not joining Reagan in any attack against them, because we think that simply poisons the atmosphere.

I have difficulty with reconciling your admiration for the Soviet Union with your strongly expressed belief in the American Bill of Rights. In terms of political rights, only one group, the Communist Party, controls the entire Soviet system. How do you justify this?

This is not as unusual or strange as you might think. Every society tends to reflect the forces of its own historical development. The Soviet Union came into being as a result of the Revolution of 1917 against the czar and the bourgeois class. As a result, they never sanctioned any bourgeois, or capitalist, political parties because that is what the new government was designed to replace.

Our own country came into being when we overthrew the British monarchy. As a result, we are pledged to maintain a republican form of government. If any political group attempted to form a monarchy in the United States, the federal government would be required to send in troops to put down that monarchist form of government. A different restriction emerged in postwar Germany after the overthrow of the Nazis. The United States is party to the Potsdam Agreement which outlaws any fascist political parties in Germany. In other words, each of these countries has placed different restrictions on various forms of political activity because of differences in their historical evolution.

But doesn't the Soviet Union restrict the most fundamental freedom of all—free and open elections which enable people to choose alternative political leaders?

I think we've got to be realistic about this. I don't claim the Soviet Union is perfect, but I certainly don't think the United States is perfect either. In many respects, our democratic rhetoric has been overshadowed by the harsh realities of our political life. We claim to be a free and open society, but minority groups, especially blacks, have been denied fundamental freedoms throughout our history. Under the Communist Control Act of 1954, my own political party, the Communist Party of the United States, was denied the rights, privileges, and immunities possessed by other political parties under state and federal law. We were infiltrated and harassed by the FBI. We were literally hounded out of the political arena to a point where we even stopped nominating presidential candidates until the 1968 election.

We can say that's all past history, but even today we have a very restrictive political system in this country. It's a built-in two-party monopoly that is designed to prop up the Republicans and the Democrats to the exclusion of all other political groups. The smaller third parties, including the Communist Party, face massive obstacles even trying to get on the ballot in many states.

I'm not trying to make a simplistic argument that the United States is all bad, and the Soviet Union is all good. We each have our faults. As a result, I think we've got to recognize our individual differences in order to avoid a nuclear holocaust that could end up destroying the entire world.

THE PRESIDENTIAL CAMPAIGNS

Since you mentioned Gus Hall's presidential bids in both 1976 and 1980, I'd like to get your views on this. First, did Gus Hall and Angela Davis both spend a lot of time campaigning in different states in the 1980 race?

They did. Gus spoke from one end of the country to the other. He was on radio talk shows. He was on television to the degree that we could get on TV. Angela, unfortunately, had a teaching schedule which kept her busy five days a week. However, on Friday nights, she would hop on a plane and crisscross the country. As a matter of fact, she got more invitations than she could accept.

In how many states were you on the ballot in 1980?

Let's see. We finally managed to get on the ballot in twenty-five states plus the District of Columbia. We've made some progress in this area, but it's a tough, uphill battle. Way back in 1932, communist votes were counted in thirty-eight of the forty-eight states. After the repression of the 1950s, we stopped running presidential candidates until 1968, when we managed to get on the ballot in only two states. We upped this to thirteen states in 1972, nineteen in 1976, and now we're on in twenty-five states and the District of Columbia.

What are some of the problems you've encountered in trying to get onto the ballot?

A sizable number of states have outright anticommunist provisions. Delaware, for example, requires that the Communist Party and its members register with the state police. Louisiana demands an anticommunist affidavit of candidates. Georgia has an antisubversive clause under which election officials can deny ballot status to communist candidates. West Virginia gives you a little more rope—enough to hang you. A canvasser needs a county clerk's certificate authorizing him to collect signatures in the magisterial district where he resides, and it was a misdemeanor for an out-of-stater, or a nonresident of that district, to circulate petitions. In addition, candidates for president and vice-president, unless they are indigents, must pay a filing fee of 1 percent of the annual salaries paid to those officers. We refused to do this, since we didn't want to waste money in a state where we probably couldn't have gotten on the ballot anyway. Finally, there are very onerous petition signature requirements in many states like California, where, as you probably know, it takes up to 100,000 signatures to get on the ballot.

Aren't these restrictive state laws subject to legal challenge?

Yes, we've challenged some. In 1980, we waited for John Anderson to challenge others. But it's a tough, tedious, expensive process. In some states, we decided it just wasn't worth the time and effort.

Many of these state laws affect all third parties. Is there any chance you could get together, perhaps with the help of the American Civil Liberties Union, in an effort to make them a little more uniform?

I'm glad you raised that question. I think the labor and progressive movements don't consider these problems sufficiently. They are organic problems of democracy, just like reapportionment or redistricting. They may seem technical to the man on the street, but as a political scientist, you know that if you rig the rules, you can control the substance. I feel that it can be overcome, but only if there's a wide united front which will include organized labor, black people, hispanics, and other minorities, plus insurgent Democrats and liberal Republicans—a movement so broad and so big that it will overcome all of the legal barriers.

What do you think would be reasonable? Would you try for more uniform state laws?

No, I think we need a federal law if we're dealing with the president and vice-president, since they're officers of the federal government. There's no question in my mind that the courts would uphold it as being constitutional. The tough problem is the political one: getting Congress to act when it could obviously hurt both of the major parties they represent. As I said, it could be done, but I suspect we're not going to have any structural reform in the election laws unless we experience some profound political crisis—a deep, long recession or a bitter struggle over the question of war and peace—which will galvanize public opinion and compel Congress to act.

Let me play devil's advocate for a minute. If the system was thrown wide open, couldn't this produce chaos? Do you see problems if hundreds of people decide to organize third parties and run for president?

Oh, yes. Actually, there is already a growing body of law about this. I don't know whether you ever read the Pratt decision.

Was that the recent Michigan District Court case, Hall *v.* Austin?

That's right. The U.S. District Court case in Michigan. The state denied our application to get on the ballot as independent candidates. Judge Pratt ruled that there can no longer be any doubt that state laws which preclude independent candidates from appearing on the ballot are unconstitutional. However, he also cited Justice Powell's opinion in the 1976 case of *McCarthy* v. *Briscoe* that the courts should be sensitive to the state legislatures' interest in preventing a laundry list of candidates who would confuse and frustrate the voters.

As a result, he referred to an even earlier case, *Bullock* v. *Carter*, where the court held that a state could require candidates to show a modicum of support before it printed their names on the ballot. Now, what is a modicum of support? Judge Pratt looked at a variety of evidence—previous campaigns, signature collections, knowledge by the public of our candidates—and he came to the conclusion that Gus Hall and Angela Davis had that modicum of public support and were not frivolous candidates. That is a reasonable standard, and we would be prepared to accept that for any candidate. The point is that we could devise reasonable standards to govern ballot access. Too many of the state standards today are totally unreasonable.

One thing that confused me about that case. Why did Judge Pratt refer to Hall and Davis as independent candidates?

Because there are two ways to get on the ballot in Michigan. One is to be nominated as a member of a party, which requires that you have to go through a primary election; the other way is to run as an independent, which doesn't involve a primary. The latter was the route we used.

It seems confusing to me for a party candidate to run as an independent. Do you think that is fair?

Well, under the present law, it's certainly easier not to have to run in both a primary and a general election. However, if the state ballot laws were made more reasonable so that it would be possible for third parties to actually get on the ballot, we'd be more than happy to run under the Communist Party label in any state.

How about campaign finances? What are your views on the Federal Election Campaign Act?

In the first place, we think that the minority parties and independent candidates should have as much access to federal funds as the major parties. It should be proportionate, of course, but they should have some reasonable access to these funds. Secondly, there's got to be some free access to the media, just as you have in France and some other countries. That's crucial.

What was your experience with the media? Did you get much coverage?

No, on the contrary, when we wanted to get onto programs like "Phil Donahue" or "Meet the Press," we were always told that these were news programs, and therefore the networks could decide what was news. So we were rebuffed. However, it's fair to say the local media was kind of anxious for copy when Gus and Angela got to medium-sized or smaller cities.

So it was the big national networks that caused you the most problems?

Yes, because they're so damned expensive. In 1976 we broke our backs to get five minutes on NBC. We spent $27,000 for the five minutes plus another $3,000 for production costs. It cost us $30,000 for 300 seconds. That's $100 a second.

What was the total amount you spent in the 1980 campaign?

They gave us the official figure for 1976, but we haven't received the 1980 figures yet. It was over $450,000 nationally in 1976. I would say in 1980 we spent less than half that amount because we decided not to get into the TV network business.

According to the figures I've gotten from the Federal Election Commission, you reported total expenditures of about $195,000 in 1980.

Yes, that sounds about right.

Was all of this money raised from your party members?

Not all. We used other methods—mail appeals, passing the hat at meetings, etc. But now we've gotten into another fight over this. We refused to turn in the names of all our contributors in 1976, and the Federal Election Commission [FEC] sued us. We got an opinion from our legal counsel, John J. Abt, that we were not required to turn in the names of all our contributors if we could prove that they might be harassed. So we went by this. Those people who sent us checks and said we could use their names, fine. Those who didn't want us to use their names—we protected their right of privacy. The FEC sued us. They sought an injunction and a $5,000 fine, and we told them no dice.

In our answering brief, John Abt quoted copiously from the Church Committee's findings on surveillance and harassment of the Communist Party by the FBI. The Federal Election Commission said that wasn't good enough. So we issued a subpoena for the records of the FBI to prove surveillance and harassment. The FBI responded with a long affidavit saying that they had 36 million pieces of paper on the Communist Party, and if they were to retrieve all those pieces of paper, it would paralyze the work of the FBI and the Department of Justice, and it would cost $26 million. They branded our demand as "oppressive." In other words, we were accused of "oppressing" the poor old FBI. Well, this was nonsense, and the federal court finally ruled in our favor.

When was this?

The decision came down within the last three months. The case was tried in Foley Square courthouse. The judge was Lee Gagliardi. But, hold on, the story is not over yet. Now, after we won the case, the Federal Election Commission has just told us that they're going to appeal. So here is this case, which is already six years old, and the FEC is still bothering us.

This leads to my final question on the campaign. There seems to be a clear record of FBI infiltration into the Communist Party in the past. Does this still take place today?

We suspect that it still goes on, and we're rather calm about it. In the first place, we don't do anything that's illegal: we don't manufacture bombs or plan any illegal actions, so a guy can come to a meeting and take notes all night.

But, let's face it, over the years, a number of FBI agents and informers have served their time in the Communist Party. They may get some names, but nothing more than that, so we're not too concerned. However, we've begun to insist that everybody has to carry a certain amount of the workload, and that tends to flush out the phonies. So we make our new members take on very visible jobs, like distributing literature early in the morning in front of a factory. It isn't too terrible, but after a while, you get suspicious of people who refuse to do anything at all.

PERSONAL IMPRESSIONS

You've been involved with the Communist Party for over half a century. How do you feel about the party today? Are you optimistic or pessimistic?

In a long-term sense, I am optimistic about the growth of the party. More particularly, I am optimistic about the growth of progressive and socialist sentiment in the country, because the laws of capitalism are leading inevitably to the collapse of the system. Now, that may sound doctrinaire, but a careful examination of the Reagan policies indicates that we are getting into deeper economic trouble; it's not only short-term, or minority-group, unemployment. This is structural, and people are going to look around more and more for basic solutions. As they do, they will move in a different direction. It won't necessarily be parroting anything that's happened elsewhere. They're going to look at different alternatives—public ownership, municipal ownership, social ownership—that will involve basic changes in fundamental economic approaches, and also in the larger social questions.

You've gone through some rough times in the last fifty years. Has it been worth it?

Well, I like to think I'm a pretty well-balanced guy. My wife and I have celebrated our golden wedding anniversary, so we're kind of stable people. We've had two children and three grandchildren, and I'm quite strong on family. We enjoy what most other Americans enjoy.

The years have not been easy, but I look back on them with a feeling of satisfaction. I've seen one-third of the world become socialist. I've seen colonial countries become independent. I've seen the growth of the labor movement in this country, the organization of unorganized industries which was deemed impossible when I was a kid. I've seen the growth of considerable progressive sentiment in this country, and some real—but far from adequate—improvement in the lot of many minority groups. I've seen the growth of science and technology. So, yes, I think it has been worth it. I've been very fortunate in my personal life, and I feel I've made at least some small contribution in helping to make the things I believe in come about.

How do you think Communists are regarded in the United States today? What kind of a reception do you get? Are people basically hostile or friendly to you?

That's another change I've seen, especially during more recent years. Quite a few people are friendly. I think most are interested; they're curious. Some are quite suspicious. A smaller group is very openly hostile. There is a substantial difference from the cold war years. Many of the younger people who are beginning to come into leadership roles today are products of the sixties. Red-baiting is unknown to them. Even if they may not like us, they don't go in for the McCarthy-era red-baiting. It isn't part of their background or their ideological baggage. This country went through some very rough experiences in the 1960s—the Vietnam War, the civil rights revolution. As a result, I think a lot of people, especially the younger people, are a little less doctrinaire and a little more open and tolerant of other people's lifestyles.

One last question. You've spent most of your life working for the communist cause. Do you ever think communism will come to America someday in the future?

I think it will, but its precise form and timing are points I wouldn't presume to suggest. I think the American people have a genius for moving in the right direction. I have faith in them. It's not a completely blind faith, because, like everyone else, we often tend to stumble around and temporarily lose our way. Eventually, however, I think Americans will see their way clear to a different world than the one we are living in today.

THE SOCIALIST WORKERS PARTY

The Socialist Workers Party (SWP) was organized in 1938 as part of the Fourth International to carry forward the principles of classical Marxism following Trotsky's call for a complete break with the Stalin regime in the Soviet Union. Isaac Deutscher, in the final volume of his Trotsky biography, *The Prophet Outcast*, notes that

the only country where Trotskyism stirred a little was the United States. In January, 1938, after various splits and mergers, the Socialist Workers' Party formed itself, and soon gained the title of "the strongest section" of the Fourth International. . . . At its head there was a fairly large team of, by American standards, experienced and able leaders, of whom James P. Cannon, Max Shachtman, and James Burnham were the best known.[17]

Deutscher goes on to explain why Trotskyism was able to appeal to the radical American intelligentsia of the time who were disillusioned by a series of shocks that included the rise of nazism, the Spanish Civil War, and Stalin's infamous Moscow purge trials:

Trotskyism appeared to them as a fresh breeze breaking into the stuffy air of the left and opening up new horizons. Men of letters responded to the dramatic pathos of Trotsky's struggle and to his eloquence and literary genius. Trotskyism became something of a vogue which was to leave many marks in American literature. Among the writers, especially critics, affected by it were Edmund Wilson, Sidney Hook, James T. Farrell, Dwight MacDonald, Charles Malamud, Philip Rahv, James Rorty, Harold Rosenberg, Clement Greenberg, Mary McCarthy, and many, many others.[18]

The Socialist Workers Party waited until after World War II to run its first candidate for president of the United States, Farrell Dobbs, who served as the party's nominee in four successive elections from 1948 to 1960. Dobbs was followed by Clifton DeBerry (1964), Fred Halstead (1968), Linda Jenness

(1972), and Peter Camejo (1976), who made the strongest party showing ever with 91,310 votes.

In 1973, the Socialist Workers Party filed a civil suit against the federal government claiming that the FBI, the CIA, and other government agencies had engaged in a prolonged period of illegal harassment and disruption against the party. The suit, which calls for $40 million in damages, finally went to trial before Federal District Judge Thomas P. Griesa in New York City on April 2, 1981. The case is still under consideration.

During the 1980 election, a black steelworker, Andrew Pulley, campaigned for president on the SWP ticket. The party's vice-presidential nominee was thirty-six-year-old Matilde Zimmerman, a writer for the party newspaper, *The Militant*. Since Pulley was only twenty-nine years old at the time, he would have been ineligible to serve as president, if elected, because Article II of the United States Constitution requires the president to "have attained the age of thirty five years." As a result, though Pulley campaigned nationwide, he only appeared on the ballot in six states, while former presidential candidate Clifton DeBerry appeared as the party's alternate nominee in twenty-two states, and Richard Congress ran as the party's candidate in Ohio. Their combined total was 49,038 votes.

Andrew Pulley, who has been active in the Socialist Workers Party since the late 1960s, had previously run as the party's nominee for vice-president in 1972 at the age of twenty-one. He offered the following observations during an interview in the SWP headquarters offices in New York City in late June 1981.

Andrew Pulley

From the very earliest days, I could see the fundamental inequality built into society.

PERSONAL BACKGROUND

Smallwood: Tell me something about your own background. I

know you were born in Sidon, Mississippi, on May 5, 1951, so let's start there.

Pulley: Well, having been born in Mississippi, being black, and living in a rural area, from the very earliest days I could see the fundamental inequality built into society. It was reflected in everything I saw in the surrounding area. For example, just one look at the quality of white housing in the area compared to my home, which was overcrowded with a total of eleven people—my grandmother and aunts and uncles—all of us living in a three-room shack-type house in a rural area. We had to earn a livelihood through agricultural work, chiefly cotton picking and chopping. During the off season, the winter, my grandfather would hunt. We survived off the little crop that we grew in our yard mainly for our own consumption.

When did you go to work?

I began working when I was eight years old. This was, of course, when school was out. School would end in May, but we were cotton choppin' after school even while school was going on.

How much did you make in your job back then?

Thirty cents an hour, up to 1963. I would earn $20 to $30 a week, and that's working half a day on Saturday. School would begin in November. This was all done to guarantee that the black worker would have the maximum amount of time to labor, that's including the black schoolchildren. So I got an early taste of the economic realities of the country, and the social inequalities of being bussed beyond the best schools, the white schools, to the worst schools, the black schools. I saw all of that right away, and it never appeared right to me. I knew no solution to the problem.

I can also remember the so-called Cuban missile crisis in 1962, when we had just gotten a television set. The whole thing was fascinating, including world events and news. I felt, like everyone else who was conscious then, that the world was at the brink of total elimination.

We moved to Cleveland, Ohio, in 1963. I was twelve years old. Conditions there did not really improve at all. Again, a large number of my immediate family lived in a real run-down area, in the ghetto of Cleveland. Unlike the South, there were no gardens, or no hunting you could do, and no real labor that young people could engage in that could bring in any kind of appreciable income. Plus the massive unemployment that existed. So in reality it was worse there, just on the level of the living standard and trying to get some kind of education. We later moved into a mixed neighborhood where we confronted racist violence and racist problems in the school.

Did you encounter white resistance in Cleveland?

Yes, the "Bisby Boys," a loose white gang in the area. The only thing that kept them together was their opposition to blacks coming there. Of course, we had to organize to defend our own people, so I began getting involved in that. It was not a conscious intention on my part. I just got forced into it to defend myself. I was about fourteen—I began to get interested in civil rights and the black power movement, casually interested. I was not a proponent of anything at the time. But when Martin Luther King was murdered, I began to radicalize. I became more active and more conscious. That was in 1968. I was involved in a protest in the school, and I got kicked out. I was given the choice of going to trial or joining the army, on the charge of inciting a riot, so I went into the army. It was there that I learned about the Socialist Workers Party and really began to become a conscious political being.

In the army you met Joe Cole, a white man from Georgia. Is that when you first learned about the Socialist Workers Party?

Yes. This was totally new to me. Another thing that was completely new was to find a white person who felt himself equal to me, rather than superior. Also to find a white person who espoused black equality forcibly, who introduced me to Malcolm X. I hadn't even heard of Malcolm X until after he was murdered, none of his ideas or anything. Joe Cole really began introducing me to black nationalism, socialism, and politics. It was through him that I read the first issues of *The Militant* newspaper, the Socialist Workers Party publication. Because he was white, his ideas had a tremendous impact on me. All of the immediate whites I dealt with were hostile. They were teachers who were hostile, or police officers, or some kind of insurance men. All "superior" men, all authority figures. This was quite different. We listened to Malcolm X tapes and discussed the Vietnam War, and we began to attract a lot of other soldiers.

As a result of this, you became involved with the "Fort Jackson Eight" protests, and you got an undesirable discharge?

Yes, an undesirable discharge. Our group was really called the "GI's Against the War," against the Vietnam War, although the press called the leadership group, including me, the "Fort Jackson Eight" because we were stationed in Fort Jackson, South Carolina. At our high point, we had a meeting of about 300 people. In the court proceedings during our army trial, the government reported that the meeting was larger than we recalled. In any case, we had planned to go down to Atlanta to march in the antiwar demonstration on April 4, 1969. There was a big meeting outside the army barracks on the base to organize the march. We did everything legal and aboveboard, but we organized against the war, and for that we were busted. I was taken to the stockade, along with four or five other soldiers, but we were never tried. We had what was the equivalent of a grand jury investigation hearing. The army then decided to drop charges against us—of course they had no case. After that, we received an undesirable discharge.

Once you got out of the army, you became actively involved with the Socialist Workers Party. You ran for vice-president of the United States, didn't you?

Yes, I ran for vice-president in 1972.

How old were you then?

I was twenty-one.

Have you been active with the party ever since?
Yes, since 1969.

POLITICAL IDEOLOGY

Tell me a little about the party. What would you like to see happen? What do you stand for?

Basically we feel that the majority of people in this country and throughout the world—since we view ourselves as part of a world perspective—exist in a world of oppressed people who are being exploited. Our view is that the majority should control their own destiny, meaning the economic functions of a given country. In our view, the politics, the culture, everything, should be designed to benefit the vast majority, as opposed to benefiting a minority of people who happen to hold title to companies, or banks, or whatever they inherited from their parents, which was all gotten as a result of the labor of working people, going all the way back to slavery.

In our view, the only way you're going to be able to end unemployment is to totally nationalize the system of banks, industry, and commerce to produce for the social good, rather than for the good of Rockefeller and a few others. This is the only way to end inflation in the last analysis, the only way to bring housing conditions up to the most available quality standards. We want to bring about free education for all, free medical care. What we see right now going on in the country is not an advance to improve these conditions, but a retreat, a drive to push the living standard of American people backward through plant closures, demands by companies that workers take pay cuts, unemployment with no end in sight, racist violence, the denial of women's rights, a war—or even two wars—for every generation because the American government chooses to maintain the economic and political status quo throughout the world.

The only way to end all of these problems, including nuclear power and the ultimate threat of the extermination of humanity through nuclear war, is for the working class and the oppressed—the farmers, the women, the blacks—all of us voting as a majority, to control things in this country, both the economic realities and the political realities. So the ultimate goal of the Socialist Workers Party is to help bring about a socialist form of government and a worldwide system of socialism. If this happens, we think democracy will flourish. This is the only way we can have real democracy in the United States.

Your party broke away in 1938 from the U.S. Communist Party to become a Trotsky-type party. Is that important? Is Trotskyite ideology a central concern to you?

Well, yes it is. Our ideological aspect is, of course, what leads us to take the position we take on specific, everyday issues and on the strategies we advocate. What we need to do, what our class needs to do, is to begin to organize our own political party. That's what we don't have in the United States—unlike the French workers, the Canadian workers, or the British. And until we get a mass labor party, we're not going to move forward in any way.

Do you think you can get together with the other parties like the Communists to build this mass labor party?

There are some very major differences between us, especially on international issues. For example, take Poland. Very fundamental differences exist between the Socialist Workers Party and the Communist Party on Poland. We think that the Polish workers are doing more to fight for socialism than any of the other worker states. We support the Solidarity movement demands that they decide the policies of the country, that genuine democracy should exist. All of this is very fundamental to socialism in general and very key to our view of socialism. However, the U.S. Communist Party sides with either the Polish government against the workers, or the Soviet government against both the Polish government and the Polish workers. There's no way that we can reconcile those differences.

How about the Workers World Party? Are they closer to the U.S. Communist Party or to your own party?

They are somewhat different from the Communist Party and also from us. The Communist Party tends to follow any line, any twists or turns, that comes from Moscow. The Workers World Party's approach on international questions tends to be one of confidence in whatever socialist government holds power in any country. That is, if there's a rebellion by workers in China, they would tend to side with the Chinese government. The same thing is true in Poland, where they side with the official views of the Polish government.

Do you see any real prospects, then, for united action between your party and the other parties on the left?

Actually, we seek some unity in action. We build coalitions around those things that we can find common agreement on, such as the current war threat that is being brought on by U.S. policies in El Salvador. During the recent Washington antiwar demonstrations, which many organizations helped build, and which we supported, 100,000 people came out. Specific issues, such as nuclear power and opposition to police brutality— these represent the beginning of unity. However, in terms of one big socialist organization, there's no way that that can be brought about because of the genuine political and strategic differences that are represented by all of these various groups. These are not simply limited to ideological differences.

THE 1980 CAMPAIGN

How did you get the nomination as candidate for president? Was this done at one of your party conventions?

We usually have a convention every two years. The main work of the convention is to discuss and advertise a general political approach to what is happening in the country, what is happening in the world. Actually, the nomination for president is one of the smallest aspects of the convention. It is done through discussion and vote.

Once the party makes a decision, does it follow the philosophy of democratic centralism in carrying out that decision?

The majority carries out its will through democratic discussion and democratic vote. Before we have a convention, we have three months of written discussion in which every member can participate, write articles, discuss different ideas. Then we have the election in the branches for our delegates to the convention. Then we have another discussion at the convention about all of the issues that are being raised. Finally, we take a majority vote, and what is decided becomes the policy of the party until the next convention. That becomes the perspective of the whole party. That doesn't mean a minority in the party has to change its mind on a given question. It's just that when the party performs publicly, which is why we exist, the view of the majority is the one that's presented. If there's a difference as to whether or not the election in France is a victory for the working people, the view of the majority is the view that would be expressed in our paper, and expressed by our candidates, not the opposing view of the minority. The minority can retain that view and fight for that view in the next convention. So that's basically what democratic centralism means to us.

The Socialist Workers Party was on the ballot in almost thirty states in 1980. Did you actually go out and campaign in all those states?

Yes, more than I care to remember. This was our biggest effort, without a doubt. We spent more money this time, we collected more signatures, hundreds of thousands, and we were kicked off the ballot in a couple of major states, like California and Texas, on the basis of technicalities, or so they claimed. Actually, in California, they violated their own law. We had more than enough signatures in each state, but we didn't have enough political influence to make them obey their own law.

In any case, we campaigned all over the country, crisscrossed the country, and we gathered tremendously favorable responses from working people. Working people would listen to what we had to say, rather than becoming hostile because we were

Socialists or Communists or whatever. This marked a big change. We asked people to sign to get us on the ballot as Socialists supporting public ownership of oil or public ownership of other industries, ending the military budget and using it for social services. We supported equal opportunity, ERA, affirmative action, and similar causes. We were very straightforward about our position.

Your party got fewer votes in 1980 than it did in 1976. Is that because you couldn't get on the ballot in states like California that were very important to you?

There were a number of reasons for our smaller vote. I think the chief one is that our party had different candidates listed for president. Since technically I was too young to run for president, I was only listed on a ballot in a few states, and that had a tendency to confuse people. But our main reason for running was trying to win peoples' views. We had no illusion about winning the election, or even getting a bigger vote. Our main problem is that most people never knew we ran. They didn't know that any of the other third-party candidates ran. Paradoxically, there were many more third-party candidates on the ballot in 1980, and the totality of this vote was larger than in 1976.

What kind of reception did you get during the campaign? Was there any personal harassment?

I think in all honesty the response I got from the workers at the plants was better, more cordial, than the response Ronald Reagan or Carter would get. I mean, people would listen to what I had to say. Sometimes there would be a few right-wing remarks, but in general most of the people would take my campaign material and shake hands with me. I was a steelworker at that time, on a leave of absence. I worked at Gary U.S. Steel, and I campaigned as a worker running for president. I think Reagan and Carter had a much rougher time when they went to plants because workers viewed them as the enemy, at least some of them did—not all of them, obviously.

There was a different degree of cordiality to me out there. I don't want to try to overstate this. The main thing was a willingness to listen to new ideas rather than hostility.

But there are groups like the Ku Klux Klan. What do they think of a black person running for president?

Fortunately, we didn't really encounter them at any plants. I mean, periodically, we were running into right-wing workers, but for the most part, there wasn't any real hostility, and certainly no fear of physical harm.

How about media coverage? Could you get on television, get in the newspapers, appear on radio?

We got a small amount, mainly in the different local areas, the local media. We never got any nationwide coverage at all. This was less than before. The media argued there were so many third-party candidates running that they could cover only a few: the Communist Party or Barry Commoner or someone like that. Then they began to retreat on the equal time law that once existed. But we did get some local coverage. It was not a total blackout. However, the bulk of the people never knew there were candidates other than Democrats and Republicans.

I'd like to ask you about your lawsuit against the federal government. The Socialist Workers Party has brought a suit against the government for $40 million in damages to cover harassment by the FBI—infiltration, informers, etc. Why did you decide to do this? Are you unique? Why has the government had all these alleged agents looking at you?

We're not unique at all. The government claims in their case that they have the right to spy on any group, regardless of their nature. They have the right to look at any political organization that espouses revolutionary change, so that they will know who's on the side of the government and who is not. Now that's a very totalitarian concept. They justify their informers in our organization, not because we're committing any illegal acts—they've been doing this for forty years—but

because of the ideas we espouse. They don't limit this to socialists. They spied on Martin Luther King. The evidence
points that they must be at least aware of who killed King.
They had agents in the Klan as well as in the King organization. They spied on Malcolm X. We know they had a mur-
derous drive against the Black Panther Party, including setting
them up. So they spied on anyone who is in opposition to the
government policies from the left. This can include congressmen like Ron Dellums and others. If you opposed the government policies from the right, you were safe. In fact, you may
even be hired by the government to work for the CIA!

What were they actually doing?

Wiretaps, mail covers, planting informers within the organization, a lot of things.

*Do you have any idea of how many informants they had in your
party?*

A total of 1,300, they say. This was during the period of the
1950s right through 1969, they say. Now, we think this type of
function still goes on today. We have evidence of collaboration
with the FBI from documented evidence that they have been
forced to turn over. All this has come out in the course of the
court trial.

Fundamentally, the case is whether or not the American
people, including Socialists, have the right to dissent. But it's
more fundamental than Socialists having the right to dissent
without government harassment, government spying, and
whatnot. We maintain that everything we do is covered by the
Bill of Rights. When we go to Cuba, Nicaragua, Grenada;
when we collaborate with revolutionists from abroad; when
we run an election campaign and urge people to join our
movement; and when we openly espouse the need for a socialist revolution in the U.S.—this is all legal. If the Bill of Rights
does not cover this, then the Bill of Rights does not mean
what it says. But what the government lawyers have been saying in court is that the president has special powers that cannot

be restricted or limited by Congress or the judiciary, which give him the authority to carry out so-called internal security intelligence operations, to fight subversion, which they never define. They cannot demonstrate what a subversive activity is. They couldn't specify what it was clearly. What they mean is to demonstrate against the policies in El Salvador is subversive, or to call for a socialist revolution in the U.S., even if you don't commit a crime, is subversive.

Therefore, they can spy on you if they want to do so. They claim that the presidential oath of office authorizes them to do that. They claim they have a right to use these police-state methods in order to preserve and defend the republican form of government here. Now, we favor the republican form of government, but we favor the workers republic, not a capitalist republic. The main issue here is whether the public in general, or the working people in general, have the right to dissent regardless of their views, without government harassment.

It seems to me the question you would be asked is, if you're for overturning the system and putting in a new revolutionary system, does the existing government have a right to defend itself?

Defend itself against whom? Against its own people? This is exactly the issue here. My answer to that is no, they don't. As long as we are engaging in lawful political activity, we're not going to change this country through some secret maneuver. It's impossible to do so.

The only people who can change this country, and the only way revolutions are made everywhere—as opposed to coup d'etats, which the U.S. government has more experience with than we do, and which we do not seek—is by mass participation and mass support. It is the government that engages in illegal acts to stop that from being brought about. Today they engage in open and illegal acts to block the development of the antiwar movement, the civil rights movement. So when it comes down to the question of whether the government and the president have the right to defend the present system, we ask, defend it against whom? Who are they talking about?

They end up talking about defending the status quo against the masses of people! And the only way they say they can do that is through illegal acts.

So your position is that as long as you are legal, as long as you're not doing something that's illegal, you have a right to dissent in an effort to change the system.

Yes. We have not engaged in unlawful acts. There has never been a conviction of us within the last forty years for any criminal act. But the government's argument is that that does not matter; whether we function within the letter of the law does not mean that we can be left alone.

Our legal suit simply has to be brought, not only on our behalf, but on behalf of all of those who have been involved in other social movements. It was filed on behalf of the American people. Here's the main thing—the government, in order to protect the present economic and political setup, must engage in these illegal acts—burglaries, wiretaps, assassinations. They're the ones who are breaking the law of the land all the time. We think the American people at a certain point have a right to defend themselves by whatever means, but clearly the violence is not coming from the movement. It was not true even in the panther days. The Panthers were not going around shooting police, attacking police stations. It was the other way around.

Is your suit mainly concerned with FBI harassment, or do you claim other agencies were involved?

It's all of them. We're suing all of them. The FBI, the CIA, the Immigration and Naturalization Service, since they claim they have the right to deport any foreign-born person in this country who is a Socialist, who is a member of our party, or who is affiliated with us, just by virtue of their agreeing with our ideas, not breaking any laws.

Do you know what it costs to bring a suit like this?

No, I don't have any real idea about that. Over the last two months we've had to raise $125,000 alone, and we've been doing the suit since 1973. The total fee for the lawyers was over half a million dollars.

How about the 1980 campaign? Was that expensive?

We spent over a couple hundred thousand dollars. That was mainly airfare and whatnot, and it came from mostly party members and sympathizers.

PERSONAL IMPRESSIONS

Let me end up with some questions about the future. You've run for vice-president, for president, and for mayor of Chicago. You haven't won any races. Do you feel the party is making progress? Are you optimistic?

Oh, sure, I'm very optimistic. I think we achieve an important victory each time a new person is won to the cause of socialism. If that's translated into votes or new members, of course, that would be the ultimate. But just to begin to break down the effects of the propaganda of the ruling class today is very important. The other thing is to use our campaigns in a way to help the other movements in general: the antinuclear movement, the black movement, to help defend mothers in the Atlanta situation, to just make gains in whatever way we can.

As for the future, because of the economic reality and the need of the U.S. government to go to war to protect the status quo, the future certainly is going to be one of convulsion and tension: the threat of war, real war, more unemployment for working people, and whatnot. We're going to continue to see a polarization develop within the country and throughout the world. In the face of this, we're confident the American people will begin to change politically, begin to radicalize more, begin to change the unions, begin to make them democratic like the coal miners, begin to move them towards a political labor party. There's an independent black party now that I think indicates the direction the labor movement as a whole should go, so I'm very confident in the future. I don't see the U.S. ruling class, or any other ruling class of the capitalist kind, making gains. What is happening is that more and more people are either fighting for their freedom or have won their freedom. I think all of the labor parties will grow. I'm confident in the way we do things, in our whole perception of what needs to be done, and in our base in the union movement today. We're trying to bring about change in that area. I think we're going to be in a good position to make gains in terms of members and influence.

If you're confident about the party, how do you feel about the country? Where do you think we are heading in the future?

In terms of the outcome of the 1980 election, I think that the opinions that have been voiced by the official media are totally wrong. I don't think the working class, or the oppressed, are moving to the right in this country at all. People voted for Reagan because they didn't see any real difference between Reagan and Carter. Carter was an incumbent who had not done anything he had promised. Reagan appealed to the idea of getting big government off your back, solving the unemployment problem, lowering the inflation problem, and so on. So Reagan won the election largely because of that, not because of his extreme right-wing position on war, black rights, or women's rights. He certainly did not win by a landslide either. The popular vote didn't show that, only the electoral vote. But today there is a drive to the right by both parties, the Democrats and Republicans, which affects everything we see in Congress, and everything we see on the local level. Cutbacks are going to force working people to begin resisting these policies. We're going to see increasing black protest and antiwar action.

Let me conclude with a few personal questions. It's hard work to be involved in politics. Realistically, you seem to have little chance of winning. Why do you do it? Is it worth it?

I'm involved in politics because I believe in what I'm doing. I believe in the program of the Socialist Workers Party. I'm motivated by the power of an idea, of an ideal. It's not a personal thing. It's not an ego thing. You're right. It involves a lot of work, but I definitely think it's worth it. As I told you, we achieve a victory every time a new person is won over to socialism, and that's what keeps me going.

When you ran for mayor of Chicago, the Sun Times *said you'd been angry for twenty-eight years. You're now thirty years old. Are you still angry?*

Oh, yes, I'm very angry. I don't know if I was angry when I was born. I was probably sour, but ever since I've been conscious, beginning when I was in the South, I was very angry at the inequality, the war, the poverty, the injustice. Certainly I'm angry. However, I hope I have matured in the sense that there's not just a gut anger. It's both that and knowing now what it takes to bring about the ultimate solution which is a socialist world.

After that incident with the gang out in Cleveland, you said that you viewed all white people as the oppressor, the enemy. How do you feel about that now? Have you changed your opinion about white people?

Oh, certainly. Of course. Having met Joe Cole and having worked with white soldiers and all kinds of soldiers in the army to build the GI antiwar movement, it really changed my opinion about whites in general. I learned who among the whites were the oppressors. It's not just any old white, but those who have the political power, those who have the economic power. You don't find many blacks in that category, although we have black elected officials who carry out the will of the other capitalists, leading the cutbacks not only against blacks but also all working people. So it's a question of understanding the source of racism and why racism exists, which is to aid in maximizing profits by the ruling class and to keep the working class divided.

Back in Cleveland when I made that general statement about whites, which expressed my view then, it was only partially correct. But that's all I saw at that point. All I saw were cops and all the rest of them. Now I think there's unity in action between black and white workers, not to the disadvantage of blacks, but rather to respect the rights of blacks.

You seem well informed. You never finished high school because you had to go into the army. Do you read a lot? Have you educated yourself on political issues?

Yes. The only way to function as a political being in any kind of movement, and especially a radical movement, is to know what you're talking about, and to be able to understand what is happening in the world. My earlier involvement in the Young Socialist Alliance really began the advancement of my education in the sense of learning to read, write, speak, and everything else. I had no real interest before then. I saw no value in school. I saw no future offered by the educational system to deal with the injustice in society. But once I had become convinced there is a way out, there is a way to change things, then I wanted to read and study to help bring about these changes. That's what keeps me going, and that's why I am so active in the Socialist Workers Party.

WORKERS WORLD PARTY

The Workers World Party was organized in 1959 when its leadership split off from the Socialist Workers Party. Workers World is an activist revolutionary group that organized many antiwar, civil rights, and related demonstrations during the 1960s and 1970s. The party supports "liberation struggles against U.S. and capitalist imperialism" in all areas of the world, but it has backed the communist regimes in Hungary, Czechoslovakia, and Poland when revolts have arisen in these countries. The party has an active youth arm, Youth Against War and Fascism.[19]

The party had never run any presidential candidates prior to the 1980 election, when it named Deirdre Griswold, the forty-four-year-old editor of its weekly newspaper and one of its founding members, as its nominee. Her running mate for vice-president was Larry Holmes, a twenty-seven-year-old black activist. They appeared on the ballot in ten states and received a total of 13,300 votes.

Griswold is well versed in the polemics of the socialist and communist ideologies. I interviewed her in a restaurant adjacent to the party's headquarters office on West 21st Street in New York City in June 1981.

Deirdre Griswold

You cannot have socialism in the fullest, free sense of the word until you have a workers' world. That's what the title of our party means.

PERSONAL BACKGROUND

Smallwood: Tell me something about yourself, particularly about how you got involved in politics.

Griswold: I have been with the Workers World Party since its founding. I was one of the people who founded it in 1959. I was born in Delaware, but I grew up in Buffalo, New York, where my father was a steelworker, a union activist, and anti-racist. He worked real hard for the rights of workers in the Bethlehem steel plant there. I have tremendous respect for him. My later ideas were shaped by the movements against the Vietnam War and against racism in the 1960s, but I was also lucky enough to have had a chance to see the powerful working-class movement of the 1950s and its ability to respond in a militant way to the kind of right-wing politics that characterized that period. I can remember some very big strikes that my father was active in during the late 1940s and the early 1950s.

This was in the Buffalo area?

Right. Most people who are younger than me never saw anything like this. They have grown up in a different period, one in which the labor movement has been pretty much an appendage to the government's foreign policy. In the 1940s and 1950s there were some tremendous struggles where workers sacrificed a great deal and showed a lot of heroic determination to protect their interests. I saw that when I grew up, so my background is different than a lot of people who came out of the student movement or the women's movement.

Did you get your education in Buffalo?

Yes. I was a philosophy major at the University of Buffalo for a couple of years, but this was during the depths of the Mc-Carthy period. As a matter of fact, I remember the only attempt to have anything progressive on my campus was around 1954. Some students put a tiny little notice in the student paper that they wanted to start a John Reed club. I didn't even know who they were. The next day, the *Buffalo Evening News* had a front-page article on how subversives were becoming active at the University of Buffalo and how the Buffalo antisubversive squad was going to be on hand to monitor this meeting. The meeting actually never took place. But that was the kind of period it was when I went to college, so I left school after a couple of years.

Were you actively involved in politics in Buffalo before you came to New York City?

Not right away. I worked for several years in Buffalo. First I was a warehouse worker and secretary of my union. Then I worked in a hospital for a couple of years as a lab technician. I held a number of different jobs as a typesetter and a meatpacker.

Were you involved with the Socialist Workers Party before you helped to organize the Workers World Party in 1959?

Yes. I had been in it.

Have you always been interested in politics? Did you study politics when you were in college?

Since I went to a very reactionary college, there wasn't much opportunity for me to study politics in school, but I was always interested in political events. At that time, the civil rights movement was opening up, and I was involved in some activities in Buffalo concerning discrimination, open housing and things like that.

When did you come to New York City?

I was twenty-three or twenty-four years old. I came at the end of 1960, about three months before the Bay of Pigs invasion. In fact, I think I came on New Year's Day, or Eve, of 1961, just when we broke diplomatic relations with Cuba after the Castro revolution. I remember I went to a session of the United Nations with a group of people, mostly Puerto Ricans, who were very inspired by the Cuban revolution. When the Cuban delegates spoke up, a group of counterrevolutionary Cubans got up and yelled. Then the U.S. ambassador announced we were breaking off relations with Cuba. A group of us got up and denounced him as speaking for the bankers in the United States, and we were thrown out. That was my introduction to New York City.

Did you come to New York specifically to work for the new Workers World Party?

Yes. We wanted to make this our strongest center because New York is really the political capital of the country.

Have you always worked for the party since you arrived in New York?

I've always been active with the party. I've served as editor of our newspaper since 1970. However, the party isn't rich; we're always pressed for funds, so I have a part-time job as a proof-reader and copy editor to bring in money to support my family. I work at that about twenty hours a week.

Do you live in the city?

No, I live across the river in Hoboken, New Jersey. I have an eleven-year-old daughter. I was married in the late 1960s, but I'm divorced now. I'm looking for a place in the city, but it's very difficult, since rents are so high.

Are your father and mother still alive?

Yes.

What do they think about your running for president of the United States?

They were all for it.

POLITICAL IDEOLOGY

There are a lot of parties on the left—Socialist, Socialist Workers, Communist, Workers World. If you were to stake out your position, how would you define it?

First of all, you don't just put a label on it and say that will explain our views. For example, we think Trotsky was a great revolutionary, but it would give a false impression of our views on contemporary world situations in China and the USSR if we categorized ourselves as a Trotskyite party. Most of the parties like us that call themselves part of the Fourth International have extremely different views than we do.

Basically, we're a multinational Marxist or Leninist party dedicated to the building of a socialist society. Our views are a continuation of the basic method of analysis that these revolutionary figures developed. We are opposed to the capitalist economic system, which we feel is at the root of the world's problems. A system which pursues profits at the expense of people is bound to lead to oppression of the workers, militarism, and war. We identify ourselves with the workers of the world—women and men, young and elderly, disabled and able-bodied, gay and straight, lesbian, black, Latin, Asian, and white.

Let me try to sum it up in another way, rather than to put a label on it. We think that there are two basic class camps in the world today: a capitalist camp and a socialist camp. The socialist camp is divided politically, very much so, especially now with China making a virtual political, and maybe even military, alliance with the United States. We put out a lot of literature giving our analysis of why the split developed between China and the Soviet Union, but we don't think the split invalidates a Marxist approach. It does not change the fact that there is a new social system alive in both countries that has the potential for moving ahead and solving basic problems for the mass of the people.

You were originally a member of the Socialist Workers Party. Why did the Workers World Party break away from the Socialist Workers?

We had a lot of differences on the world issues, particularly the developments in eastern Europe, such as Hungary in 1956, Czechoslovakia in 1968, and in Poland today. The Socialist Workers see this as a renewal of working-class democracy, a move to the left. We don't objectively believe that this is what's happening in eastern Europe. We think that the leadership of these movements and rebellions has been reactionary and counterrevolutionary, despite the valid grievances that many people had there about living conditions, equality, bureaucracy, and bureaucratic methods.

We think that these are primarily right-wing movements very much encouraged by Western imperialism. Poland, as you know, is $27 billion in debt to the West, and this gives us a tremendous lever on their economy. The big strikes and demonstrations of the past year broke out because the banks demanded that the Polish government raise the price of food and generally impose an austerity program. The Socialist workers Party supports the Solidarity movement, but we think the issue is much more complicated than this, so there are big issues which separate the two of us.

All of the parties on the left seem fairly small. Is it possible for you to form some sort of coalition?

Not on issues such as the one I've just described. However, there are different coalitions and coalition efforts that will bring together parties of different views on some specific issues, such as an antiwar demonstration or a campaign against harassment of black people. So we work together on specific issues. However, there are very big ideological differences between many of the socialist political parties; they're not just petty.

Can you describe these differences a little more clearly?

If you look at historical periods when there are revolutionary potential and movements among the people, you'll see that some parties are able to grasp that and to provide leadership, while other parties can't do this. They will call themselves socialist. They may even say they are all followers of Marx, but they're all very different. These differences become apparent in how they respond and how they organize.

We believe in worldwide revolution. We think the Soviet Union provides an invaluable, if imperfect, model. We back other revolutionary movements. For example, we initiated the first demonstration in the United States in support of Arab liberation in 1967 during the Israeli-provoked war in the Mideast. We have also supported liberation struggles against U.S. imperialism in Chile, Indonesia, Angola, Ethiopia, Nicaragua, Iran, Grenada, and El Salvador. We are sympathetic with the IRA in Ireland and with the PLO's attempt to gain a decent homeland for the Palestinian refugees.

If you believe in worldwide revolution, do you think you can work within the existing political system, or do you think the system has to be overthrown to achieve your objectives?

First of all, revolutionaries don't make revolutions. It's the conditions created by society that make revolutions. Revolutionaries can only provide some guidance, some direction, some organizational experience so that the revolution can actually accomplish a change in society.

Of course, every ruling class has viewed the revolutionary movement as a sort of conspiracy. Look today at how the Reagan administration views El Salvador. It doesn't solve anything. It will just maintain the same system of oppression and starvation, and they'll be able to go on indefinitely as long as they can nip off the revolutionary leadership.

Let me rephrase my question. You seem to be talking about revolutionary activity in an abstract, intellectual, almost utopian sort of way. However, revolutions can involve terrorism, violence, brutality, and bloodshed. How do you feel about this? Do you think direct confrontation is justified to achieve your objectives?

Not necessarily one confrontation. There will be a million confrontations down the line. Every strike is a confrontation. Every demonstration is one. I've seen a lot of confrontations in my life. I think the most meaningful are the ones where what is needed is political courage, rather than physical courage. We're too used to everything being in terms of violent physical confrontation. I don't underestimate that as a factor, but how that turns out depends on political courage. The Russian Revolution was not some big bloody clash. It was primarily a political struggle for power. Later they had a civil war which was a much more violent struggle, but that was because the imperialist countries invaded, and the revolution was isolated.

So, in the final analysis, I think the key ingredient is political courage. Take our recent antiwar demonstration in Washington. People were saying that we couldn't do it at the Pentagon because it would be confrontational. We said we didn't think it would be and explained that we were applying for permits. It was like a war of nerves based on different political perspectives. In the end, we felt that our view was vindicated by the result. It was the first big antiwar demonstration of the 1980s, yet it was done by kind of dragging along a lot of people who considered themselves leaders in the antiwar movement.

It seems to me that there is a basic contradiction in your ideological position. You don't support revolutionary movements in socialist countries, such as Solidarity in Poland. However, you do support revolutions in nonsocialist countries, like the Democratic Revolutionary Front in El Salvador. Why is revolution desirable in one situation but not in the other?

Well, I wouldn't put it quite that way, but I see what you're driving at. We think the creation of a truly socialist state involves a long transitional period. It takes time. As a matter of fact, the USSR itself went through many different phases when it veered back and forth. This may surprise you, but fundamentally, we think this came from weakness. The USSR, like China, was a country where the revolution took place because the old system was the weakest. Both Russia and China were backward, agrarian countries. That's why the revolutions were able to succeed there, rather than in some other places like Germany or the United States.

Because of this inherited backwardness, it's extremely difficult to reorganize society on a more advanced socialist level. It can't be done overnight, and sometimes there are even periods of backward slippage. There are times when some remnants of the old system may return. This isn't just confined to socialist revolutions. This was also true of the earlier bourgeois revolutions against the old feudal order. Take the French Revolution of 1789. There was a period of political reaction after the monarchy was overturned. However, it didn't actually revert back to the old system of feudal monarchy. It was a transitional phase. We think the same transitional problems are occurring in socialist countries today, but we also think these countries deserve our support, even though they are not yet perfect, because they are moving in a forward direction.

But what about the capitalist countries? Why do you support revolutionary movements against them? Don't you think they are capable of moving in a forward direction?

That's the real contradiction. We think countries like the United States verify the Marxist predictions about the inherent contradictions of the capitalist system. Look at how irrational it is. A society that can be so productive, that can attain such a high level of technology, that can create such a superabundance of goods, and yet our social problems are intensifying rather than easing because of the deep inequalities created by the capitalist system.

You see, capitalism is based on one criterion—producing goods for profit—not necessarily to fulfill real social needs or to achieve more equality among the disadvantaged, but to make more profits. If they can't produce goods for a profit, they have to stop producing goods because they don't have a market for them. For a while they can make a lot of silly little things that nobody really needs, but eventually they have to build up for another war to take care of all the slack in the economy. War is the only thing that ended the capitalist depression of the 1930s, and we're heading in this same direction today with the new Reagan military buildup. This will provide a temporary shot in the arm to the economy, like heroin or something. However, the more money we spend on missiles, submarines, and aircraft carriers, the less we have for social programs. So we're overspending on arms to stimulate the economy, and we're producing useless goods from the standpoint of satisfying human needs.

That's the illogic of the capitalist system. That's the real contradiction. It was Eisenhower, of all people, who warned us to beware of the power of the industrial-military complex. Eventually, the United States will have to do something with all these arms, either by starting a war or by selling them overseas to other countries which also have unfilled social needs of their own. So we've become the great arms merchant of the world. It's completely chaotic. It's going nowhere in terms of improving the basic living conditions of the mass of the people.

You've spoken quite a bit about international issues and socialist theory. What is the party's position on domestic issues?

Our long-range goal is a system which will enable the workers to control the means of production. However, we don't think this can happen overnight. In the meantime, we'll settle for less. We favor an immediate people's takeover of the oil companies in this country; we think nuclear plants should be shut down; we support a shorter workweek with no cut in pay to alleviate unemployment; and we support full benefits for all who are still unemployed.

We're also very active on a great variety of social issues. As a matter of fact, our youth arm, called Youth Against War and Fascism, held its very first demonstration back in the early 1960s against George Lincoln Rockwell, who was then the leader of the American Nazi Party. We don't support Zionism, but we're opposed to anti-Semitism and all other forms of bigotry, racism, and chauvinism. As a result, we favor the strengthening of affirmative action and an end to all forms of racism, passage of the Equal Rights Amendment, free abortion on demand, an end to oppression of lesbian and gay people, and support for equal educational and employment opportunities for all.

How is your party organized?

We have one leadership body called the national committee which has representatives from all our branches on it. We now have nineteen branch offices throughout the country. Most of them are east of the Mississippi, because we started on the east coast, but we've now opened branches in Austin and San Antonio, Tucson, and San Francisco.

Does the party follow the philosophy of democratic centralism?

Yes. We think to function effectively we have to have a unity of purpose. When a decision is made, the membership must carry out that decision until the time comes to review it. If there's a change to be made, the membership has the right to do that. However, we don't have competing factions, or views, expressed by our party. We feel that the workers have to know what the party stands for in order to trust the party. It can't have five different positions on the same issue, like the Democratic Party or the Republican Party. It can't be all things to all people. It's not that type of party.

THE 1980 CAMPAIGN

Although the Workers World Party was organized in 1959, you never ran any presidential candidates until the 1980 election. Why did the party decide to get involved in presidential politics at this time?

It was primarily an educational objective—to get our program across. Prior to 1980, we had spent our efforts organizing on specific issues. We were the first group to organize street demonstrations against the Vietnam War back in the early 1960s, and we have organized many different protests over the past two decades.

In 1980, we felt there were a lot of questions because of the prolonged economic crisis in this country, the high inflation and unemployment. Eventually, this shakes people up. They will listen, even if they don't agree. We felt that millions of people are disillusioned with the system, but they're also fed up with elections because they feel they are not relevant to their situations at all. They don't even vote, and they are among the most oppressed people.

So we decided we would really try to speak out through the presidential campaign in order to reach these people. We were offering a real alternative. We told people they did not just have to vote for the lesser of two evils—the Democrats or the Republicans.

How did you try to do this? What kind of campaign did you run?

I worked very closely with Larry Holmes, our vice-presidential candidate. He's a black activist who has been involved in many social causes. We campaigned together in many different states. Not big monster rallies with a lot of hoopla and balloons. We appeared at tenant organization meetings, union picket lines, antinuclear meetings, even in people's kitchens for small, informal gatherings.

We went everywhere we could get a chance to speak. We did a lot of interviews, especially on radio. We got a few on television, but that was much more difficult, even though we were national candidates. We particularly enjoyed being on radio programs where people can call in. You can feel what they have to say, and hear their questions. You can debate, and converse with them. I remember one particular program in Mississippi where we got more people calling in who were sympathetic to our ideas rather than hostile.

Did you run into a lot of hostility and harassment?

It depended on the area. I think San Antonio, Texas, was the hardest. We had to actually walk off a program there.

How about press coverage? Did you get much of that?

We got some good, serious coverage. We got a very good article in the *Los Angeles Times* and a grudging article in the *New York Times*. We were covered in hundreds of local newspapers. Everywhere we went, we had an active crew of people who were setting up interviews for us. We visited about seventy different cities during the course of the campaign.

Was money a limiting factor?

Well, we didn't have any big contributors, since I don't think our program appeals to them. A party like ours depends on the fact that the members are very dedicated. Even though they don't have much, they make very large contributions relative to their income. However, we didn't have enough money to afford paid advertising. Our method was to be visible with posters which we did ourselves, with leaflets, and to try and get as much press and radio coverage as we could, whether it was the establishment press, college papers, black community papers, or whatever.

We had to file several financial statements as we went along. I don't remember the final one, but I think we spent between $30,000 and $50,000. We probably spent more on transportation than anything else, although we tried to be economical about it.

Did you have trouble getting on the ballot in different states?

It depended on a combination of factors—election laws, whether we had a core of supporters in the state who would work to get us on the ballot. The election laws varied tremendously. In New Jersey, a big industrial state, you only have to have 800 signatures from registered voters. In other states, like Georgia, you have to have 60,000, or in California, 100,000, signatures. We couldn't handle that, so we missed those states.

As you know, the Socialist Workers Party has brought a lawsuit against alleged government harassment by the FBI, the CIA, and other agencies. Have you run into any of this type of harassment?

I think any party on the left which is halfway serious is going to get harassed. The government is going to try to send in agents. You're going to have your phones tapped, your offices burglarized, sometimes even bombed. We've had all this happen to us. We don't go around looking for informers in our party. We feel the most important thing is to keep your mind on your objective, which is to organize the working people. I hope the Socialist Workers Party wins its suit. I think that all organizations on the left should support them. However, tactically, I think it's a mistake to divert so much of their time, attention, and funds to this when there's so much else that could be done.

You've got to understand that the government represents the ruling class in this country, which wants to protect the status quo—to protect its privileges, its power and interests. You can gain some temporary advantage, but the main concern is to get out to the people who are being hurt by the system and help them organize to bring about real political change because, in the long run, the government only respects the strength of mass organization.

PERSONAL IMPRESSIONS

How about the future? Do you think your party is making any real progress in meeting its objectives?

Yes. I think we gained a great deal from the campaign. We helped many people understand some rudimentary ideas about our program for socialism and our programs against racism and bigotry of all kinds. There would have been much more of a vacuum if we had not run as candidates. We ran a vigorous campaign. We went to many parts of the country where none of the other parties on the left had appeared, so I think we reached a lot of people.

What do you think your political base is?

We don't view ourselves as a political party that's just trying to think in terms of how to get this constituency or how to get that constituency. We don't look at it that way at all. We look at what kind of a program do you put forward that's a real answer to all these problems we face today.

Our position is generally one of self-determination for the oppressed. The people who have suffered are the ones who have to be in a position to formulate the way out of it. So we don't look at it from the point of view of a narrow political program that, if you come up with enough promises to enough people, you will get a bigger vote. We're really trying to develop a program for a working-class movement in this country that can say this is the way to end these historical evils; this is the only way to do it.

Are you optimistic about the future? Do you think a Marxist-Leninist party will succeed in the United States in your lifetime?

One thing I've learned from our party is to have a longer view of history. In that sense I'm optimistic for humanity, for the survival of humanity, and for the development of a superior social system to anything we've ever known. It's not based on faith that people are born basically good. It's based on looking at the development of humanity and the practical and theoretical knowledge that has emerged over thousands of years. The human race is now capable of sustaining a comfortable existence for all. It's certainly possible, given our understanding of nature and technology, of how to grow and produce the things that are necessary for decent human survival and cultural development. However, I think that this is a terribly dangerous period of great struggles and conflicts because the world is still predominantly capitalist. See, that's the hard thing. You cannot have socialism in the fullest, free sense of the word until you have a workers' world. That's what the title of our party means.

When Marx and Engels wrote about socialism, they talked about the withering away of the state. They predicted that when class antagonisms begin to diminish, and there's more equality in the sense of people being able to share material abundance, there won't be the need for one segment of society to impose its order on the rest. Therefore, the state, which carries out this function, will disappear. Well, that hasn't happened at all. But the next question to ask is why hasn't it happened? Is it just because evil men have gotten the leadership? No. We don't think that. We think that the reason it hasn't happened yet is because the socialist parties can only be imperfect as long as capitalism has the preponderance of the world's natural resources and controls the world market. This poses the constant threat of intervention and subversion, even of a new war. We think that these are very real dangers.

It's hard work to campaign for president. Do you think it was worth it?

Actually, it's not that hard to campaign. It's very interesting. You learn a lot doing it. It's a great opportunity to test your ideas out on different people, to sharpen your own ability to articulate your views. I've had a lot of different jobs in my life, and I think that most people who work for a living work very hard. I felt that being a candidate for this party was a great privilege. It's not any harder than if you work as a waitress somewhere, or you work on a nine-to-five job and then have to come home at night to take care of three kids, which is the life most people have. So I would have to say, in terms of personal satisfaction, it was definitely worth it.

5 VOICES FROM THE RIGHT AND THE LIBERTARIANS

Three of the third-party candidates who ran in the 1980 election represented political movements that first emerged during the late 1960s and early 1970s—the American Independents (1968), the American Party (1972), and the Libertarians (1972). These three parties tend to speak for the right end of the political spectrum, though the Libertarians resist classification under any single ideological heading.

The ideologies of the right, including traditional conservatism, are more loosely structured and ambiguous than communism or scientific socialism. Historically, conservatism grew out of a desire to maintain, or to conserve, the existing order. It has been defined as "a set of beliefs about society and government, among them an attitude of respect towards the existing social and political arrangements, especially when these have been gradually formed over a long period of time."[1]

The conservative movement emerged in Europe in response to the massive political and social upheavals that occurred during the French Revolution of 1789, and its two earliest spokesmen were the British political writer and statesman, Edmund Burke (1729–1797), and the French writer and diplomat, Joseph de Maistre (1754–1821).

Burke's essay, "Reflections on the Revolution in France" (1790), initiated a tradition of more moderate conservatism in which the importance of continuity in political experience and the necessity of protecting and preserving traditional liberties in the face of radical change were emphasized. Joseph de Maistre, who was an ardent Royalist and a Roman Catholic, advocated a much more reactionary conservative philosophy that stressed almost unquestioning allegiance to traditional authority.[2]

The Burkean form of conservatism was nurtured in England by such nineteenth-century statesmen as Sir Robert Peel and Benjamin Disraeli. During more recent times, one of Britain's leading conservative theorists, Professor Michael Oakeshott, described this type of conservatism as an attitude, rather than a dogma. According to Oakeshott, "it is not a creed or a doctrine, but a disposition. To be conservative is to be disposed to think and behave in certain manners . . . to prefer the familiar to the unknown, the tried to the untried, the actual to the possible."[3] The American historian Peter Viereck has characterized this conservative temperament as distrustful of untested innovations, and believing in historical continuity and the need for some traditional framework to tame human nature.[4] On the other hand, the reactionary conservatism of the de Maistre school is more zealous than Burke's in its emphasis on the authority of traditional values and its allegiance to traditional institutions.

Both types of conservatism, however, shared an attitude of suspicion and caution toward social and political change. As a result, most present-day conservatives are skeptical (if not actually distrustful) of governmental intervention into the existing social order, and many of them place a high value on private (nongovernmental) institutions such as the club and the church, and volunteer associations.

Many conservatives also subscribe to the free-market approach that was set forth by the Scottish economist Adam Smith (1723–1790) in *The Wealth of Nations* (1776). However, conservative ideology is not necessarily, or inevitably, wedded to the concept of capitalism or complete laissez-faire economics. As Peter Viereck points out, "the conservative temperament may be, but need not be, identical with conservative politics or with right-wing politics or economics."[5] In a similar vein, British philosopher Roger Scruton holds that "conservatism is a stance that may be defined without identifying it with the politics of any party."[6]

An interesting variant of the more moderate conservative

approach in the United States is to be found in the so-called neo-conservative movement that has emerged during the past two decades. In 1965, Irving Kristol and Daniel Bell launched a new journal, *The Public Interest*, with the aim of translating social science knowledge into a form that would be accessible to public policy makers. During ensuing years, however, they became increasingly disillusioned with the failure of many Great Society initiatives, with the widespread social unrest that accompanied the student revolt against intellectualism during the Vietnam War, and with what they perceived to be the growing excesses of the New Left. A number of other prominent figures in academia and journalism began to share their disillusionment, including Daniel Patrick Moynihan, Seymour Martin Lipset, Michael Novak, Ben Wattenberg, Norman Podhoretz, Nathan Glazer, and James Q. Wilson. Over time, this group identified a number of potential causes for the failure of governmental programs: the unintended negative consequences of many policies; the limits of knowledge; pursuit of conflicting and contradictory policies; the growth of a new governmental class with a vested interest in expanding the role of the state; the weakening of traditional mediating structures such as the family and the church; and an overly utopian view of the ability of government to change the nature of man and society. As a result, they began to advocate a new neo-conservative approach to politics that called for the revival of mediating structures, the use of a corrected market mechanism for the promotion of social ends, and the restoration of more traditional approaches to political change through coalition building, bargaining, and incrementalism.[7]

While the neo-conservative philosophy grew out of liberal disillusionment with the government's Great Society initiatives, a second, totally different example of a more reactionary, authoritarian conservative ideology is to be found in the so-called radical right (or, more recently, New Right) groups. This ultraconservative approach emerged in the United States during the late 1950s with the appearance of one of the most prominent of the extreme right-wing groups, the John Birch Society. Founded in 1958 by Robert Welch, a wealthy candy manufacturer, and named after John Birch, an American intelligence officer who was killed by the Communists in China in 1945, the society was originally organized to fight communist subversion in America. However, it also advocated abolition of the graduated income tax, repeal of social security legislation, and opposition to forced busing.

The ideology of the radical right organizations of more recent vintage consists of a strong revulsion toward any form of collectivism, especially communism; a fundamentalist interpretation of the Bible; and a conspiratorial view of world events that leads to ultrapatriotism and stronger national defense, and calls for the purification of American society through a return to the values that characterized "the golden age" of the founding fathers.[8] This ideology is promoted today by such groups as the Moral Majority, the National Conservative Political Action Committee (NICPAC), and the Committee for the Survival of a Free Congress. Although these groups favor lower taxes and a more limited role for government in such areas as welfare services, they support stronger defense expenditures and major governmental intervention into many social areas, including tougher drug laws, a constitutional amendment to prohibit abortion, and other measures that they consider to be necessary to restore traditional moral values.

A third political group that has drawn upon some strains of conservative thought, but disagrees with both the neoconservatives and the radical right, is the Libertarian Party, which was organized in Denver, Colorado, in 1972. It is difficult to categorize the Libertarians under any one ideological label. The central creed of the Libertarian Party is individualism and individual freedom. As a result, they support a free-market approach in economic affairs, but they also strongly oppose what they view as unwarranted governmental intrusion in the area of personal and civil liberties.

In light of this wide range of viewpoints, it is hardly surprising that none of the third-party candidates who ran in 1980 described themselves as conservatives (the closest any candidate came to this was when Benjamin Bubar indicated the Prohibition Party was "a conservative, Christian-oriented party"). John R. Rarick, the American Independent Party candidate, indicated that he didn't call himself a conservative; he just felt people were fed up with being told what was good for them. Percy Greaves of the American Party, who viewed himself as a "free-market, free-minded" person, was opposed to being described as conservative because conservatives do not favor change and he did. Ed Clark, the libertarian candidate, favored a free-market view, but he indicated his party reached back to the classical liberal tradition of John Locke in its defense of civil and personal liberties.

Under these circumstances, is it possible to classify any of the third parties as "voices of the right"? There are two different rationales that can be used to justify such an approach. First, one of the central axioms of the traditional political parties of the right is a strong belief in individualism, coupled with a skeptical view of the power of the governmental institutions to influence or determine human conduct—a position that has been advocated, in varying degrees, by the American Independent, the American, and the Libertarian Parties. Second, all three of these parties are directly opposed to the ideologies of the leftist parties—the Socialists, the Communists, and the Trotskyites—who believe in varying degrees of collective action to achieve social reform.

Hence, while they certainly do not fit into any one mold, each of the parties presented in this chapter favors less governmental intervention into economic and/or social affairs. The three parties differ quite markedly, however, on a variety of specific issues, and the nature of these differences becomes quite clear during the course of the interviews.

THE AMERICAN INDEPENDENT PARTY

The American Independent Party (AIP) was organized in 1968 to support the presidential campaign of Alabama Governor George C. Wallace. Wallace based his presidential bid on a broad appeal to white voters who feared the changes in race relations growing out of the civil rights acts of 1964 and 1965, and who were disillusioned with the government's failure to use sufficient military force to win the Vietnam war. While serving as governor of Alabama, Wallace had achieved national recognition as an outspoken opponent of racial integration, and his campaign centered on issues of segregation, law and order, and patriotism.

Wallace received 9,906,473 votes in 1968, the highest popular vote total achieved by any third-party candidate in American history, carrying five southern states with forty-six electoral college votes. Bolstered by his 1968 showing, Wallace decided to seek the Democratic Party nomination for president in 1972. However, he was shot and seriously paralyzed on May 15, while on a campaign stop in Laurel, Maryland.

Following the Wallace shooting, the AIP cooperated with the newly organized American Party in the 1972 election, when it supported John G. Schmitz of California, the American Party candidate, who received over one million popular votes. After 1972, however, the two parties broke apart, and in 1976, the American Independents' presidential candidate was former Georgia governor, Lester B. Maddox, whose vote total dropped to 170,000.

In 1980, the American Independent Party nominated John R. Rarick, a former congressman from Louisiana, who was on the ballot in only eight states. Rarick received a total of 41,268 popular votes. Most of his support came from Alabama (15,010), plus his home state of Louisiana (10,333), and California (9,856), the home state of his vice-presidential running mate, Eileen M. Shearer.

I interviewed John Rarick in January 1982 at his law office in St. Francisville, Louisiana, a small town thirty miles north of Baton Rouge and about ten miles south of the Mississippi border. Rarick described the area as "the Deep South. We're south of Mississippi. You can't get much further south than this."

John C. Rarick

I was always very outspoken. I always told everybody what I felt.

PERSONAL BACKGROUND

Smallwood: I'd like to start out with a little background information. As I understand it, you were not originally from Louisiana. I think you were born in Indiana.

Rarick: That's right. I was born and raised in Waterford, Indiana. It's a farming area. My ancestors date back to the early settlers. I was born in 1924, and I will be fifty-eight next week on January 29. After attending grade school and high school in that area, I entered Ball State Teachers College in 1942 in Muncie, Indiana. While I was in college, I joined the enlisted reserves, so I ended up being called to active duty.

Once I finished basic, they sent me to the Army Specialized Training Program at LSU—Louisiana State University—in Baton Rouge, which was the first time I'd been in Louisiana. Eventually, I was assigned to the infantry. In 1944, we were sent to England. We landed in the heart of France after D-Day in the fall. I was a BAR man in Company C, 393d Infantry, 99th Regiment, captured on the first day of the Battle of the Bulge on December 16, 1944. After spending four months as a German prisoner, I got sick and tired of living on a potato a day, so I escaped. I made it back to the American lines in thirteen days, where I promptly got put back in jail as a suspect by my own army. The FBI fingerprinted me and interviewed my parents before they eventually decided that I was an American.

Did they think you were a German spy when you first came back?

Yes. After thirteen days hiding out with some Poles, Greeks, and Czechs—I think there were eleven of us—we captured an American command post. That was the only way we could surrender. None of us had on American uniforms. I had a French uniform with my hair clear down my back and lice all over me. So we captured a guard at an outpost, took his gun from him, and then we marched him in to surrender.

They were immediately suspicious that we were some kind of a nazi outfit, so they locked us up. I was in an army jail in France for something like three months. The FBI interviewed me, and of course, in those days we didn't get any special treatment. In fact, you remember Eisenhower finally got teed off at it, and he ordered that all former prisoners, escaped prisoners, and repatriates be given triple A priority. So suddenly, man, I couldn't do anything wrong!

Were you involved in any more fighting after that?

No. I got a Bronze Star, a Purple Heart, and even a decoration from the Belgian government. I wasn't interested in any more fighting. They flew me back to Indianapolis, and I spent time in different hospitals—Billings General and then Ashford General in White Sulphur Springs, where I used to sit and play Hearts with Skinny Wainwright. I had lost a lot of weight when I was a prisoner. When I escaped, I weighed probably about ninety pounds, and I was having difficulty with my circulation, especially in my feet. After my discharge, I qualified as a disabled veteran so I applied to law school.

Originally I wanted to go to Notre Dame, but they told me it would be six years before I could get in because they had to give priority to all those naval officers who attended their programs during the war because they were alums. That's when I decided to go back to LSU in Baton Rouge where I had met Marguerite, my wife, when I was in the army. We were married on December 27 in 1945, so '45 was quite an important year for me. Marguerite was from New Orleans, and even though she had gone to LSU, she encouraged me to apply to

Tulane Law School. They accepted me. That's how I got back south again. I graduated from Tulane in 1949.

How did you first get involved in politics?

I guess I've always had some interest in politics. My parents, who were Democrats, were very active in the farmers union back in the old depression days. My mother had been the county secretary and treasurer. I had an uncle—John, he's my namesake—who had been on the city council in Goshen, Indiana. When I graduated from Tulane back in 1949, they didn't know what to do with lawyers. You could get a $50-a-month job emptying wastebaskets in a law firm. So I went back to Indiana where I became city chairman of the Democratic Party in Goshen.

Eventually, I ended up taking a job with an insurance company in South Bend, working as an adjuster. I never will forget it. I thought it was the biggest job I had in my life. I was paid $200 a month, and they gave me a car—even paid for some of the gas. But they wouldn't give me a promotion, so I got another job with State Farm Mutual. They were getting ready to go into Louisiana, because up until 1952, the state never had compulsory insurance. When they found out I was a graduate of Tulane Law School and also a member of the Louisiana bar, they sent me down here as the first claim adjuster they ever had in the state.

Was this when you moved to St. Francisville?

No. We lived in New Orleans at that time. In fact, two of our children—we have three—were born in New Orleans; the other was born in South Bend. I moved around with State Farm to Birmingham and Dallas, but I still handled a lot of personal injury litigation all over Louisiana. It was my job to try to settle as many cases and lawsuits as I could, so I used to pick up a whole bunch of files and fly to Louisiana over the weekend to try to horse-trade with lawyers to see if we could settle six cases for the price of five.

One of the most active lawyers lived in St. Francisville.

While I was here trying to settle a case, he had a heart attack. He didn't have anyone else working with him. At that time, I think we had three lawyers in this whole parish; today we've got about twenty. He offered me a junior partnership, and I moved my family to St. Francisville.

When was this?

In 1957. Within three months after I arrived, my partner got indicted. My first case in the state supreme court was defending my law partner. After he was acquitted, we promptly severed our relationship. Shortly after that, the district judge had a stroke and died, so there was a vacancy. He was quite a character with a southern flavor. My former law partner announced for the office, but more and more people started to drop by to tell me they wanted me to run. I was a young lawyer, having only been in the community a couple of years, but I was very active in youth programs—Boy Scouts and things of that sort. So I decided to run. On the first ballot, I came within seventeen votes, and in the runoff I was elected.

Was this the real beginning of your career in state politics?

Well, actually, I wasn't accepted by the establishment. After I was elected district judge, I promptly got sued on the basis that the law says I had to practice for five years to qualify, although I'd been a graduate of Tulane Law School and member of the Louisiana bar since 1949. I won the law suit and was finally installed as district judge, but I wasn't one of the chosen few in the state Democratic hierarchy from the governor's group on down. Every time there was a case that some other district judge didn't want because it threatened to upset the political apple cart, I'd be assigned by the supreme court to drive a hundred miles or so to hear it. I had to shut down my court, and go to some other parish to hold court. During the first couple of years, I must have ended up holding court in twelve different parishes. Of course, the state politicians didn't know what they were doing. I mean, I was getting around, people were liking me, and I was really enjoying this new stature.

Was this when you decided to run for Congress?

Not immediately. I served as a district judge for five years before I ran for Congress in 1966. The incumbent was Jimmy Morrison, who was very much in line with LBJ and all the new liberal Great Society programs. He'd been in Congress for twenty-six years, and most people thought he was unbeatable. But I was riding around the judicial circuit, and people kept telling me, "We've got to get us a man to run against Morrison." The trouble was that nobody was about to sacrifice their political career to run against a guy who'd been twenty-six years in Congress, who was the darling of all the news media, and who had both the state and national party's support. At that time, there were twelve parishes in the congressional district, including Baton Rouge, which is the state capital, and it would involve a big effort.

It ended up they couldn't get anybody else to run for Congress, and people kept coming up to me and saying, "You run. We're gonna give you help; we're gonna campaign for you." I finally decided to run. I went to the chief justice of our supreme court to get a leave of absence as a judge to run for Congress, figuring, you know, hell, this was going to be a bust. But somebody needed to run.

Was the chief justice sympathetic?

He told me that Jimmy Morrison was one of the greatest friends he ever had. He made it clear that he didn't want me to run against him. He said, "I'm not granting any leave of absence. If you're going to run against my beloved friend, I want you to quit the bench, and quit right now. I don't even want you talking about this." But, I did go home to talk with my wife about it, and she said, "Let's quit." So I resigned as district judge and announced for Congress.

How did you beat a twenty-six-year veteran congressman?

I guess I campaigned for ten months. I wore out about three cars, and never drank so much coffee in my life. I had a real base in the rural parishes because everybody knew me from my work as a district judge. My real problem was Baton Rouge, a big city where I had to get some television exposure and publicity.

One day I received a call from my old company commander who owned a hotel in Baton Rouge and wanted me to come down there. Once I arrived at his office, in marched about five big contractors from Baton Rouge, all Republicans, who told me they wanted to help finance my campaign. One of them said to me, "Don't think I'm doing this because I love you or the Democratic Party. But listen, I hate Jimmy Morrison so bad that I'll sell my business and everything else I've got because I think you have a real good chance to beat him."

He was right. This put us on TV. I beat Jimmy Morrison pretty good; I don't know, about 5,000 or 10,000 votes. In 1967, I went to Washington as the new Sixth District congressman from Louisiana.

POLITICAL IDEOLOGY

Once you were in Congress, did you try to represent the new conservatism that was emerging in the South?

I don't think we were really conservative. The people were just fed up being told what was good for them. The old congressman used to come down here from Washington and announce that he voted this way or that way because he knew what was good for people. This kind of stuff infuriated them whether they were conservative or not. So I ran as an anti-LBJ candidate. I still got those tapes around where I said that Jimmy Morrison even had LBJ printed on his pajama britches.

If you don't describe yourself as a conservative, how would you summarize your own political position?

I simply ran as an independent Democrat. I didn't campaign with the politicians, who were all against me, but by trying to give the people what they told me they wanted. I'm not sure many of them thought I could deliver, but at least they felt it would be a refreshing change to have someone say that he wanted to try to represent the people of the Sixth Louisiana Congressional District rather than representing people in New York or California because they were giving him money.

What did you think the people wanted? Let's start with a domestic issue like the government's role in the economy.

I was violently opposed to any more encroachment by the federal system on the states and also by the states on the local governments. I felt, almost like your New Hampshire rural-type meetings, that we should have more people involved. We should try to get the government as close to the people as we can. People in Louisiana have no more interest in what happens in New Hampshire than the average New Hampshire person cares about what happens in Louisiana. As long as you leave us alone, we'll leave you alone.

When you were running for president in 1980 was this the basic message you were trying to get across?

It was one of the major issues. I think we've had too much government in our lives for a long time. A strong government makes weak people and families. The trouble is they don't feel they can do anything for themselves. They have to go to the food stamp office or the unemployment office to find someone to get a job for them. They don't feel they can do these things themselves because they have been trained—or the word may be educated—to think the federal government has to do it for them.

Of course, if we listen to the economists, we can see what the federal government has done for us. It has cost us all about a hundred thousand times what we could have done for ourselves. But the whole new generation seems to be dependent upon the politicians and the system. You ask kids today why they're going to college—well, they want to make more money. When I went to college, I never did it with the idea of making money. I felt it was my duty to try to improve myself to be able to help the rest of society. But the idea we have today, that the more education you get, the more money you're supposed to make, is going to crumble sooner or later because we're going to have too many college professors and too many college graduates. Then the next thing you know, you're going to have people saying it's discriminatory to give a man a job merely because he's got a college education. That's discrimination, if you want to get into that field.

As a matter of fact, I do. What is your position on civil rights issues—busing, affirmative action, and the rest?

It's counterproductive. It's not accomplishing anything. In Baton Rouge, we're now going into the third phase of desegregation. The last federal judge just threw up his hands. Every time he tried to force people to desegregate the schools or to bus, they either opened up private schools or they moved. They just resegregated themselves. So it looks to me that there might be much better ways to spend our money than to try to force school kids into situations that adults won't accept. It just doesn't work.

The South is far more integrated—always has been—than the North. You're sitting here in the blackest parish in Louisiana. Our population of Negroes is probably 67 percent. Always has been that way. If you'd been here a little earlier, I had to take my grandkids to the babysitter, and, of course, there just isn't enough white people to do babysitting. We've always had black people. I know this is what you northerners say is paternalism. But we live closer to the black people than anyplace else in the country.

The American Independent Party grew out of the George Wallace movement in 1968, and critics have charged it is racist. I assume from your last comment that you don't agree with this.

It's not even in the picture. Race is not in this. You're either an American or you're nothing. If you're not producing, then you're a nonproducer—you're a dreg—and we try to help you. But it's not based on race. This country's not going to rise or fall on race. It's going to rise or fall on whether the people are proud to be an American under the system and theory of limited government.

But you said that 67 percent of the people in this county are black. Does the government have any role in helping them if they need help?

The government in this parish has been given extra sums for aid to dependent children, extra aid for food stamps. The government has also been opening up all these new industries, but when you go down the river to the nuclear plant, almost all the workers are from out of Boston, Massachusetts. Stone and Webster is the general contractor. They're not hiring many local people. They're bringing all the people in from outside. And this is a program that is supposed to help us. Well, I mean the unemployment is as bad here now as it was before. It's just third and fourth generation now depending on handouts and federal assistance.

Let's turn to some other domestic issues. In your campaign literature, you talked about returning to traditional American values. How do you feel about issues such as abortion and the Equal Rights Amendment?

The government, of course, has been trying to control everything from the cradle to the grave. It has now entered into morality, although the government itself is the perpetrator of all the problems we have. I have never been endeared by the right-to-life people. I don't believe in abortion, but I've always thought that it's a matter for the states. If the people in New York want wholesale abortion on demand, that is their business. The people in Louisiana—and I'm not a Catholic, I'm a Baptist—the people down here have always felt that there are certain areas where there was a justification for abortion—in cases such as miscegenation, incest, or forcible rape, although, of course, it had to be proven. Other than that, they regard it as murder.

As the American Independent Party candidate, I accepted their platform, which was completely opposed to any abortion with tax money, federally funded abortion. Many times when you're the candidate—and I'm not the candidate now—you have to accept their platform.

How about ERA?

I was one of only a handful of congressmen who voted against it. My main opposition was that they were going to try to make a political football out of it, which is what has been done. I see that now Georgia and Oklahoma have just turned it down. I don't think it will ever come to anything except to stir up more litigation. I'm not saying that women don't have some legitimate complaints about salaries and the like. One of my daughters is divorced with two kids, and she complains to me about this, so, of course, I'm helping pick up her costs. But if you start letting politicians handle ERA with a constitutional amendment, it would end up as a litigated matter in the Supreme Court that would take twenty years before anybody would know what they meant.

What's your position on international issues? Do you think Reagan is right to increase the military budget and defense expenditures?

I wouldn't relish living under communism, but when I was a German prisoner, I wouldn't have been able to get through that winter if it wasn't for the Russians who were imprisoned with me. We had our troubles communicating and all, but they sure taught me how to live under that type of system: how to steal, how to survive. When the war was over, of course, a lot of them wanted to come to this country. But, our policy under "Operation Keelhaul" was to round them up, and we forced them to be sent back in cattle cars to Russia, where they completed their statistics. That is, the Soviets took them out and shot them.

The Russians all think that we are capitalists, and this is a bad word to them. The average American doesn't realize that they're not talking about the American people. They're talking about the financial system which controls us. I agree with a lot that Mr. Reagan says he's trying to do, but I can also see that he's already captured by the idea that we have to protect the big banks and money interests in this country by protecting their foreign investments. I can't understand why our interests in the Middle East are more important than our interests in Cuba or Central America or Canada. As far as national defense, I can't see why we have to arm the whole world. I mean, somebody else has got to help.

Does this mean you are opposed to foreign aid?

Let me finish on the national defense, because this may surprise you. I'm a combat veteran, but I'm against the draft. I never voted for the draft while I was in Congress. I feel the only way we're going to be able to afford the increase in defense that Mr. Reagan's talking about is through the National Guard. The real strength of our military in the past has always been through the use of the reserves and the National Guard. If we could beef up our National Guard, we would be nearer to accomplishing what we're told we're after, rather than by sending our boys to Japan, Italy, and Germany, especially when Europeans are marching up and down the street telling us they don't want our nuclear power in their backyard. If they don't want our nuclear power, then why should they want our boys? Why should we sit here and be controlled by the international cartel that some people call the United Nations? Americans have to start worrying about their own country and their own boys, and if we have a strong country back home, then the people overseas will worry about us.

As for foreign aid, I never voted for that in Congress. To me, this deficit thing is unbelievable. You know that we have to balance our budget with what some other people buy from us, and then we give them foreign aid to make up for it. I'm opposed to foreign aid, so why should I believe in the draft and sending our boys overseas, which is only another form of foreign aid?

Let me ask you a couple of final questions about your personal political beliefs. When you were in Congress from 1967 to 1975, the Almanac of American Politics *described you as the most rabidly right-wing member of the House, who championed "any far-right, anti-Semitic, or antiblack bilge that came across your desk."*[9] *How do you feel about this kind of comment?*

That really makes it sound like I've got smoke coming out of my ears, doesn't it? I don't know why they'd say those things, nor who said them. The Anti-Defamation League took after me because I never voted for any foreign aid, and that includes Israel. I sure wasn't going to defend any Germans or Israelis or anyone else. Of course, being a southern judge, it was real easy to say I was a racist, especially when I opposed the Voting Rights Act and open housing. Isn't that a beauty? They talk about equal rights and justice, but eight southern states can't even pass their own laws under the Voting Rights Act.

I was always very outspoken. I always told everybody what I felt. In fact, I voted for prayer. I'm a Mason, and the organized Masons were all for outlawing prayer in public schools, but I voted against them because I want to let kids pray where they want to pray. Yet, they never called me an anti-Mason. I think comments like this were a political gimmick. In 1972, I was the only Democrat on the AFL-CIO Committee of Political Education hit list even though I wasn't antilabor. I guess my problem was that I never was a politician. I didn't go to Congress to politick. I went there to try to do something, not to wet-nurse this group or that group.

The same article indicates your strength was in the rural areas where memories of the Ku Klux Klan are still alive. Is the Klan still active in Louisiana politics?

I wouldn't know. How does one know? I never heard of any TV, radio, or newspaper chains they control. Reagan got into an argument with Carter about this in the 1980 campaign. I've never been involved with the Klan. They tried to get me to repudiate Klan support, but I've never repudiated any support from any group of voters, any more than I would expect my opponents to repudiate liberal support or socialist support. Drew Pearson came down here once and accused me of being a neo-Nazi. How do you like that? Here I was, a prisoner of war in Germany while he was sitting in Washington, and he accused me of being a neo-Nazi. Politics used to be a dirty, dirty game. I don't know whether it is anymore, but after a while, they'll get you just by repeating things over and over again.

THE 1980 CAMPAIGN

When did you first get involved with the American Independent Party? Did you support George Wallace in the 1968 election?

I supported Wallace for president in 1968. He actually ran as a democratic independent in Louisiana, and 75 percent of my constituency voted for him. Louisiana gave its electoral votes to Strom Thurmond as a States' Rights Democrat in 1948 and also to George Wallace in 1968. Wallace beat Humphrey in this state.

After the 1968 election, I was punished by the House Democratic Caucus for not supporting Humphrey. It was a joke. They had to get somebody, and since Mendell Rivers and the other Wallace supporters in Congress were too powerful, they got me. They stripped me of my seniority. It was a big deal. Since I had just finished my first term as a freshman congressman, I didn't have much to lose. But they had to get somebody, so they singled out me for the treatment.

I'm still not clear how you got involved with the AIP. When did you leave the Democrtic Party?

After I left Congress in 1974, I ran for the American Independent nomination at the party's presidential convention in Chicago in 1976. There were three of us—Lester Maddox, a fellow named Robert Morris from New York, and me—and I was defeated for the nomination at that time. Then, four years later in 1980, some of the very same people who didn't support me in '76 asked me to run as the American Independent candidate for president. So I accepted the nomination, and Eileen Shearer, a businesswoman from California, who was one of the founders of the party back in 1968, agreed to run as vice-president.

During the 1980 campaign, did you actually go out to visit different states? Did you spend much time giving speeches?

I campaigned quite heavily in California, Idaho, South Carolina, Wisconsin, and here in Louisiana. I got into Alabama a couple of times. Of course, with the American Independents, you're dealing mainly with amateurs. You don't have money to hire PR people. Some of the meetings were very discouraging, a downright bust. The party people think that if they line you up to fly into San Diego or Madison to speak at six o'clock in the afternoon, everybody's supposed to know it. They don't realize that you have to make phone calls. You have to get out flyers. You've got to have contacts. So the campaign was run by amateur people. They were all heart and all talk, but they lacked understanding as far as sitting down and organizing.

You were only on the ballot in eight states. Did this present a problem for you?

Actually, I think the American Independent Party was only active in about three states. We were listed under different names in other places. In Wisconsin we were called the Constitution Party; in South Carolina I think we were called the Conservative Party. In Michigan they divided us into the American Party and the American Independent Party, and neither of us got on the ballot. When I went from state to state, I almost had to rehearse my lines to be sure how I was running in that state.

Do you think the state ballot access laws are fair?

This was why we didn't try to change the names of the parties in the different states. We ran under different parties because they already had a position on the state ballot. You remember George Wallace never would allow the American Independent Party in Alabama. He always ran as a Democrat in his own state. We couldn't get on the ballot at all in some places. In Mississippi we were turned down until we filed suit. However, we didn't have money to file many suits, so we were left off the ballot in a lot of states.

Would you like to see more uniformity in the state laws?

No. The minute you say you want to nationalize, then you're taking other gambles. I would leave it up to the states. I think we've had every one of the third-party candidates on our ballot here in Louisiana. That was unusual, because I can remember when the Communist Party tried to get on in Louisiana, there were threats to take them out and lynch them. But if you try to standardize it, it's all going to end up being controlled by the federal government.

How do you feel about the Federal Election Campaign Act?

I voted against it. Old Hale Boggs was the whip. All they were doing was creating more regulations to make the major parties stronger. It was a free ride. They've given more control to the PAC's—the political action committees—by taking it away from the individual. When I ran, of course, I never got any support from the party, so I had to go out and raise my own money. In fact, I was a Louisiana congressman for eight years, and I never had a penny from any oil company. Can you imagine that?

I think that if the federal government's going to do anything about elections, they ought to limit or outlaw the use of television and radio and go back to stump oratory. The major parties don't offer any real choices. Politicians today come on like they're being sold as a jar of jam or Campbell's soup. At least we attempted to force them to deal with the issues.

Do you think you received good media coverage in 1980?

I got some, but the media's interested in selling their product. They're interested in emotionalism and sensationalism, so I certainly didn't get much national coverage.

One last question about the campaign. I'm not clear why the American Party and the American Independent Party split after the 1972 election. Do you know what happened here?

The idea seemed to be if you don't control it, you destroy it or you walk out. It was like the Baptist church. One guy, the deacon, says, "I want piano music." The other deacon says, "I want to have a trumpet and a piano." They can't get together, so they both separate and start their own church. Then they both lose membership, and the next thing you know, they both go broke and there's little unity left.

PERSONAL IMPRESSIONS

What about the future? Are you optimistic or pessimistic about the American Independent Party?

I hope that the leaders of the party—conservative, independents, and constitutionalists, the ones that have been doing all the squawking in the party—will be able to mend their fences. They all seem to think, "You join my team, but I'm not going to join your team." I hope in the future we can get them all under the same roof.

How do you feel about the country? Are you optimistic or pessimistic about Ronald Reagan's policies?

The American Independent party believes in limited constitutional government, and Mr. Reagan's rhetoric has set many of them back. Many of my friends think he's so much better than Carter that they want to give him a chance. So I think he's still pretty strong, but I don't know how long it's going to last, because I'm afraid he's going to stub his toe pretty soon. I will say this: he's the only president we've ever had that talks like an American. However, he's trying to carry water on both shoulders.

The key question is whether he will keep us out of war. He's already come out for draft registration. This is obviously to be the big stick to let the Soviet Union know we've got troops, but I don't know what he's going to draft them for. I have eight grandchildren. My son has never been in the service. He was too young for Korea and too old for Vietnam. I just hate the idea that we've got to pick up everybody else's marbles all over the world.

Let me conclude with a few personal questions. Why did you want to run for president? Isn't it a long shot for any third-party candidate?

I never did want to run for president, but somebody had to do it. The people in the American Party selected Mr. Greaves as their candidate. He's an author and an economist, apparently a very learned man from New York State—figuring, I guess, that they'd be able to pick up more money in the East. When the American Independent Party called their convention, they said, "We just can't go along with this New York guy. We've heard him, and he won't get us any votes." At the time, they led me to believe they had a pretty strong nucleus, and they persuaded me to accept their nomination.

Was it worth it? Are you glad you ran?

I guess it's a great experience and honor. Everybody should run for president at least once, especially with no money and very little organization. It's mighty lonely, and it doesn't help your income, I'll guarantee you that. You really have to believe in what you're doing. Of course, it hurt me. I practically had to shut my law office down. A lot of my clients said, "Well, you're just traipsing around all over the country, and I'll have to get another lawyer." So the key question is, what did we really accomplish? Were we really being gadflies for the two national parties? I'm not sure.

Would you ever run again for president?

I say no. I've said that many times before. I'll be fifty-eight next week, and I enjoy my life here. I've got all my grandkids with me here. But no one knows what's down the road. We just don't know what is going to happen in the future.

I've tried to cover a lot of different areas. Are there any final thoughts you'd like to express?

Well, I think the greatest problem the American people are going to face is the one-world threat—the idea that Americans have now become such egalitarians that they feel everybody in the world is equal, and we should all have the same jobs, the same incomes. This isn't what made America the target for the world. It's ridiculous for the American people to go along with the one-world thought—you know, the idea that we can raise everybody to our standard of living—because the only way we're going to help the world under that theory is to reduce our standard of living.

I was a prisoner in the Second World War, but I have no hatred for the Germans. In fact, my ancestors originally came from Germany. Just look at the Germans and the Japanese. The Germans have made real progress since the war, but to this day we're still pistol whipping them and trying to keep them divided.

We have to get our budget under control, reduce our unemployment, and take care of ourselves. I've talked with my kids about this, and they worry about the poor Chinaman over there making $30 a month in communist China. They feel he should be making a union wage. But if we move our factories over there, what's going to happen to America? We can't take care of everybody in the world. We can't be the policeman for the whole world. To me, the greatest threat we've got to face today is the internationalist one-world concept.

THE AMERICAN PARTY

The American Party came into being after Governor George C. Wallace was forced to withdraw from the 1972 race. A group of his supporters held a convention in Louisville, Kentucky, in August and nominated John G. Schmitz, a Republican congressman from California, and Tennessee journalist Thomas J. Anderson as the American Party candidates for president and vice-president. Although Wallace was not able to be active in the campaign as a result of his shooting, Schmitz did quite well, receiving 1,099,482 popular votes.

Following the 1972 election, the newly organized American Party began to split apart. One faction, centered in California, resurrected the original American Independent Party label, and this group nominated the former Georgia governor, Lester Maddox, for president in 1976. A second faction, centered in Utah, retained the American Party name, and nominated Thomas Anderson for president. The bickering between the two groups took its toll, since Maddox received only 170,000 votes, while Anderson dropped to 160,000 votes in the 1976 election.

The American Party continued to deteriorate after 1976. By the late 1970s, its financing had dried up, and it was fragmented by internal divisions. Percy L. Greaves, Jr., of New York, a seventy-four-year-old economics lecturer and author, was the party's nominee for president in 1980. Although Greaves attempted to pull the party back together, he was only able to get on the ballot in five states, and his popular vote dropped to 6,647. In addition, Frank Shelton received 1,555 votes as an American Party candidate in Kansas and 6,139 votes were cast in Minnesota for American Party electors without designated national nominees.

I interviewed Greaves in his home in Irvington, a picturesque and historic Hudson River community in upper Westchester County about forty miles north of New York City in late June 1981. Greaves gave the following account of his lengthy involvement in American politics, beginning with the earliest days of the New Deal.

Percy Greaves

My basic desire in the remaining years of my life is to try to give some of my ideas about freedom to the young people who are going to have to face these problems in the future. They think I invented these ideas. They've never heard them before.

PERSONAL BACKGROUND

Smallwood: I would like to learn a little about your background. When did you first get involved in politics?

Greaves: It was a long time ago, more than half a century ago. I first got interested in political problems because of the depression. I graduated from the College of Business Administration at Syracuse University in 1929 just before the great stock market crash. Fortunately, I was close to the top of my class, so I was able to get a good job, but then a few years later I lost my job and my father also lost his job. I wanted to know why people were suffering through no fault of their own, so I went back to school and did graduate work in economics at Columbia University.

In 1934, I got a chance to work with David Lawrence on the *United States News* in Washington. I was their economist and financial editor for a while. I had a desk in the treasury press room. I went to Roosevelt's press conferences and to the press conferences of his cabinet officers. I got a good background exposure to the New Deal, and I was both intellectually and emotionally opposed to it.

Why were you opposed to the New Deal? Didn't you think Roosevelt's policies were directed at the problems of unemployment that concerned you?

I was very much a student of free enterprise. Roosevelt was interested in government intervention and in short-term gimmicks. He was opposed to the free-enterprise system. As a result, the New Deal never solved the unemployment problem. It was as bad in 1939 as it was in 1933 when Roosevelt took office. The only thing that solved unemployment was World War II.

I left Washington in 1936 to work for a private company in Europe. I saw the socialism and the sit-down strikes of the Popular Front in France, and the rise of the Nazis in Germany. I had contact with national socialism over there, and it increased my mistrust in the power of government.

After I returned to the United States in 1938, I worked for a large insurance company until 1943. At that time, I offered my services to the Republican National Committee, and was appointed research director of the committee in 1943.

How long did you work for the Republican Party?

About two years. After the 1944 nomination of Dewey, I had differences with Herb Brownell, who was our national chairman. Following the election, he told me that the Republican Party was now divided on such issues as public housing, federal aid to education, and socialized medicine. As an employee of the party, I could no longer take positions in opposition to these proposals. In other words, the Republican Party was no longer opposed to the New Deal.

I felt this was very unfortunate because we no longer had a major opposition party, no real alternative. This is bad for a constitutional republic which is, or which should be, based on free choices. If you and I disagree, we should be able to express our disagreements through the political process. However, the Republican Party took the expedient route and began to embrace the Democratic programs, so I resigned after the 1944 presidential election. It was a matter of principle to me.

I remained in Washington for a number of years to work on different assignments. I served as chief of the minority staff of the Joint Congressional Committee for the Investigation of the Pearl Harbor Attack, and after that I worked with the House Committee on Education and Labor when I wrote the first draft of what became the Taft-Hartley law. Then I had another disagreement, this time with Joe Martin, who was the Republican leader in the House, so I resigned from that position.

Where did you go after that?

I finally came to New York as an economist and columnist for the Christian Freedom Foundation. They sponsored a publication called *Christian Economics*, which was circulated to 200,000 Protestant ministers. It was largely subsidized by Mr. J. Howard Pew, who was head of the Sun Oil Company. I spent eight years on that from 1950 to 1958.

Were you still a Republican at that time?

In 1952 I started the Constitution Party in New York State. We backed General MacArthur for president. I felt he was sort of the last grand old American who wanted to return to the virtues of the Constitution as originally construed.

After the 1952 election, I joined the Conservative Party of New York, serving on their executive board in Westchester County. I became engaged in free-lance writing, plus some lecturing and teaching on economic issues, which I have been doing since that time.

Why did you leave the Conservative Party?

In 1968, the Republicans refused to allow us to have any electors pledged to Nixon. Actually, I was in sympathy with that. I had a personal dispute with Nixon way back in the 1940s. He served on the House Committee on Education and Labor when I was on the staff. John Kennedy was also on the committee. They were both freshmen congressmen then. Personally, I liked Kennedy much more than I liked Nixon. I had a scrap with Nixon over the Un-American Activities Committee, which he actually sabotaged for his own personal ends.

The upshot of all of this was that Nixon won the presidency in 1968, but he lost New York State to Humphrey. As a result, the Republicans changed their minds when the 1972 election came around. This time, they wanted the Conservative Party to nominate Nixon. We had quite a battle. I was against endorsing Nixon. I lost. The Conservative Party nominated Nixon, and I resigned. So this left me with no party at all.

Was this when you joined the American Party?

It was shortly after this that I was approached by some American Party people. It was called the Courage Party in New York State, since state law doesn't permit the use of the word American in any party name. The American Party people wanted me to run for governor of New York. They knew I couldn't win, but they wanted me to run because the way you get on the ballot in this state is by the number of votes a party gets for governor. I wasn't interested in running for governor, so they finally nominated another person, but I got drawn into the party. In 1976, I campaigned for the American Party nominees for president and vice-president—Tom Anderson and Rufus Shackleford—even though they weren't on the ballot in New York.

Tell me a little about the American Party. What does it stand for?

The American Party stands for the United States Constitution as originally interpreted.

What does that mean? Doesn't every party say they stand for the U.S. Constitution?

Oh yes, they all say it, but we really mean it. We believe in a free-market economy and a free society without federal government intervention or regulation of personal affairs. All of the leftist socialist parties favor strong central government, and both the Republican and Democratic Parties favor strong government in Washington at the expense of the states and the people. The Constitution, as originally written, called for a federal system in which the central government could only regulate interstate commerce. We have eliminated competition by regulation and social programs, and become a monolithic society which is dominated by the national government in Washington.

When did the American Party get started?

It was an outgrowth of the George Wallace presidential campaign in 1968. Four years later, in 1972, when they ran John Schmitz for president, they did very well, since Schmitz got over a million votes. The party had a fair amount of money in those days. Then it began to get torn apart by internal dissension, which led to a split into two different parties in the 1976 election. The American Party nominated Tom Anderson, while the other group, the American Independent Party, nominated Lester Maddox of Georgia.

Was this split caused by a personality clash within the party?

Yes, in part. The American Independent strength was mainly based in California, while we were getting stronger in other states, particularly Utah. The split was the beginning of hard times for both parties.

POLITICAL IDEOLOGY

Before we get to the 1980 presidential campaign, I'd like to be a little clearer about your own personal views. I assume you would describe yourself as a conservative.

I've been involved in what is popularly called the conservative side, but personally I don't like the term. I'm more interested in concepts like the free market. I am freedom minded. I consider conservative to be a bad name because conservatives don't want to change, and I certainly favor change. Conservatives are bound to lose in the long run because change is inevitable.

If you want to call me a conservative in my economic views, that's all right, although I don't think it's accurate. I want to move toward the free market. The federal government should stop meddling with the free market. Instead it should do its job by restoring the value of our currency, which is a scandal. You can label that a conservative position, but I'd simply call it common sense.

How about social issues? Where do you consider yourself to be in this area?

Interestingly enough, I got into real trouble with some members of the American Party who feel I'm too liberal on some social issues. I had the worst time with the abortion issue, which some of them seem to think is murder. My feeling is that this is a religious matter and not a matter for the government to decide. I feel the government shouldn't subsidize it, and the government shouldn't ban it. It's a personal matter. People have different opinions about it, and they're entitled to their opinions. No group should be able to force their position on others.

Then do you subscribe to the Libertarian Party position that we should have minimum governmental intervention in both the economic and social spheres?

Good Lord, no. I mean the Libertarian Party is almost a licentious party. They go across the board. They believe prostitution and all those other things should be permitted in public places. We agree in wanting limited government, but I think about a third of their members are anarchists and many are also atheists.

Where do you draw the line? What do you think is the proper role of government?

It is the duty of government to protect life, property, and our borders; to settle disputes; and to back a sound currency. It's the government's duty to define the currency, because if I owe you a couple of hundred dollars and we disagree on what is a dollar, they've got to decide in court what satisfies that debt.

I've been concerned about inflation and the debasement of our currency for a long time. Back in the 1950s I told a joke about a man who went to his doctor to get a checkup, and the doctor told him that he was as sound as a dollar. "Oh, no," the man replied, "I'm not really that bad, am I?" People were skeptical about inflation in the 1950s, but when I go back to them today, they say this is the fellow who warned us about those things.

Take the price of anything today. The Democrats and the Republicans keep telling us that prices are going up. They say the price of gas is going up. Actually, last year you could still buy gas for ten cents a gallon, if you paid with an old silver dime. The problem is not that prices have gone up, but that the value of the dollar has gone down. It's gone down because the Democrats and Republicans keep pumping more money into the economy to finance the welfare state. It's an outgrowth of the Keynesian theories of "pump priming" to stimulate the economy that started back in the New Deal. I studied and worked closely with the free-market economist Ludwig von Mises, and I am opposed to the Keynesian approach—which is economic nonsense.

Historically, inflation was always defined as an increase in the quantity of money. The new definition of inflation is higher prices, which is one of the effects of an increase in the quantity of money. However, this new definition shifts the blame to the businessman for raising prices when the real problem is that the government is creating too much artificial money. Government, not business, creates the money that bids up prices.

Prices haven't gone up anywhere near as much as the value of the dollar has gone down. It has gone down because the government—the Federal Reserve Board and the Treasury—keeps pumping out dollars into the economy to pay for all these socialist programs which started way back in the 1930s. So today we have both inflation and unemployment, and everybody is worse off. This is the message I've tried to get across.

Do you think Ronald Reagan will be able to deal with this problem?

In 1968, some of my friends who heard me lecturing about economics invited me out to California. I spent three days in Sacramento, where I met Reagan and the top people around him. I got a good opinion of Reagan personally, but not the people around him. They all wanted bigger jobs in Washington.

In private discussions, they found out that I was against the

New Deal, and they didn't want the press to know about my views. They were embarrassed, like I was from some foreign planet, because I opposed the New Deal. Even Reagan himself has indicated that he favors Roosevelt, so I don't think things are going to change very much.

You talked a lot about the economy. Is this the only issue that interests you?

I think that it's the single most important issue. The three main problems we face today are inflation, mass unemployment, and the energy crisis. All three are the result of the policies endorsed by both major parties, and the remedies are the adoption of free-market principles. To cure inflation, we need to stop the political creation of dollars by adopting the gold standard. In order to deal with unemployment, we need to repeal labor union privileges, such as minimum wage laws, that prevent open competition for jobs. For the energy crisis, we need to remove government interference with free market processes in the form of special taxes on energy and profits earned in providing energy. If we could straighten out the economy, we could solve most of our other domestic problems.

We would also be in a strong position internationally. I agree with George Washington that we shouldn't become involved in foreign entanglements. We should be strong enough to defend ourselves, but we should not try to serve as the policemen for the world. We should never have gotten involved in Vietnam, which was an unconstitutional war, since it was never approved by Congress. It was a stupid mistake. We still have tremendous vitality in this country, despite the fact that the government has botched things up for years. If we can get our economy back in order, we will be the strongest nation in the world once again, internationally as well as domestically.

You argue that the government has no role in the free market except to back a sound currency. Is it really this simple? If a business pollutes the environment, shouldn't it be regulated? Many businessmen favor government subsidies. How do you feel about this issue?

My campaign slogan was equal justice for all and privileges for none. When I said privileges for none, I meant it. I didn't even favor federal funding to pay for my own campaign expenses.

If a business pollutes the environment or creates other problems, these matters should be settled by law suits in the courts just like any other injury. It's true that businessmen have gotten privileges, and the unions have certainly gotten privileges, from the government. This is wrong. However, I don't think you can say that business has been a big favorite of the politicians during the past half a century when government first taxes their profits and then taxes them again when paid out as dividends. Historically, business got a lot of privileges in the earlier days, but I think this has been turned around the other way since the 1930s.

One last question about your personal philosophy. You indicated that the American Party grew out of the George Wallace campaign in 1968. Some of your earlier candidates were involved with the John Birch Society. How do you feel about issues such as racism and the Birch Society?

When I first joined the party, I was concerned about the old Wallace-type image. This is one of the things I started fighting, one of the differences I had with Tom Anderson, our 1976 presidential nominee. Tom is a southerner who tended to look down on blacks. He started putting some of his ideas in the party paper. He was editor at the time. I told him he shouldn't do it, since the paper represented the party's views and not his own personal opinions. Tom resigned from the party chairmanship, so racism wasn't involved in our 1980 campaign. I don't consider myself to be racist, and I certainly didn't raise this issue. Back in 1952, the Constitution Party was infiltrated by some anti-Semites, and that's why I resigned as national chairman. I don't regard myself as a bigot of any kind.

As for the other part of your question, John Schmitz, our 1972 presidential candidate, and Tom Anderson were both members of the John Birch Society. I've never been a member.

I've had some differences with Robert Welch, whom I know quite well. He's a brilliant man. I don't agree with him on everything, but I admire him. He's made great sacrifices for his beliefs. He published one of my earlier books, and he contributed to my campaign; but that was the extent of his involvement.

THE 1980 CAMPAIGN

Let's turn to the 1980 campaign. When did the party start working on this?

Quite early. After the 1976 election, we began to contact Meldrim Thomson, your governor up there in New Hampshire, about the possibility of his running as our candidate in 1980. .We invited him to speak around the country, and had him to a national committee meeting. He wanted $1,000 every time he spoke; so he bled the party and probably got some $10,000 to $12,000 out of us. I opposed him after I read his book in mid-1979, which I thought was very poor. He was bragging about some of the interventions he had done in New Hampshire, about how he had gotten some federal money for the state and how you had to have a life belt on if you went out in a rowboat. I wasn't impressed with it.

When did Thomson refuse the party's nomination?

He told us he wouldn't be our candidate in the summer of 1979. Our executive board had a late September meeting. We asked Rufus Shackleford, our national chairman, to set up plans for a party convention in Pasadena, California, in December, since we had to get moving if we wanted to make the ballots in different states. About the middle of October, Rufus called to tell me and other board members he was resigning from the party. A week later, Thomson announced he was running on the Constitution Party ticket and Rufus Shackleford was his campaign manager! So we went to California with this real mess on our hands. Some of the delegates wanted to join the Thomson crew, while others wanted to nominate our own candidate.

It must have been a pretty wild convention.

Yes. There was a drag-out fight. The delegates were dead-locked. A majority could not agree on any one person. My name was put in nomination, but I withdrew it. I was seventy-three years old. I didn't want to run for president. We went to a number of ballots, when a group of us went off to see if we couldn't reach a middle ground. But we didn't. I was challenged on my abortion position. I got up and stated it. They knew what my position was; there was no secret about it. Finally, after many ballots, I received a majority vote and was nominated. Frank Varnum, a retired airline pilot from California, agreed to run as vice-president.

All this bickering split the party badly. Some stayed, some left, and some tried to resurrect the Thomson candidacy, although he finally decided not to run for president on any ticket. So the party started off badly split, without funds. That's how I got into the campaign, without any funds and with a badly split party. When I was nominated, I didn't want to accept it. But I was persuaded that it was the only way to save the party because if I had refused to accept, that would have been the end of the party. We had to get out of the hotel that night. It was already around two or three in the afternoon, and we still had a platform to adopt, so I felt that this was the only way to save the party, and I agreed to run. That's the way I got into the campaign.

It must have looked like a long uphill climb to you. What were your top campaign priorities once you got the nomination?

We tried to get on the ballot in as many states as we could. We had real ballot problems, so we had to spend half our meager funds on lawyers' fees. In two states we were removed from the ballot on the last day. In South Carolina we were taken off because they said I hadn't submitted my financial statement, even though it was on record in Washington, and I was never told it was needed. In Kansas we were disqualified because the signature of the party's secretary was not notarized. I was not informed of the incomplete applications until it was too late to do anything about it.

We had a problem in Michigan, where the American Independent Party submitted John Rarick's name, while my name was submitted by our group. The Michigan secretary of state wouldn't put either of us on the ballot. We went to court, and things looked good, but he refused to put either Rarick or me on the ballot. When the filing date closed, our party was on the ballot, but my name never appeared, so I didn't get any votes at all in Michigan.

We had trouble in Minnesota, and we weren't able to get on any ballots in New England. I could go on and on, but the point is that, in the end, I could only make it onto five state ballots—Indiana, Iowa, North Dakota, Delaware, and Utah.

But didn't you have any professional staff to help you? What was your campaign budget?

Our total budget was only about $30,000. I refused to spend any money until we actually raised it, since I'm opposed to deficit financing.

Our staff was made up of amateur volunteers. The American Party had only one paid staff member, a secretary who worked in the national party headquarters in Utah for the national party chairman, Earl Jeppson. My campaign manager was a professor of astronomy from the University of Kentucky, a well-meaning and intelligent man; but he had very little political experience, and he needed his wife to prod him a good deal. As a matter of fact, we didn't even get on the ballot in Kentucky because of a last-minute technical foul-up down there.

Did you actually go out and campaign in many states?

Oh yes. I began campaigning during the petition drives to get on the state ballots. I started in North Carolina. I really campaigned quite hard in about fifteen states, but I was in more than twenty states overall just to give one or two speeches.

I went wherever they could raise funds to bring me. I told you that half our budget went to lawyers' fees. The other half went to the airlines for the trips I made. They botched up a colored folder they were going to get out on me, so we lost a thousand dollars there. It finally came out in black and white in the middle of October. We also printed up some campaign buttons which I thought were pretty corny. They said, "I Dig Greaves for President." You see, "graves" is the way you pronounce my name. I thought they were kind of corny, but they said the buttons might attract some attention, so I went along with it.

Do you think you were treated fairly by the media and the public during the campaign?

Yes I do. My only complaint is all those ridiculous technicalities involved in getting on the state ballots.

In terms of the media, I got quite a bit of local coverage in the various places I visited. I had three half-hour television interview shows in Kentucky. I'd have to say, in justification of the media, that our party didn't have a big membership, we didn't have money, and we didn't hold large meetings. In addition, they felt I had no chance of winning, so the large national media ignored me. I did receive a tiny bit of coverage in the *New York Times* when I was nominated, but I don't know if I was ever mentioned again. Of course, I wasn't on the ballot in New York. It is one of the worst places to get on the ballot since the law prohibits the use of the word American in a party name. This law had been passed to get rid of the American Labor Party, which was communist. I thought our lawyers were going to fight it, since we certainly weren't communistic. However, they found out it was too expensive to fight anything like that in New York.

The audiences I talked to were usually small, informal gatherings, but they were quite receptive. I particularly enjoyed talking with the college students, especially in Utah, where I met quite a few of them.

No, I can't say I was treated unfairly except for all of those ballot technicalities. We just had too many things going against us. The party was too fragmented. We didn't have enough money to make any impact on the final election results.

PERSONAL IMPRESSIONS

What about the future? Do you see the American Party going anywhere in the years ahead?

To be honest, I'm not very optimistic about either the party or the country. No one really knows the future. I certainly don't know the future. However, I'm worried about the way we're going.

I'm very concerned that Reagan may take us into another war once he realizes that his present policies are going to fail. He's getting set to defend the whole world—fleets in the Indian Ocean and everything. I'm afraid he's preparing for something big overseas to cover his economic failures. I'm not very optimistic about the future of either the country or the American Party. The party's badly split. We don't have the funds. I don't see much of a future for us.

Do you think the American people share your sense of pessimism about the country?

Well, during my campaign, I saw a tremendous amount of vitality and creativity out there. We shouldn't underestimate it. We're still very powerful even though we've made a lot of foolish mistakes during the past fifty years.

However, when you look just beneath the surface, I think many people are pretty close to a crisis of confidence. They're willing to give Reagan the benefit of the doubt, to give him a chance, but many people don't know where to turn right now. The older people are worried about their retirement security. Middle-income families are racked by inflation. The younger people are being told they're going to have to prop up a social security system that's an absolute shambles. And then, there's always the threat of another war, possibly a nuclear war, which could finish us all.

The vitality is still there. I could sense it when I went to speak in different places all over the country. Maybe the young people will be able to turn things around because I feel that many of them are losing their sense of confidence in the welfare state.

You've been remarkably open with me, so I would like to ask just one final question. Now that you can reflect back on the 1980 campaign, was it worth it? Was it worth all the time and effort you put into it?

I've thought a lot about that question. See those two plaques over there on the wall? They were given to me by the American Party. Those plaques, plus a scrapbook of clippings my wife put together for me, are the only tangible things I got out of the whole campaign.

I have to admit I was pretty discouraged. At one point, our local newspaper here in Westchester County ran an article on me. One of my close neighbors was quoted as saying she was surprised to hear that I was a candidate. It hurts when you try to speak out, but people don't seem to be listening.

However, I also have to think about it in another way. I'm going to be seventy-five years old in a couple of months. The question is, would it have been better for me to sit down in my basement reading or not doing anything at all, or did I help to educate at least some of the people on the issues this country faces?

My basic desire in the remaining years of my life is to try to give some of my ideas about freedom to the young people who are going to have to face these problems in the future. At my age I've acquired a certain background and knowledge that I want to leave behind. I want to leave behind some of these ideas about freedom and free-market principles which the younger people have never heard about. They've never had a chance to see what a free market is. They don't have any idea what it's like to work in a free-market system. They think I invented these ideas. They've never heard them before.

I hope I got some of my message across to these younger

people. It was difficult trying to express my views through the American Party in the face of all our divisions and internal problems. Our party is basically an older traditional party. It's a party where I would have to say the old folks are dying out. It's kind of passing in that sense.

It's funny, but I don't seem to fit anywhere any more. I'm too anti-New Deal on economic issues for the Reaganites and the Republicans, and I'm too liberal on social issues for some people in the American Party. Politicians learn to compromise, to be less outspoken, but as a professional economist I could not compromise on principle. I didn't want to run for president. I did the best I could under the circumstances. So yes, I would have to conclude that it was worth it.

THE LIBERTARIAN PARTY

The Libertarian Party was formally organized in Denver, Colorado, in June 1972. The modern libertarian movement actually came of age a few years prior to this at the August 1969 convention of the Young Americans for Freedom (YAF) in St. Louis when a minority "Libertarian Caucus" split away from the YAF over the issue of the draft, which the caucus regarded as a form of slavery. A number of caucus groups began to organize in different states, such as the California Libertarian Alliance and the Maryland-based Society for Rational Individualism. In late 1969, the two groups formed the Society for Individual Liberty, with approximately 3,000 members. There were a number of other early libertarian groups, however, that advocated a variety of other ideologies, ranging from anarchism to old-fashioned laissez-faire Randian and neo-Randian philosophies (based on the books of the late Ayn Rand, especially her 1957 novel, *Atlas Shrugged*).

In the 1972 presidential election, the Libertarian Party nominated John Hospers, a professor of philosophy at the University of Southern California, as its first presidential candidate. Since the new party had just been organized in June, Hospers received only 3,600 popular votes, though Roger McBride, an elector from the state of Virginia, cast his electoral college vote for Hospers.

The following year, in 1973, Murray N. Rothbard, an economics professor, wrote *For a New Liberty*, a book that set forth the basic tenets of libertarian ideology. According to Rothbard, the central core of the libertarian creed is based on the crucial "nonaggression" axiom which holds that:

no man or group of men have the right to aggress against the person or property of anyone else. . . . "Aggression" is defined as the initiation of the use or threat of physical violence against the person or property of someone else.[10]

Rothbard defined freedom and liberty as "the absence of invasion," and the Libertarian Party defends individual freedom in a vigorous and rigorously consistent fashion, opposing governmental intervention in both economic and civil affairs.

In 1976, the party nominated Roger McBride of Virginia as its presidential candidate, and McBride received 173,000 popular votes. By this point the Libertarians were well on the way to building party organizations on the state level, though signs of internal dissension were appearing within the national organization. In 1977, Edward Crane, the chairman of the California Libertarian Party, was named president of the Cato Institute, a public policy research organization in San Francisco funded by wealthy New York industrialists Charles and David Koch. The institute, which was named after the conservative Roman stoic and statesman, Cato the Younger, began to publish pamphlets and, more recently, an interdisciplinary public policy journal on a semiannual basis.[11] When Edward Crane and Murry Rothbard began to disagree over different issues of party strategy, the Libertarians turned to Ed Clark as their 1980 presidential candidate.

Clark, an antitrust lawyer for Atlantic Richfield Company in Los Angeles and an ardent party activist, had made a strong showing as the Libertarian Party candidate for governor of California in the 1978 election, receiving almost 380,000 votes. In addition, the Libertarians nominated David Koch of New York as their 1980 vice-presidential candidate after Koch "in an open letter to convention delegates . . . pledged to contribute $500,000 to the national campaign if nominated" (Koch "proved to be even more generous than he promised, providing the Libertarian ticket . . . with $2.1 million of the $3.5 million it raised").[12]

Clark and Koch appeared on the ballot in all fifty states, plus the District of Columbia, and the Libertarians also ran candidates at the state and local levels in the 1980 election. During the campaign, Clark, a Dartmouth and Harvard Law School graduate, outlined his positions in a book entitled *A New Beginning*.[13] He received 921,299 popular votes for president in

1980, and, more recently, his wife, Alicia, was elected to serve as the new chair of the Libertarian Party at its 1981 convention.

I interviewed Clark outside the United States Federal Court for the District of Columbia in Washington during a business trip that Clark made to the east coast early in January 1982.

Ed Clark

The entire libertarian philosophy is based on the concept of individual liberty and freedom. We believe that each individual has the inalienable right, and the capability, to make the decisions to control his or her own life.

PERSONAL BACKGROUND

Smallwood: Tell me a little bit about your personal background.

Clark: I grew up in Middleboro, Massachusetts, where my father was active in local affairs. He served as town moderator for fifty-two years, which I believe was the longest period of service in the history of the state. My family was Republican, and I started off being a Republican, although I was never sure whether I belonged in the more liberal or the more conservative stream of the party. Since I was a teenager, I've always been a very hard-core free-market person in all areas. Moreover, I've always taken the position that American involvement in World War I was a complete disaster, and that, while World War II may have been inevitable, the Roosevelt administration took a lot of steps that led us into that war. I view war, and the growth of government which is involved in war, as the primary enemy of liberty. So I had these two views—a very strong free-market view, and a not quite pacifist, but very strong, antiwar view—for a long, long time.

Where did this leave you in the Republican Party?

My free-market, laissez-faire views led me to a liberal position on social issues and a conservative position on economic issues. But I was never really comfortable with this, and I never was very active in the Republican Party. I did a little work occasionally, and I made a very modest financial contribution each year.

When did you finally decide to break away from the Republican Party?

I remember, very vividly, the exact time, place, and date. On August 15, 1971, while watching television in Dallas, Texas, I saw Richard Nixon give a speech in which he imposed wage and price controls during peacetime for the first time in our history. I view wage and price controls as disastrous for the economy and also as a basic denial of civil liberties. Both labor and business have the right to try to get higher wages, to try to sell apples and oranges, or any other product, for any price they want that people are willing to pay. This was a very strong emotional experience for me. I remember calling up my wife and yelling at her on the telephone for half an hour after watching it. I was very upset, and there was nobody else to listen to me rant and rave.

Where were you living at the time?

I was living in New York, practicing law for the Atlantic Richfield Company, but I was in Dallas working on a case for the company. Nixon came on television and said he was not only imposing wage and price controls for the first time in the United States during peacetime, but he was also cutting all ties between the dollar and gold. When you cut the ties between the dollar and gold, or some other kind of basic commodity, you just invite the government to expand the money supply endlessly, as they've done in the 1970s. That is what, in my view, is the principal cause of inflation. So at that moment, I left the Republican Party. I felt betrayed.

How did you get involved with the Libertarian Party?

A few months later, in the fall of 1971, I went to an educational conference sponsored by a libertarian educational group at Columbia University in New York. There were a lot of libertarian speakers. They were talking about exactly the kind of

philosophy I believe in: limited government, free-market economics, and a noninterventionist foreign policy. I felt I had
discovered my new political home.

Did you immediately become active with the Libertarian Party?

The party was just beginning to get off the ground. In January 1972, I was reading the *New York Times* on my way to work
and saw that the Libertarian Party had been officially organized in Denver. I immediately got in touch with them. When
they responded, they asked me what I wanted to do. I told
them I'd be willing to organize the New York party, so I ended
up organizing the Free Libertarian Party of New York in my
living room in April 1972.

When did you move to California?

Seven months later, in September 1972, I moved to the Atlantic Richfield Los Angeles office. As soon as I arrived, I became active in the California party, which was just getting
started at that time. I served as chairman of the California
party in 1973 and 1974. I also served as vice-chairman of the
national party, and I was a member of the national executive
committee from the date of our very first meeting in 1972. Incidentally, as an interesting aside, that very first convention of
the national party was held in Denver on Watergate weekend
in June of 1972.

*Up until 1978, you were active in party organizational matters.
Was your race for governor of California your first try for political
office?*

Yes. I ran as the Libertarian Party candidate for governor of
California in 1978. My opponents were Jerry Brown for the
Democrats and Evelle Younger for the Republicans. It was the
first time the party had actively campaigned for the office, and
we got almost 400,000 votes. I think it was about 378,000
votes.

*That's a pretty strong showing for a new third party. Were you
then drafted as the libertarian candidate for president in 1980, or
did you have to fight to get the nomination?*

Oh, I had to fight for it. Absolutely. It was a contested—a very heavily contested—nomination. The person who ran against me was a businessman from New Hampshire, Bill Hunscher. He announced his candidacy at the end of 1978 and started campaigning vigorously then. I announced my candidacy in February 1979. We campaigned across the country all during the late winter, spring, and summer. The party held its nominating convention in Los Angeles in early September of 1979, since we wanted to get an early head start on the 1980 race. I won the nomination at the convention.

Did you begin your campaign that early? What about your job with Atlantic Richfield?

I took a full-time leave from the company, but it was not until July first of 1980. Prior to that, I campaigned quite extensively, but it was on a part-time basis—weekends, or during a holiday or short vacation. Of course, California is a big, and very important state, and I could campaign there quite easily. And a lot of the preliminary work was organizational, developing position papers and the like, which I could do on a part-time basis.

POLITICAL IDEOLOGY

O.K., let's turn to the positions you advocated in the 1980 race. As a start, let me quote one of your statements that intrigues me: "Libertarians are different than most other parties in that we didn't start out as a group of people already in politics. We started out as a group of people who had some philosophic ideas about what was right and wrong in life."[14] What does this mean? What are your ideas about what is right and wrong in life?

Actually, we're guided by one very powerful central idea, which is a very old idea. Although there are different shades of ideology within our movement, the entire libertarian philosophy is based on the concept of individual liberty and freedom. We believe that each individual has the inalienable right, and the capability, to make the decisions to control his or her own life. We believe that no one else has either the right to make such decisions nor is so wise as to be able to make them better than the individual can. We believe the individual is the basic unit in society, and governmental organizations ought to reflect that by not interfering with an individual's freedom to make decisions.

You say this is an old political idea. Isn't it exactly what the conservatives talk about when they say they want less government in their lives?

Many of them say it, but they don't really mean it, and they certainly don't practice it in any consistent fashion. Many of them want less taxes, but they want bigger governmental subsidies for business; they want all sorts of rules and regulations that restrict free competition and interfere with other people's social freedom and private morality. Many of them advocate restrictions, for example, on abortion or on the use of drugs and alcohol. We think these are inappropriate, unethical areas of governmental action, except in special situations involving young children, or perhaps the mentally retarded.

So Libertarians believe in individual freedom in both the economic sector—the free-market idea—and also in the social sector—the area of civil liberties and private morality. Our central axiom is based on a broad definition of freedom—the right to choose in the full range of human activity so long as this freedom doesn't involve the use of force or fraud which could encroach on the freedom of someone else. It's an old political idea because it reaches back to the beginning of the classical liberal tradition: back to John Locke and the concept of property rights, back to Adam Smith and Spencer and John Stuart Mill. It was also very much part of our own American Revolution, and it reflects the thinking of Thomas Jefferson and many of the other founding fathers.

Does the government have any role at all under your ideology?

The only possibly legitimate role of government is to defend individual rights; to defend a person against the imposition of force or fraud by others; to defend that person and that person's property against such illegal encroachments. Hence, the sole functions of government should be defensive: to defend the freedom of individual decision making.

It's important to point out, however that we are only talking here about the limited role of government. Under our philosophy, there is plenty of room for both social leadership and for philosophical, religious, or moral restrictions on actions, based on what individuals may freely decide is right or wrong. The government's function is to establish and maintain freedom. Beyond that, individuals can freely choose to place all kinds of constraints or disciplines on themselves, whether it is the discipline of a family, or of a church or temple, or whatever else they may choose.

Why is so much of your concern directed toward the government?

Because, in our view, the very definition of the state is force. The state has a monopoly on legalized force, and this powerful force can be used, and in the past has almost invariably been used, to coerce others to act against their own free will. Liberty is our highest value, and government is always the strongest enemy of liberty.

But there are other very powerful institutions in modern society—large multinational corporations like your own company, big labor, even big organized crime. Who is supposed to control these groups in the absence of the government?

I've already indicated that it is a legitimate role of government to defend individuals against the imposition of force or fraud by others. If a corporation, or a labor union, or any criminal element encroaches on the freedom of others, it is appropriate for government to defend these freedoms. Paradoxically, however, big government actually fosters much of the bigness in other elements of modern society. In my view, big government is one of the principal motivating forces that generates big business. High income taxes, for example, are a massive force toward the consolidation of the economy. They make it virtually impossible for small businesses to accumulate the capital necessary to survive. A second motivating factor is found in large governmental deficits, which drive up the interest rates, and once again make it difficult, if not impossible, for small companies to assemble capital. A third influence is governmental subsidies, which tend to favor large companies and drive out small competition. In addition, there is the whole bewildering area of governmental regulations, many of which, such as licensing laws, are designed to eliminate competition. Big companies are much better able to stand the expense and overhead of regulations than small companies, and therefore governmental regulation tends to promote the growth of big business. Finally, tariffs, subsidies, and other government intervention in the marketplace almost always favors big business over small business.

How about big labor? Should it be free to go its own way?

Absolutely, providing that individuals are really free to decide whether or not they want to support big labor. Once again, however, the government has tended to artificially prop up big labor. We're completely opposed, for example, to a government-imposed closed shop where people are forced to join unions in order to get or hold a job. This is a complete violation of individual freedom of choice. In the absence of such artificial props, the American public has, by and large, rejected unions. The percentage of American workers who belong to unions today is about 22 percent, and that has been declining, despite the existence of many laws that are very favorable to union organization, such as compulsory collective bargaining. So the level of unionism depends on the desires of the people. If people want to belong to unions, they'll be very important. However, if people don't like unions, they will decline in influence.

Let's complete the trilogy. Do you think big government contributes to the growth of big crime?

It most certainly does this through the imposition of improper and unwise regulation. Organized crime has always been in favor of prohibiting drugs, alcohol, and gambling because that's the only way they can make money. We believe that all voluntary acts involving consenting adults should be permitted.

The counterproductive nature of governmental intervention in this area of victimless crimes is clearly shown by Prohibition, which, during the 1920s, corrupted virtually every major city police force, expanded organized crime, and led to untold deaths from unsafe, contaminated alcohol usage, particularly among younger people, because the desire to break rules is part of growing up for many people. Without victimless crime laws, organized crime would be poorer and smaller.

If you were elected president, what specific policies would you follow to carry out these philosophical goals?

In 1980, I issued a white paper of some eighty pages which outlined our proposed budget for the first full year, fiscal year 1982. It had a balance of $400 billion in expenditures and $400 billion in revenues. That's a lot of money, but it's nowhere near as much as the $725.3 billion budget, and the huge deficit, we're actually ending up with in fiscal year 1982. Our proposed budget called for the abolition of all subsidies to business and agriculture. About $50 billion of the federal budget is spent on subsidies to shipping, agriculture, airlines—you name it. We would eliminate all of these immediately. We would also eliminate virtually all regulations and regulatory agencies, which cost hundred of billions of dollars a year in administrative costs and in lost productivity. We would have much stronger cuts in welfare spending than the Reaganites have proposed. In addition, we would reorient American foreign policy immediately towards the defense of the United States and phase out of our alliances with Western Europe and Japan. In future years we would continue to make radical reductions in the size of government.

Is this your position in international affairs? What do you advocate in the area of foreign policy?

We want to do a lot of things. A high priority is to establish a Libertarian International movement that will promote activism and political action groups in every nation of the world. The goal of this movement is to produce a worldwide Libertarian society to reduce the level and size of governments, and particularly military spending, all around the world, including military expenditures behind the iron curtain. Our aim here is to create a worldwide society of small governments to reduce the threat of nuclear war, which may well be the worst threat facing mankind today.

That is an interesting long-range goal, but what do we do in the interim?

In the interim we work for an actual reduction in the existing supply of nuclear weapons which have already been stockpiled by the nuclear powers. We should take very strong steps against proliferation. In my view, the United States should stop the taxpayer-supported export of its nuclear technology.

But you indicated earlier that you wanted to do away with governmental regulations. Aren't private companies exporting this technology? Isn't the free market leading to this? How can we halt nuclear proliferation unless the government steps in and orders an end to it?

We don't need any government regulations to do this; we just need to stop subsidies like those provided in the form of below-market loans by the Export-Import Bank. In my opinion, the nuclear industry has only a very slight connection with the free market. Government subsidies are keeping it alive. It wouldn't survive without the Price-Anderson Act, subsidized research, subsidized protective services, and all the rest.

How about our defense policy? What should we do in this area?

Unfortunately, I think we need to maintain a strong nuclear deterrence until we can get the Soviets to agree to arms reductions. However, we should cut overall defense expenditures drastically and destroy some nuclear weapons. We adamantly oppose the draft as an encroachment on individual freedom. Since we should phase out all of our overseas military alliances and devote our efforts to the defense of our own borders, we do not need a large conventional army.

How can we protect our vital interests overseas? What should we do, for example, if there's a take-over of the Saudi oil fields?

First, we should recognize that ethically it is not our oil. In dealing with a possible cutoff, we should deregulate natural gas, which provides a third of all our energy. That will reduce demand and increase supply. Beyond that, we will simply have to adjust through pricing, free-market pricing, to the situation by conserving more if there is a cut-off of Middle East oil. Pragmatically, there is no way the United States is going to have any positive impact on Middle East politics by supplying American troops in that area.

Isn't this basically an isolationist policy?

No. We should take advantage of our geographical location and not get involved in Europe's quarrels. This is the original foreign policy of George Washington: a noninterventionist policy. But Libertarians are internationalists, not isolationists. We believe in free trade; we support massive people-to-people contacts; we believe in free immigration. These are not isolationist policies, but laissez-faire, internationalist policies.

Let me ask one last question about libertarian ideology. It's attractive to talk about individualism and freedom, but couldn't this lead to selfishness, and even hedonism, in both international and domestic life? Who will take care of the less fortunate? Couldn't this lead to a new manifestation of social Darwinism—the survival of the fittest?

It's not social Darwinism at all, unless you assume the government is the only institution which is capable of showing compassion, which is certainly not our assumption. The Libertarian International is designed to reduce military expenditures which are bleeding the poor nations to death to a point where these societies have no resources left to improve the lot of their own people.

In the domestic area, we believe the benevolent impulse exists outside of government. The problem today is that a family can't afford to take care of their own elderly because they pay taxes which are used by the government to send their parents to institutions for the aged. We would give direct tax incentives to families to take care of their own. We would encourage all sorts of collective action, beginning with the family, the church and temple, the neighborhood, and the community association. We think this would improve the quality of care by providing a more personalized, compassionate approach. So we certainly don't think we are advocating a hedonistic, or self-serving, philosophy at all by encouraging people, rather than the government, to care about other people.

THE 1980 CAMPAIGN

We spent a lot of time on ideology, so let me ask a brief set of questions on the campaign. In 1980, you managed to get on the ballot in all fifty states. Do you have any comments on the ballot access issue?

Ballot access laws are completely unfair. Many states have laws to prevent new parties from getting on the ballot. The Libertarian Party is big enough now to jump these hurdles, so it's no longer a serious obstacle to us, but it is a very undesirable set of laws and rules. I think it ought to be a constitutional right to be on the ballot, and therefore there should only be a very minimal financial, or signature, requirement.

In terms of campaign financing, you actually raised a sizable amount of money. I think you spent $3 or $4 million.

We spent three and a half million.

How did you raise this money?

It came from party members. Our vice-presidential nominee pledged to contribute at least $500,000 to the campaign, and he provided a lot of his own money.

Was this permissible under the Federal Election Campaign Act? How do you feel about this act?

It's perfectly legal under the act for candidates to contribute as much as they want to their own campaign. Moreover, I don't think there should be federal election laws that limit contributions by others in any way. To limit what anybody can contribute to a party is both unconstitutional and very detrimental to the appearance of new parties. New parties are usually composed of small groups of people who care very intensely about their particular points of view, and the laws impinge most heavily on these parties. The Republicans and Democrats have huge constituencies; they can raise hundreds of millions of dollars in relatively small contributions. New parties cannot. The Federal Campaign Act directly restricts competition and abets the two-party monopoly by limiting individual contributions and requiring very detailed accounting and reporting.

Would you get the federal government out of financing elections?

Absolutely. It's very undesirable to use the tax collection mechanism to help finance election campaigns. The government has no business in this area at all. Its actions almost invariably act to entrench incumbents.

Do you think the media treated you fairly?

They gave us a decent amount of coverage. I can't say it was adequate, since I certainly felt we deserved more. In a free society, of course, the media is free to make their own decisions. In 1980 they seemed to be less interested in ideas or the emergence of new parties than in competitive aspects of the campaign—how many votes a candidate expected to get in this or that state. For parties like ours, this creates a chicken-and-egg problem. To overcome it, you have to campaign hard to get a little coverage. Then you campaign even harder to get a little more coverage. You have to build up step by step. In Alaska, where we are a substantial party, we received substantial coverage. In other states, we received less coverage.

What about the national media?

We got very minor coverage from the big networks, the six o'clock television news. I think we certainly deserved more, and we'll get more if we keep working hard in future elections.

There was one incident involving NBC news where you were accused by some party members of agreeing to compromise libertarian principles. What was this controversy all about?

Some members were upset, and they may be right. We contacted NBC to buy television time to run ads, and they were slow in giving us this time. We had the money to pay for the ads, and we thought we were being delayed and delayed and delayed. We felt that we should bring suit on the grounds that they were a monopoly that had violated FCC regulations, which limits their monopoly powers.

The FCC has consistently limited new stations, opposed pay TV, put roadblocks in front of new methods of communication. So in our view, suing a network was like suing an electric utility to have them hook up electricity to your house. They are given a monopoly, and if there's going to be a monopoly, it's not unlibertarian to sue in order to force them to do what they are supposed to do under that monopoly grant. Actually, I think we reached an agreement on running the ads without bringing the suit.

You got over 900,000 votes, which isn't bad if you look at third parties historically. Were you disappointed in that? Did you hope to get more?

We had hoped to get more votes, and without John Anderson in the race, I think we would have. In 1978, when I ran for governor of California, we were the alternative. People were unhappy with Jerry Brown and Evelle Younger, and I was the logical alternative. In the 1980 race, John Anderson had a great deal more money to spend than we did, and he became the logical alternative. Therefore, he got much of the attention that would have otherwise gone to us in terms of media coverage and public interest and votes.

PERSONAL IMPRESSIONS

This brings us to the future. Are you optimistic or pessimistic about the Libertarian Party?

I'm very optimistic—extremely optimistic—about the future of the party. Our goal is to become as big a party as the Republicans and the Democrats by the end of the decade. In 1980, we elected twenty-two candidates to office in different states. In 1982, we hope to run 1,000 candidates for local, state, and congressional offices.

Why do you think you will succeed in doing this when all the other third-party efforts have failed?

The problems with third parties are generally twofold. Some are built around a single individual, such as George Wallace and the American Independent Party, and they are not able to develop viable long-term organizational strength at the state and local levels. Others are devoted to a single issue, like the Prohibition Party, so they're not able to develop a mass constituency. We are a broad-based party; we have a comprehensive view of society; and we are not organized around any single issue or individual.

As a result, I believe we have the same opportunity to become a mass party as the Republicans did in the 1850s. We have come on the scene at a time when both the Republicans and Democrats are disintegrating; when only half of the people vote; and when most of those who do vote are voting against rather than for, one of the other traditional party candidates. Therefore, we have the same type of fluid situation as in the 1850s, and we think we can take advantage of that, as the Republicans did, to become a major party.

Do you have any evidence that the libertarian philosophy has great mass appeal?

We took some research polls in the last election. We asked younger people—these were people under age forty—whether they would support a third party whose principal positions were a noninterventionist foreign policy, which we defined for them, and major cuts in taxes and spending. Forty-eight percent of those under forty said they would. A very large proportion of the younger generation also supports our views on civil liberties. They have a much less hawkish foreign policy than older people, and they have lost faith in government as the leader of the economy. So we feel the younger generation has a great deal of philosophical and emotional empathy with our views, and this is the group that will determine the future course of American politics.

You really do seem to be extremely optimistic about the party.

Yes, because I'm convinced there is no party that is more American, that can contribute more to our society, than the Libertarian Party.

What do you mean by that?

The thing that distinguishes our society from all others is individual rights and the individualistic point of view of the American people. There is no other country in the world where as many races and religions live together harmoniously. Our views on civil rights, immigration, the economy, and foreign policy reflect this individualism of the American people, this concept of freedom which brought this country into being.

If this is the case, where do you think we strayed off the path? Why do we have so much big government today?

I originally came from southeastern Massachusetts, and I'm afraid it all started in that area of the country. Way back in the early 1790s, a bill was introduced in Congress at the request of the Cape Cod fishermen. They wanted the government to provide protection against the Canadians and British fishing close to the United States and landing goods in New England ports, since this was reducing the price of fish. This was the beginning of governmental intervention in private affairs.

There are certain costs of freedom, and one of these is that you have to work hard and be efficient and take care of yourself. Many people would like to slough off that burden and have the government do this for them. Then, after awhile, the government gets to be an independent force, always building its own power through its own sense of internal momentum. Eventually, people lose sight of their original goals, and the government ends up running their lives for them.

A couple of final questions. How do you feel about national and international affairs today? Are things better or worse than when you ran in 1980?

On the domestic front, I don't think there's any chance for any real improvement in the economy unless Reagan makes major cuts in military spending, and he's just proposed a massive 18 percent increase. The military economy is the least productive part of our society; it basically makes goods that you hope you'll never have to use. Unless there are major cuts in military spending, there will be no real economic revival in the United States.

I also think Reagan's foreign policy is much too militaristic. In my view, his strident anticommunist point of view is dangerous because it raises unnecessary dangers of nuclear war. As I have already said, I think we could improve our defense by de-escalating our military commitments. Western Europe is capable of defending itself by itself, and they're much more likely to do a capable job of it. There are more people, more wealth, and higher technology in Western Europe than in the Soviet Union. The French got out of NATO because they thought it was being used by the United States for its own purposes, while they wanted an alliance whose sole goal was to defend Western Europe, their homeland. The first effect of a U.S. withdrawal from NATO would be to bring the French back in, which would replace all the American troops in Western Europe. As a result, they would be in a better position to defend themselves than they are today.

What are your own plans for the future? Are you going to run again in 1984?

I am certainly not going to be a candidate in 1984. I've already issued my Sherman statement on that. As far as the 1988 and 1992 elections, I haven't reached my decision. It would depend on whether I thought I could make a contribution, and whether the Libertarian Party thought I could. I certainly will stay very active in the party. I've already committed myself to do a substantial amount of speaking at libertarian conventions this year, and I will also do some writing. I really believe in our goals. They are very rewarding goals. That's why I am participating in the Libertarian Party.

6 NEW VOICES OF 1980

Virtually every presidential election is characterized by the appearance of new third parties, most of which quickly disappear from the political arena and are then virtually impossible to track down.[1]

Three new political coalitions that appeared in the 1980 election were the Right-to-Life Party, with Ellen McCormack as its candidate; the Citizens Party, which nominated Barry Commoner; and the National Unity Campaign, which was organized by independent candidate John B. Anderson.

Since Ellen McCormack was only on the ballot in three states to push a single issue (antiabortion), it is doubtful whether the Right-to-Life Party will contest future presidential elections. Basically, it is interested in pressing the major parties to carry out its program against abortion, a classic pressure strategy that has been used by other single-issue parties in the past.

The Citizens Party may develop into a more viable, long-term political coalition. Since the 1980 election, it has already won a number of contests at the local level, and it is now attempting to build both a national party organization as well as strong party organizations at the state level.

At the time this was written, John Anderson had not yet decided on his plans for 1984, but he indicates in his interview that he will establish a new third party if he makes another bid for the White House. After the 1980 election Anderson received $4.2 million in retroactive federal funds under the provisions of the Federal Election Campaign Act because he got over 5 percent of the total popular votes cast while running as an independent candidate. If Anderson decides to run for the presidency again in 1984, he may qualify for over $4 million in federal funds prior to the election if the Federal Election Commission certifies that any new third party he might organize is eligible for such funds based on his 1980 performance as an independent candidate.

THE RIGHT-TO-LIFE PARTY

The Right-to-Life Party was organized in New York State in 1970 by a group of women from the town of Merrick, about forty miles east of New York City, on the south shore of Long Island. It is a classic example of a single-issue party, since its entire focus is dedicated to opposition to abortion. The leadership of the party, which is heavily Catholic, is entirely female.

The party has focused its major efforts on New York State elections. New York State has long had a highly competitive group of third parties as a result of what Daniel Mazmanian calls its "modified two-party system." Like other states, New York has both of the two major parties—the Republicans and the Democrats. As Mazmanian explains, the state's election laws also enable other parties "to pursue a variety of strategies and thus provide the voters with a wide range of choice. In New York the party, not the candidate, establishes a ballot position, and more than one officially recognized party may endorse a candidate. The candidate is listed under each party heading. Consequently, a third party that endorses a major-party nominee does not have its name withdrawn from the ballot, but simply inserts the candidate's name in its own line."[2]

The two most important third parties in New York during the postwar period have been the Conservatives and the Liberals. The former often endorse Republican nominees, and the latter, Democratic nominees, but both parties are free to designate their own candidates. Thus, they retain their party identity, and they are in a strong position to influence major-party nominees and policies.

In 1978, the Right-to-Life Party qualified as an official party in New York by polling 130,193 votes in the gubernatorial election to place fourth behind the Democratic, Republican, and Conservative Parties, but ahead of the Liberal Party. Under New York State's election law, an "independent body" qualifies as a political party "when it receives at least 50,000 votes in the last preceding gubernatorial election."[3]

Ellen McCormack, one of the founders of the Right-to-Life Party, ran as a Democratic Party candidate for president of the United States in the 1976 primary elections in order to dramatize the abortion issue. Although she had never before sought elective office, Mrs. McCormack received over 250,000 votes in the various 1976 state primary contests that she entered.

In 1980, McCormack ran for president of the United States as a Right-to-Life Party candidate in New York State. She also ran as an independent candidate in New Jersey and Kentucky with Carroll Driscoll, a forty-four-year-old teacher from New Jersey, as her vice-presidential nominee. She received a total of 32,327 popular votes in these three states.

McCormack, a fifty-four-year-old homemaker, has raised four children. I interviewed her in late June 1981 in her home in North Bellmore, Long Island, located about five miles north of Jones Beach State Park. She offered the following comments on her involvement in politics.

Ellen McCormack

You know how it is. If you have a job that has to be done, sometimes you have to do it yourself.

GENERAL BACKGROUND

Smallwood: Let's begin with some background information. Tell me a little about how you got started in politics.

McCormack: Back in 1966, some local friends and I started a dialogue group. I was a young mother with four young children. It was an outlet for the ladies of the town I lived in. Different local issues would come up, like the new sewage plant in town, the new buildings that were being constructed—just the general things that anyone in the community would be interested in. But mainly we discussed different books. It was basically a book discussion group.

At one of our meetings, the issue of abortion was raised. One of our members had watched a panel show on television.

She was genuinely concerned that Blumenthal's bill might be passed by the state legislature. Someone else in the group agreed that this sounded like a serious problem, but when we discussed it, we realized we didn't know much about the issue of abortion. So we decided to investigate it, to do a little research.

We had to refer to medical books to understand what an abortion actually was. We followed the abortion issue on television and in the newspapers, and we realized that it was becoming quite possible that abortion could be legalized in New York State and that it would be an extreme abortion bill; not just abortion within the first few months, but abortion across the board. Since we all shared a common concern, we became more involved at that point. We found we had to do more research. The more we found out, the more it became evident to us that abortion was taking the life of a baby, so we decided we would reach out to the professionals for help. We went to some lawyers for advice. We thought that if we brought them our findings, they would be inspired and they would do something, or they would advise us to do something. But we found them lackadaisical. Then we approached some doctors. They were genuinely concerned, because they had to deal with it. They knew they would have to deal with it, but they were busy. So finally we went to the politicians.

When did you first approach the politicians? Were you living in Bellmore at the time?

It was in 1968. There was a big push to get an abortion bill through the state legislature, so we began to approach the politicians in 1968. I was living in Merrick at the time, the very next town to Bellmore.

Initially, we went to our local politician, who was a very big man in the area, to discuss the issue with him. He advised us he was opposed to abortion, but his research staff told him that it would be better if he voted for abortion. That was our first introduction to politics, and we were shocked! We couldn't believe that a man would say, "Well, yes, you know personally I am opposed to it, but my research staff has advised me to behave in a different way." We asked him how he could do that, realizing that he was an important man on Long Island, next to Margiotta, who was a really big politician in Nassau County. How could he make such a decision?

So we didn't stop with him. We went to see other politicians who represented Long Islanders. We found that they didn't know as much about the issue as we did. We didn't think we were very knowledgeable at that point, so we were always looking for new evidence. We felt that if we could bring new evidence to the politicians, they would fight for the unborn. So we went from the professionals—the lawyers and the doctors—to the politicians, and then we remained in the political arena to fight because we realized they were making the decisions.

Can you tell me a little more about your group at this point? Who was involved in this effort?

We represented a variety of different interests. We were local friends. We're still friends, and we work together. It all started when we first met at the library to discuss books. I worked for the Girl Scouts in town. Somebody else was a social worker. Another woman worked part-time. We got together informally. We had reading interests, and we shared them.

Then we just moved on to the abortion issue. It gave us a little extra to do, this research work that we did. We were shocked at what we found, and we thought this is it. We'll present this evidence, and there won't be any problem any more. We were surprised to find that no matter how much evidence we brought forward, we had problems because the politicians weren't interested in our material. We found that we were more knowledgeable about the development of the unborn baby. We were more knowledgeable, and they were uncomfortable.

Is this when you organized the Right-to-Life Party?

We formed the Right-to-Life Party in 1970. I was one of the original founders of the party. We attempted to run two candidates in the 1970 election. The first was Jane Gilroy for governor of New York. However, we weren't successful in gathering enough petitions, and she was disqualified. She never made it on the ballot.

Our second candidate, Vincent Carey, ran for the United States Congress. We were in the Fifth Congressional District then. Our congressman was Allard Lowenstein, a nationally known figure because he had been active in the dump President Johnson movement in 1968. Lowenstein ran as a Democrat-Liberal. The Republicans and the Conservative Party nominated Norman Lent, and we ran Vincent Carey as the right-to-life candidate.

Norman Lent won the seat, and he's been in Congress ever since 1970. However, he only beat Lowenstein by about 10,000 votes. Since Vincent Carey got over 5,000 votes in our very first election, Norman Lent paid attention to us. Vincent Carey was a very good candidate, a very caring and intelligent man, who could encourage dialogue and the sharing of information. The campaign led to a better understanding of the abortion issue. Norman Lent had formerly been proabortion, but he changed his position and became prolife. He felt that since he was elected to represent us, this would be the way his vote would go. He has been consistently pro life since he's been in Congress. So even though we lost the election, we felt we had been successful.

POLITICAL IDEOLOGY

I'd like to get a better understanding of your position. Your party appears to be a classic example of a single-issue party. Is abortion the only issue that concerns you, or are there a range of issues?

We were—and still are—interested in abortion. When we first organized the Right-to-Life Party in New York State, our platform dealt only with abortion.

Why is this issue so much more important than all the other issues? Why do you place such heavy weight on this particular issue?

Because it's dealing with life. Life is something that—whether you live or die, whether I live or die—is critically important to you and to me. It should be important to everybody.

There are different kinds of groups in politics. You have groups that are interested in helping the poor to have a better life. They want them to have a decent education and better jobs, and they fight for these things very hard. That's a very important issue, so they should work very hard for it.

Well, our fight is to allow even the smallest baby to be allowed to be born. I'm interested in all the other issues you're interested in. I've always had a concern, a genuine concern, for the poor. But there are groups that specialize, and my major concern is about abortion. If I ever finish with the abortion issue, I hope I can get back and help the poor.

Some people argue that the abortion issue is related to the problems of the poor; that overpopulation and an inability to care for children can lead to starvation and deprivation.

I utterly reject this argument. It is extremely dangerous. I think a lot of people kind of close their eyes. They don't look for solutions to these problems because they believe they have abortion. For example, the head of Planned Parenthood in New York City said if we don't abort them, we're just going to increase the welfare rolls. I think that's an abominable statement! I don't know how anyone could go on television and make such a statement. He's equating money with lives. What he's saying, as far as I'm concerned, is if we're not capable of finding solutions to the problems of the poor, we should kill them.

Once we start this, where do we stop? If we can't solve the problems of the aged, do we have to kill them too? We've got big problems in nursing homes today. If the problems are too great, will we slip them a pill? Will we put them to sleep? If we accept the theory that problems can no longer be solved unless we kill off people, we can move quite rapidly to the handicapped. This is a terribly dangerous idea.

It's very obvious that you have extremely deep feelings about this issue. Can you give me some idea where these feelings come from? Is this a religious issue with you?

Well, the Catholic church has always been strongly against

abortion, and I agree with the church. But it goes beyond this. It's really a fundamental issue of our democracy, of the kind of country we want to be, the kind of people we want to be.

You know, the Declaration of Independence guarantees "life, liberty and the pursuit of happiness." Which comes first? Life. You can't have liberty, and you can't pursue happiness, or anything else, unless you have life.

The issue appears to be very clear-cut to you, but others may disagree with your interpretation. Don't people say to you, why are you trying to impose your morality on us? Shouldn't this be a private choice between the parents? Do you have some special insight into "the truth" that enables you to tell other people what is right?

I don't think I'm saying I know what's right. I'm certainly not saying you can't do what you believe is right. I'm saying that everyone is an individual who has a right to work, to live, to do anything in the world they choose to do that society will allow them to do. But there is one thing you cannot do. You cannot destroy a baby, because that baby is a separate life. If a woman and her baby sat on the couch next to me, and she started to beat that baby or to kill it outright, I would be outraged. I would do anything I could to stop her, and that's why she cannot destroy the baby within her, because it's another life.

So I'm concerned that we allow that baby to be born. If babies are handicapped, if poor ladies are having babies, let's help the handicapped and the poor. But let's not destroy the babies, because we are teaching society that some people are expendable. It's one generation dictating the power of life and death over the following generation. And that's total slavery.

What about birth control prior to conception? Are you opposed to that?

You can put birth control into another category of big problems. I don't know a lot about it. I'm often asked why can't they find something that will help us, some kind of contraceptive that will be safe.

I don't know. I really don't know. The IUD is a problem. The pill is a problem because of the side effects. There are problems with other forms of birth control—foam—they don't work. I don't get into contraceptives at all. The only contraceptive I would be opposed to are the ones that would bring about an abortion. If it works as such and destroys a baby that is already conceived, I would oppose that kind of contraceptive.

One last question on your attitude towards abortion. Some people argue that the state has no right to dictate an official position on this issue because they feel it is a matter of private choice. I once ran for political office myself. Let's assume you agreed with me on every conceivable issue except abortion. Would you vote against me under these circumstances?

Yes. I'm sorry, but I think you would be wrong. You actually know more about this than I do because you're a professor of political science, and I never even went to college at all. But our reading group tried to look into this issue, to find out about how far the authority of the state should extend.

As I remember it, our society is based on the idea that the state agrees to protect us as members of society. So we have all sorts of laws on the books to protect ourselves from harming each other. We have laws against murder, laws against other violent crimes. I certainly think the state has a right to protect unborn babies. Indeed, I think it has a duty to protect unborn babies, since they can't protect themselves. As I said earlier, we're dealing with the issue of one generation dictating the power of life or death over the following generation.

I'm sorry, but I could never vote for you if you were a pro-abortion candidate.

THE 1976 AND 1980 CAMPAIGNS

Let's get back to your political activities. In 1976, you ran in the Democratic Party primaries for president of the United States, and in 1980 you ran as the Right-to-Life candidate for president. This was certainly a big jump from local politics into the national arena. How did this come about?

When we finished with Vincent Carey's congressional campaign in 1970, we went back to the educational part of our research. We were trying to learn more, trying to promote dialogue in order to open up the issue. I realized that it was a big job. Many professional people opposed us, professionals who were very big in the media. They appeared in all the major newspapers and in many of the magazines my own children used to read. So I realized that we were in for a very hard struggle. The professionals were the ones who were opposing our position on abortion, yet the average person was not comfortable with it. Some people didn't want to eliminate abortion entirely, but they were frightened by it; they were uncomfortable with it.

I looked forward to a situation like that, because I saw some room for dialogue here. If we could discuss the issue, I felt that we could win them over. I felt we could remind them that if they're a little optimistic, a little creative and hopeful, we can solve the social problems we're all so interested in. We'll have to do it by being creative and not destructive, because abortion is destructive. So I looked forward to dialogue like that. However, I didn't have access to the public. I didn't have access to television. That was a major problem. I might get on TV once a year, but I was restricted, and I was also censored. I wasn't allowed to show any pictures of the unborn babies they were destroying. If I owned a newspaper, or if I was the editor of the *New York Times*, I would have a chance to educate the people on the issue as I see it. But we never really had that opportunity, so we went back again into the political field.

In 1976, we looked over the presidential candidates, and we realized that we would never have any candidates who would discuss abortion if they could avoid it, because they knew it was controversial. Politicians realize in order to be elected, they've got to somehow convince the people who disagree with them that they're not so harmful. In order to win people from both sides of any issue, they've got to avoid the issue. They've got to somehow answer questions so that people on both sides of the issue think the candidate agrees with them. We realized that we didn't have a candidate who would ever discuss abortion, so we decided we would put together a campaign to see if someone would agree to run in the Democratic Party primaries. We interviewed a number of people. Some of them thought we were a little harsh in our statements, since we wanted to challenge the decision of the Supreme Court during the campaign.

This was the Roe *v.* Wade *decision of 1973?*

Right. Some people felt we were a little too strong. They didn't like to question the justices. We interviewed several people, but none of them worked out. That's when we decided I would be the candidate. It was our idea. We all had strong feelings on how it should be done. We didn't want it neutralized in any way. You know how it is. If you have a job that has to be done, you sometimes have to do it yourself.

This must have been quite a decision for you. Ten years earlier you had joined an informal book discussion group, and now you're running in the Democratic primaries for president of the United States. Did you actually go out and campaign in different states?

Yes. I visited twenty-two states.

Was abortion the only issue that really concerned you?

Yes.

What did you say when people asked you about foreign policy and all the other issues involved in a presidential campaign?

I had to deal with all the issues. I realized I would have to do that as a presidential candidate, so I sat down and put together everything in an opinion sheet. However, I found that the reporters were very interested in the abortion issue. I went into different states and met with rooms full of newspapermen, pretty much what you see on TV. When I went into a state, the press came from all over to interview me. They really came out. They asked me a few questions about problems that were current at the time, but then they would get onto abortion.

Once they started to ask me about abortion, I found they stayed with it. I found that they were surprised at my answers. They were inquisitive. I felt that this was the purpose of my whole campaign. This is what we wanted. We wanted the issue opened up. Our problem is that we have always been silenced or misrepresented. Sometimes there is a little twist here and there which can change the whole thing. But here I was on TV, and they couldn't change my words. If I appeared inadequate, or if I appeared less than presidential, I wasn't concerned about that. My interest was in discussing the abortion issue. The reporters were not as knowledgeable as me because they never had access to some of the information I had. As a result, they were genuinely interested, and the interviews became interesting for me, partly because they were difficult. Actually, in all honesty, however, I was frightened the first time I held a press conference.

When was this?

I'll tell you something about that first time. It was in Massachusetts. I had been invited to Boston by our people there. They were very anxious to have me come. They got terribly excited about the whole thing, about being in politics. They wanted bumper stickers; they wanted to get buttons and hats and pens and everything. We said no, don't do that; don't spend your money on that; we're not selling a candidate, really; we're not selling a personality. We want an opportunity to get commercials, which are very expensive, because it's going to be educational. We want people to understand that this is a baby that they are destroying, and there's another way to go. They agreed to some of what was suggested, but there was one thing that they became adamant about, persistent about. They wanted me to visit the state. They promised if I came, they would raise more money.

I finally agreed, so we flew to Boston. We got to the hotel and went upstairs. The girls who were working with me, the ones who were running the campaign, it was all new to them.

They had to go down and set up a big room to meet with the reporters. Finally, a friend came up to tell me the room was full. It was full of reporters. She asked me if I was ready to go down. I thought, OK, it's time to go down. We left the room and closed the door. I'm walking through the hotel in the upstairs corridors. I felt as if I'm going to the Green Room—you know, going to my electrocution. I was terrified. I felt like the priest was there with my last . . . all I can liken it to was a very frightening and awesome feeling.

When we got downstairs, sure enough, the room was filled with reporters. Some were hostile and angry. They were angry with me simply because I was a candidate for president; that I dared to be a candidate. They challenged me with that—how dare you be a candidate? I said, that's the American way. If I can follow all the election rules, if I can raise the money, if I can make the effort to campaign, that means I am a candidate. Regardless of what that issue is, I'm free to campaign on it. When they thought about it a little, they could see that, well, that is true. Then most of them asked me about the abortion issue. So, I got through that first press conference, but it was a terrifying experience.

I assume you didn't think you were going to win the Democratic Party nomination for president. Were you trying to get the other candidates to face this issue?

Yes. I wanted them to deal with it.

So your objective was to get this issue on the agenda in the 1976 presidential election?

Yes. I felt it was a terrible thing that both the Democratic and the Republican Parties had many candidates who would ignore an issue as important as abortion. It made me angry to think they would all ignore such an issue. It was important for me to be there, and because I existed, they had to deal with it. At the same time, I was able to unite all right-to-life people all over the country. We were never as united as we were at that time, because they felt they had somebody who would represent them, at least on one issue. They felt there was somebody they could vote for; that was what they told me during my travels from state to state. They were not thrilled with the professional candidates, and they said at last they had somebody they could vote for. You see, I had to convince them to vote for someone who others would say was not a winner. They had to vote for someone who was not a winner, but somebody who stood for a principle they believed in. That's a hard thing to do with voters. It's a very hard thing to do. The other politicians would remind them, Ellen McCormack can't win; don't throw your vote away. But, of course, what they were doing when they voted for me was saying, all right, we'll still vote for her because we agree with her.

Once you finished the 1976 campaign, do you think you achieved your objective?

Oh, yes, I'm sure we did. I got over 250,000 votes in the different democratic primary elections, so there were a lot of people out there who listened, and agreed, with me.

After the 1976 presidential primaries, did you continue to run for office?

Yes. In 1978 Mary Jane Tobin ran for governor in New York State, and I ran for lieutenant governor, so I was involved in that campaign. It was very important for the party. We got enough votes in that election to allow us to be an official party, to hold a place on the ballot right after the Conservatives, Democrats, and Republicans, or vice versa. We got more votes than the Liberal Party in 1978, and we earned a line on the state ballot until 1982. It was a gigantic step for the Right-to-Life Party in New York state.

This brings us to the 1980 presidential campaign. This time you didn't enter the Democratic Party primaries, but you ran directly as a Right-to-Life Party candidate in New York, New Jersey, and Kentucky. Was this a decision of the party that they wanted you to run as their own candidate for president?

Actually, I could only run on the Right-to-Life Party ticket in New York State, because that was the only state where we had an official party. I ran as an independent in Kentucky and in New Jersey.

I had a real problem in all three states. Ronald Reagan appealed to the right-to-life people throughout the country because he presented himself as a prolife candidate. This caused division, a great deal of division, as far as I was concerned. Many people thought I was just interested in running for the sake of running, or that I had a problem with my ego when I wouldn't support Ronald Reagan. As a result, I never really could get as much momentum as a right-to-life candidate in 1980 as I did in the Democratic primaries in 1976.

Why did you run in 1980? Did you feel Ronald Reagan wasn't strong enough on the right-to-life issue?

Reagan's record on right to life was not a good record. His record in California was poor, where he consistently supported proabortion Republicans. He also supported Senator Percy in Illinois and Senator Javits in New York, simply because they are Republicans. These people hurt right-to-life efforts in Congress. They would never support right-to-life legislation. That was the message I sent to Reagan's people. If he was continuing to support proabortion Republicans, then I could not support him. All of us were concerned about his vice-presidential candidate. He assured us he would choose a candidate who would support his views, and then he chose Bush, who has consistently supported abortion. There were good reasons to question Reagan's prolife support, but people simply wouldn't listen to me.

Then the 1980 campaign was a disappointment for you?

It certainly was frustrating, although I think we did pretty well under the circumstances. Remember, I was only on the ballot in three states, but I got more votes than four or five of the other third-party candidates. I got over 25,000 votes in New

York State, where I ran behind John Anderson and the Libertarians, but ahead of all the other third-party candidates, including Barry Commoner. The same thing happened in Kentucky. I think if Reagan hadn't confused the prolife voters, I could have done better, so the campaign wasn't a total disappointment.

IMPRESSIONS OF THE FUTURE

What about the future? Would you like to see a constitutional amendment to prohibit abortion?

Yes. We are working for that. I would like to see a constitutional amendment giving the right to babies to be born. The Supreme Court didn't really deal with the issue in 1973. They didn't deal with the issue of the baby. They only dealt with the rights of the woman. That's why we need a constitutional amendment and new legislation that specifies that a baby is a human being. We have to get back to recognizing that a baby is a baby. We've been confused by proabortionists who say it's a fetus and who use slogans such as prochoice, which only cloud the issue.

There appear to be a number of other groups who are interested in this issue, groups like the Moral Majority. Do you plan to work with them?

Well, the Moral Majority, obviously they are playing an active role. I don't know how it will develop. I don't know, but obviously they are concerned. I do know one thing. I've always campaigned for an amendment. I'll continue to work for that. We'll only achieve it when we have enough votes in Congress, and we don't have the votes now, so we have to be committed. We have to continually educate. You see, the goal is really a simple goal. I think in the years ahead, when the abortion problem is solved and society recognizes the baby as human, I think they're going to call us simpletons.

Do you think you will run again for political office?

I would never say that. No, I choose not to run. I truly choose not to run again.

But you'll remain active with this issue?

Yes. I'm vice-chairman of the Right-to-Life Party here in New York State. I've been involved politically for a number of years now. I think it's an issue I'll have to remain with. It's not a comfortable issue. You're at the forefront when you become involved in politics. The average volunteer—because we're all volunteers—is often frightened by politics and may shy away from it. I've had terrible threats. I've had to change my phone number because I've had obscene phone calls. Down through the years when my children were young, it was a frightening thing. But I'll remain active. The issue is too important for me to give up on it now after working so hard all these years.

THE CITIZENS PARTY

In the spring of 1979, a group of dissident liberals who were disillusioned with Jimmy Carter's presidency began exploratory discussions about the feasibility of organizing a new political party. The movement gained momentum, and in December 1979 an organizing committee filed papers with the Federal Election Commission to establish the Citizens Party.

The party had its founding convention in Cleveland, Ohio, in April 1980, with author Studs Terkel serving as convenor. Representatives from thirty-two states attended the convention, where they nominated Barry Commoner for president and LaDonna Harris for vice-president.

Although the party experienced difficulty raising funds as a result of its late start, it did receive a number of endorsements from former attorney general, Ramsay Clark; former Oklahoma senator and 1976 democratic presidential aspirant, Fred Harris (the husband of LaDonna Harris); and William Winpisinger, president of the International Association of Machinists. The party, which appeared on the ballot in thirty states, received 234,294 votes, with over one-quarter of the total coming from California.

Commoner, a sixty-two-year-old biologist and international spokesman on environmental issues, has authored many books, including *The Closing Circle* (1971), *The Poverty of Power* (1976), and *The Politics of Energy* (1979). LaDonna Harris was the forty-nine-year-old president of Americans for Indian Opportunity. I interviewed Barry Commoner in his office in the Center for the Biology of Natural Systems at Queens College in New York in late June 1981. He offered the following comments on his involvement with the Citizens Party.

Barry Commoner

> *I'm a congenital optimist . . . I'm absolutely convinced that 1980 will be looked on as the first year of a new political realignment in this country.*

PERSONAL BACKGROUND

Smallwood: I'd like to start with a little background informa-tion. When and how did you first get involved in politics?

Commoner: My approach to politics has been through the route of what you might call the responsibility of the scientist. I was always interested in science. I was born in Brooklyn, and I received my undergraduate education at Columbia and my graduate education at Harvard. In 1942, after I had taught bi-ology for a couple of years at Queens College, I went into the navy. Although I was only twenty-five years old at the time, I became engaged in a number of interesting assignments which clarified the public implications of science. The last assignment I had was as the navy's liaison with the Senate Military Service Committee. I was intimately involved in writing the National Science Foundation bill in its original form, and I also partici-pated in organizing the first hearings when Robert Oppen-heimer testified immediately after the release of the informa-tion on the Manhattan District (atomic bomb) project. This early involvement reinforced my feelings as a professional sci-entist that we have a social responsibility, which goes beyond just doing our own work, because of the enormous social im-plications of modern scientific research.

Did you become actively involved in politics after you left the service?

No, not immediately, but after the war, I became very active in dealing with a variety of social issues. Before joining the fac-ulty at Washington University in St. Louis, I worked for a year as associate editor of *Science Illustrated* which gave me a back-ground in the public information dimensions of science educa-tion. I spent many years in the Scientist's Institute for Public Information and in the American Association for the Advance-ment of Science working with people like Margaret Mead get-ting social issues discussed by scientific groups. What I'm say-ing is that my concern with social and political issues is very long-standing. However, my earlier concerns were focused more on public education than on active politics.

What influenced you to help organize the new Citizens Party?

The question of why my own activity in this area shifted from analysis and public education into the creation of a new political party is described in the last chapter of my latest book, *The Politics of Energy*.[+] What I have been doing in recent years is to look for the reasons for such problems as the energy crisis and the environmental crisis. I've ended up concluding that the reasons have to do with the governance of production decisions: who decides how we use our resources; what we produce and how we produce it. The crucial issue is what I call democratic social governance of the means of production. These decisions should not be made in the interests of maximizing private profits. This is the most critical issue of our era, and it requires a whole new approach to politics.

I'm involved in politics because it's become crystal clear that the issues I've been concerned with—nuclear issues, environmental issues, energy issues—are not going to be solved simply by protest. We have to make some fundamental changes in our production system. In order to make these changes, we're going to have to develop a new approach to politics in this country.

POLITICAL IDEOLOGY

Could you clarify this new approach? What changes do you advocate, and why do these changes involve the creation of an entirely new political party?

Well, I think the first point is to analyze the country's political situation in such a way as to discover what political vehicle is appropriate to the new situation; whether or not a third party is needed. A lot of people say third parties will not succeed, but I think the reason why they haven't succeeded, with the one exception of the Republican Party back in 1860, is that there has never been an adequate analysis of the political / economic reasons for third parties. When an issue that confronts the country becomes so profound that discussing it threatens the possibility of winning elections, the major parties shy away from it. The best example in the past is the slavery issue. If you'll look at the history of the campaigns that preceded the election of Lincoln, you'll find what historians call "the ignominious period of American politics." This was the period in which we elected all the presidents whose names you don't remember: Harrison, Tyler, Polk, Taylor, Fillmore, Pierce, Buchanan. The question is: why did we have this rash of nonentities as presidents? The answer is: they were carefully chosen as nonentities because none of the political parties wanted to discuss slavery in a national campaign for fear of losing the election. It was too hot to handle, too difficult an issue. When Lincoln prepared his Lincoln-Douglas debate speech, he wrote into it opposition to the extension of slavery. But his friends advised him to steer clear of this because they said he'd lose votes. He did not follow their advice; he opposed extension of slavery, and of course he lost that election. The creation of the Republican Party was really almost forced on the country by the abdication of politics by the Whigs and the Democrats who were not willing to deal with the slavery issue. That explains why the Republican Party grew so fast.

Do you think a similar situation exists in the United States today?

Generalizing from this historical experience, I believe that a third party is called for when the two major parties are incapable of confronting critical issues and conduct charades instead of campaigns. That's exactly the situation we have in America today. There is an enormous amount of evidence that the American people are turning away from both the Democrats and the Republicans: the declining participation in elections, the fact that issues aren't discussed in campaigns. This is the analysis that led to the creation of the Citizens Party.

The reason for the collapse of two-party politics is that there is a fundamental issue facing the country that neither party is willing to touch because of their unquestioning acceptance of the basic premises of capitalism, in particular, that the owner of capital is free to decide how to use it—what to produce and how to produce it—on the sole criterion of maximizing profit. But, it is no longer in the national interest for production decisions to be made on this single criterion, never asking what's good for the country, what will create jobs, what will protect the environment, what will conserve energy. The new Citizens Party believes that from now on these decisions are going to have to be made in the national interest. This is what I mean by social governance of the means of production, a position which is obviously contradictory to the basic premise of the capitalistic economic system. I think that the two major parties are afraid to discuss almost any issue because just below the surface is this one. For example, any deep analysis of the energy question leads to the fact that our dependence on foreign oil was brought about by the oil companies because it maximized their profits.

So the first thing is the analysis. A lot of people thought that those of us who were involved with creating the Citizens Party were just another one of these spasms trying to create a third party—a People's Party, the Wallace thing, and so on. A sort of "here we go again" politics. This is far from the truth. Those of us who decided to create a new party acted on the basis of the rationale I've just described in the conviction that it *had* to be done. That was the first step.

It appears that the central thrust of the Citizens Party is the corporate power issue. What are your proposed remedies? Do you advocate public control of the energy industries, the multinationals, and the large corporations?

You're right on target. The key word is control, which is a very flexible concept. I mean we followed a kind of principle of political parsimony. For example, if the issue is social control of the production decisions, that does not necessarily require social ownership. What you look for is the simplest way to achieve control. We are basically in favor of public control of the structure of the economy. But you can achieve this in a lot of different ways depending on the circumstances. You can achieve this without telling a local ice cream parlor what flavor of ice cream to sell. In cases like this, you don't need public ownership.

In other cases, however, it may be impossible to achieve control without ownership. For example, take the railroads. Since they certainly make lower profits than other enterprises, what capitalist would want to own them? So we came out for nationalizing the railroads. On the other hand, with respect to the oil companies, a different form of control might be appropriate. We discussed that in the Citizens Party through position papers and so on, and the simplest way of doing it would be to set up a federal energy corporation that would take complete control over import, production, and distribution of energy. Now does that mean nationalization? Not necessarily. For example, the government could write contracts with various oil companies to produce oil in Texas and sell it at a fixed price, making the oil companies public utilities. Nothing very strange about that.

How does your position differ from the older parties on the left— for example, the Socialist Party?

We developed our positions quite empirically, quite in contrast with any of the socialist parties. We were not being guided by what you might call a historic theory. Clearly we understood what socialism was all about. The theory of socialism calls for public ownership and control of the means of production. We stressed control, not ownership. In the Soviet Union, for example, the problem is that you have social ownership without adequate social control. I regard our position as a very valuable idea. I still think this is exactly what the world is about. It seems to me that the campaign worked. There was no question about it. With very little support—we had no brain trust to speak of, just a few of us—with this idea in our heads, we could go from one local situation to another and made a hell of a lot of sense out of it.

Wouldn't the system of public control you're advocating require a lot of money? How do you plan to get the funds to support this concept?

It's self-evident. We should make productive use of government funds that are now being wasted on foolish military expenditures. Military spending has zero productivity. It's ridiculous. We should take that money and put it into productive outlets, rebuilding the railroads and other socially useful activities. It's obvious that we have the money if we want to spend it this way.

In terms of your political ideology, you've placed a lot of emphasis on economic issues and corporate control. What about other social issues such as equal opportunity and the like? Is the Citizens Party a single-issue group?

No, no. Not at all. The corporate power issue is related to every other issue. Take the problems of racial and sexual discrimination. Of course, in both cases there are psychological, social, and institutional issues involved. But I believe that the driving force is economic. Both blacks and women get 40 percent less pay than whites and men. Why is this the case? It means that the corporations are making that much more profit. We argue that we've got to exercise control over the corporations to prevent this type of discrimination. As I said in my campaign, the old idea that what's good for General Motors is good for the country has to be challenged. The public must get control over its economic destiny in order to deal with these social issues.

The guiding principle is that the multifarious problems in the country—whether we are dealing with the environment, energy, racial discrimination, sexual discrimination, the decay of the cities, any one of these things—go back to a fundamental fault. They're all connected to the basic problem that the resources of this country are not used in the people's interest. They are managed, used (or rather, misused), and guided by the single criterion of maximizing a corporation's profits. It would be a blooming miracle if the thousands and thousands of production decisions that have determined how the country lives, all of which are being made on the criterion of maximizing profits, happened to turn out to be good for women, blacks, children, and so on. And they don't. They turn out to be good for the corporations. Any one of these issues is related to this very fundamental power of the corporations. This is what we tried to explain in the campaign, based on the intellectual pattern that had been worked out.

THE 1980 CAMPAIGN

Tell me a little about the 1980 campaign.

Let's start with the creation of the Citizens Party. A small group of us began preliminary discussions in 1979. It was a marvelous dialectic. We decided that we had to have a new party to deal with the country's problems, but there was a big disagreement whether we should be involved in the 1980 presidential campaign at all. Wouldn't it be better to develop local parties and maybe four years from now build up to a national campaign? It was a very lively debate, and those of us who felt we ought to have a national campaign won.

Once some of us decided we wanted to create a new party, we formed an organizing group—about 100 people—which we called the Citizens Committee. Members were recruited from what you might call the public interest constituency: environmental groups, some rank and file union leaders, people interested in energy and the decentralization of resources. The idea was that these types of people would be our natural constituents.

Did this committee organize the new Citizens Party?

Yes. The first job we faced was to create the party in compliance with the federal election laws because our long-range hope—an extreme hope, you might say—was that if we got 5 percent of the vote, we would then be entitled to federal matching funds. According to our reading of the federal election laws, only a regularly organized party receiving 5 percent of the vote would qualify for matching funds. So we went to great lengths to conform to the requirements of the federal laws as to what a party is. For example, there had to be a national convention, we had to organize a certain number of state groups and the like. We did all of that in order to be sure that we qualified. One of the great ironies of the 1980 campaign is that Mr. Anderson qualified for matching funds even though he clearly did not conform to the election laws because he did not establish a political party. That was one of the great bitter ironies of the campaign.

Somehow we did organize the party. It was an enormous job. We had to have a national convention far too early in our young life. It was held in Cleveland in April 1980, since we couldn't delay it, which would have been smart. My guess is between 300 to 500 people attended the national convention. I would say half of them had been members of the Citizens Party for less than a few weeks. At that point, there was no real communion of ideas, but we had to have it that early because we had to nominate our candidates in order to get on the ballot. In fact, one of the problems we faced was that the Ohio law required that we have our candidates nominated in March. This led to all kinds of difficulties, because we were very concerned with internal democracy. The question arose in March as to whether I would respond to a request of the Ohio party and declare that I was a candidate for president, even though we hadn't had our convention and we hadn't democratically decided whether I or someone else should be a candidate. So, we held our convention in April, and LaDonna Harris and I were nominated.

I'm not entirely clear exactly where the party stood at this point. Did you adopt a platform at your convention?

Let me tell you about the platform. One of the problems the Citizens Party has wrestled with from the very beginning is internal democracy. The people who were instrumental in the first organization of the party were convinced that we had to be different from all other political parties and have very strong internal democracy. So the decision was made that the convention would adopt a draft platform based on input from all of the local parties. Position papers and resolutions were sent in on the theory that a draft platform would be constructed at the convention which would then be voted on by the entire membership of the party by mail. It was an insane idea, which utterly failed, utterly. In the first place, what we got out of the convention was such a mishmash of contradictory opinions, contradictory ideas, that it took a committee of six people a week locked up in a room in Washington just to make a 300-item program out of that. There were completely bizarre things like abolishing the border between Mexico and the United States. The upshot was that the committee in Washington produced this thing, about 300 items, some of which were alternatives which were sent out to the membership for voting. That happened some time in late summer. I don't know how many members voted, but it was a complete bust. The huge 300-item platform was never officially adopted. What happened instead was that the state groups would write their own, very brief pointed platforms which explained what we stood for.

I'm sorry, but I find this confusing. Did the party adopt a consistent central position, or did you present your own positions on the issues?

That's right, that came out of discussions in the executive committee. We learned as I went along. And let me tell you, you're a professor, did the students ever come up to you after class and say that was an interesting lecture, but let me tell you how to improve it next time? That doesn't happen to you in class, right, and it didn't happen to me in class either. But when I started campaigning that was an everyday occurrence. I was their property. I gave pretty good speeches, and people would come up to me and say, "Well now, you know the way you put that position on the women's question, that's not good." They would write me long letters. It was quite a shock to find people didn't say, "Gee, that was a great speech." They'd say, "That was a pretty good speech, but I think you can do better." It's still true. Yesterday I spoke at a rally, and the head of the New York Citizens Party said to me, "Hey, that was pretty good, that was the best speech you've given in recent weeks." It was a powerful experience and forced me to learn how best to present the party's position in ways that made sense to its members and supporters.

After the April convention was over, did you start to campaign right away?

No. The first enormous job we faced was trying to get on the ballot in the different states. Most of our financial resources were used up in that effort, and we came out of the ballot access campaign with practically no money at all. We attempted to get on the different state ballots through completely local effort because, as you know, the federal election laws are not national, they're local. The way we did it was by locating half a dozen people in each state who looked as if they were interested in organizing the party. We called them the convenors of the state party. They would then get together and find a lawyer who would figure out what the state laws required. The task was enormously variable. It only takes 800 signatures to get on the ballot in New Jersey, but several hundred thousand in California. All kinds of queer things. They would work it out on the local level, and then it was their responsibility to get the party on the ballot. We gave them a certain amount of legal help. We had some lawyers who would help their local lawyers. We followed this up with visits by LaDonna Harris and myself in different states to encourage people to join the party and participate in the ballot access campaign.

Beginning in April, I spent an awful lot of time just traveling around making speeches in order to help the local party groups organize to get us on the ballot. And we did pretty well. We also spent some money in getting full-time people to go out and collect signatures because the time was so short that very often that was the only way in which it could be done. It's a very difficult logistical problem to collect signatures. A lot of people think you just go out and you ask friends to sign a petition, but when you need a lot of signatures, it just can't be done that way. You have to figure out exactly where the people are and where they'll be moving slowly enough so they'll sign something.

So, in effect, were you sort of learning through experience?

That's right. I still remember the opening of the petition campaign here in New York. I agreed to participate in the opening festivities, and I traveled out to Long Island somewhere. The idea was that I was going to campaign through a commuter train, but, of course, it was so jammed you couldn't move, so that was that. Then we got to Penn Station. The big campaign signature collection was to be at the mouth of Penn Station at rush hour. It was the most amazing scene in the world. We had people standing there, and they were like rocks in a rushing stream with people just whizzing past them. Nobody wanted to stop and sign petitions. Finally, we looked around and across the street there was a line at a bus stop. Some of us went over there and finally we got some signatures. Of course, the people there were standing still waiting for the next bus. It took us a little time to learn where you go for signatures. There was a lot to be learned. I think it's remarkable that we got on thirty state ballots, which is a record for a really new, independent party on its first time out. I think the Libertarians only got on two state ballots in their first election. What we did was to create the local parties; and the campaign was run by the local parties as well. There was no national campaign in the sense that we had a national headquarters that sent out advance people and publicity. Hundreds of election materials were published, fascinating posters, leaflets, brochures, not one of them published by the national party, all done locally. It was an amazing thing. By the end of July or August, we had functioning state and local groups, and they did the campaigning.

How did you organize your own campaign schedule under such a decentralized arrangement?

The national office did my scheduling. They scheduled La-Donna Harris and me to go out and speak; they planned ways of raising money and that was about it. We didn't even have a national press secretary until October. The schedule was set up, and I would travel, half the time alone or sometimes with one person helping me. I would come into the next town and the local schedule was completely organized by the local people. They decided where to have the press conferences, fund-raisers or rallies. I simply did my thing and then went off to another town. What may surprise you is that those activities were uniformly successful. The rallies were jammed, we got good local press coverage. You probably didn't see any of that unless you visited a town where we were. I remember a day in Grand Rapids, Michigan. There was live local television coverage of a press conference we held at noon. We were on the front page of the newspaper. There was good local coverage. The coverage that we didn't get was from the big television networks and the major national newspapers. That was devastatingly harmful, no question about it.

Why do you think you were virtually ignored by the television networks and the major national newspapers?

It's very simple. I'll tell you why exactly. This is a true story. In Albuquerque, New Mexico, I was interviewed by a reporter, and he said to me, "Dr. Commoner, I want to ask you an impertinent question. Are you really a serious candidate or are you just running on the issues?" I'm not kidding! That's literally what he said, and this is the explanation of the behavior of the big media.

I met with the editorial board of the *New York Times*. I met with the editorial board of the *Washington Post*, as well as with a number of other newspapers. It had zero impact on anything they did. The reason is—you ask any of them; you go and talk with them—the only thing they regard as serious is your chance of being elected. The reason Anderson was given coverage is that there was some chance that he might have been elected. I had no intention of being elected. It was obvious that I wasn't going to be elected. The result was that the major news media participated in making the campaign a charade in which the real issues were avoided. I can be pretty bitter about it because the galling thing is that the predicament we're in now, in which we elected Reagan to office without making the consequences at all clear to the country, can be laid at the door of the media. Did you see the recent CBS broadcast on war and defense? It opened up with the statement that this is a terribly important issue which no one is discussing, and then it shows Reagan during the campaign making these wild claims about the military and so on. This was never really discussed in the campaign. Why in God's name didn't they do this type of broadcast during the campaign?

So your major problem was with the national media?

Yes. We received practically no coverage from the networks. I finally got on the phone and made some appointments with the vice-presidents in charge of news and met with Bud Benjamin of CBS and with Les Crystal of NBC. The other major network, ABC, refused to meet for quite a while until I pressed them. The upshot was that CBS and NBC sent crews out to cover us for several days when I made speeches about nuclear war and other crucial issues. What they showed was a four-minute sequence of me getting in and out of private cars to indicate that I didn't have secret service protection! There was practically no substantive coverage. At ABC they didn't even do that. When I met with them, I said, you know, the issues are not being discussed in this campaign. It's up to you to show that some of us are discussing the issues. And they said, "Yeah, yeah, that's an interesting idea." One of them turned to the other and said, "We ought to do a program on that after the campaign." I know from the reporters at the *Washington Post* and the *New York Times* who did cover us that they tried very hard to get assigned on a long-term basis, but they were held back by their editors. Finally, they were given a chance to go on one trip or something like that. You should talk with some of the reporters. It was disappointing.

PERSONAL IMPRESSIONS

In spite of your disappointments, it seems to me you can claim some solid accomplishments. You got on the ballot in thirty states. You began to build a state and local party organization. Where do you think the Citizens Party is going in the years ahead?

Well, in the first place, you have to take a look at what the campaign taught us about our constituency. I've got a county-by-county record of our vote which is very interesting. It turns out that our strength lay not where we thought it was, not in the highly politically organized places like New York City and Detroit. Our strongest votes were in outlying areas. In four counties in Appalachia in the western part of Virginia, we beat Anderson. I didn't even know about it because we had no Citizens Party there. In January I went down to speak at Emory and Henry College which is in southwestern Virginia just above the Tennessee border. After the election, I discovered that we had gotten a very considerable vote down there, around 8 percent. As a result, some people put an ad in the local paper and said let's organize a Citizens Party. That turns out to be a very significant aspect of the pattern of our vote. For example, take Burlington, Vermont. As you know, we ran four candidates for the city council in April 1981; and as I recall the figures, one of them won with 60 percent of the vote. The other three averaged 30 percent of the vote.* We also helped elect a coalition socialist candidate, Bernie Sanders, as mayor of Burlington. You're familiar with him. Now people may say, "Well, that's only Burlington, Vermont." Yet that's the kind of place where I think our strength lies.

Do you think the party's future strength may come from the small cities and rural areas?

Here's what's going on. Take a city like Detroit where we had a strong party effort, and a very difficult task of getting on the ballot, which we did. After we got on the ballot, however,

---

*Citizens Party candidates won additional seats on the Burlington City Board of Aldermen in the March 1982 elections.

we were just one of a number of very highly organized political groups. You know, every one of the political splinter groups is very active in Detroit. They're all highly organized, which makes it hard for our party to find a way to move. So that's one point.

The second point is that we misjudged our base of support. What we thought was our natural constituency, the public interest organizations, turned out *not* to be big supporters of our organization. We made a fundamental mistake here. In hindsight, you can see why, though we didn't realize it at the time. The public interest groups are interested in lobbying people who are in power. When I got up and said I wasn't going to get elected, why should they vote for me? I wasn't going to be there to be lobbied. These groups are in a certain sense symbiotically related to the conventional political power base. The people who supported us were what you might call the autonomous, independently minded voters who are not in organizations. Who are they? Miners, farmers, craftspeople. In southwest Virginia I was told that our typical supporters don't like to join organizations. In other words, we had touched what you might call the historical populist base of the country. It's very interesting what's happening. We are appealing to basically unorganized voters. We also work with the unions as best we can, where people like William Winpisinger supported us very courageously.

Some critics look at us and say we only got 230,000 votes in 1980, so we're not going anywhere. But our constituency is larger. In November 1980, wherever we ran local candidates, they did much better—6 to 20 percent of the vote—than the national ticket. Many people who supported the party locally ended up voting for Carter, because they were so afraid of Reagan, but we didn't expect to win this election, just as the Republican Party didn't win its first election in 1856. That's not what this was all about. What we are really doing is establishing a political position for the future. I'm absolutely convinced that 1980 will be looked on as the first year of a new political realignment in this country.

Let me conclude with a couple of personal questions. You're an academic, a professional scientist. When I was active in state politics, I found that a lot of the social dimensions of politics involves small talk and compromise. Did you find this frustrating?

Nope. You have to understand, I've been a public speaker for many years. I mean, I've done the university circuit, and that was part of my social responsibility as a scientist. I get a great kick out of taking my understanding of the intellectual content of the problem and making it accessible to ordinary people. I've done that with abstract scientific matters as well as political matters.

That's the public education function of politics, but what about all the inconsequential chitchat? The solicitation of other people? How do you feel about that?

Oh, you mean fund raising and so on. Well, it's not particularly frustrating. I'm no good at remembering names and faces, but I just try to behave in a natural way at fund raisers, to tell people what's on my mind. I speak in a plain way. We didn't make any political deals, so that wasn't frustrating.

Fairly late in the campaign, in mid-October, you began running nationwide ads that included the word "bullshit" to describe what your major opponents were saying. Doesn't this indicate a degree of frustration on your part?

Well, the frustration was due to the failure of not getting any national publicity. Sure. But overall I have very positive feelings about the campaign.

O.K. Here's my last question. You spent a great deal of time and energy on this effort. Was it worth it?

Oh, I'm very glad about it; it was a year of very intense activity, and well worth it. Personally, because my purpose in getting involved—I didn't want to run for president—I mean, that's not my intent. All I wanted to do is to create what I think the country badly needs, which is a new political party. I ran because I was convinced that that was the best way in which I could serve that purpose. It worked. It absolutely worked. We created a new political party. The ideas behind it make sense, so it certainly was worthwhile.

Anyone who's worked with me knows that I'm a congenital optimist. Of course, I'm optimistic. I am, because I think this is the issue, and I think we've at last put our finger on what has to be done. I'm encouraged that as people begin to understand it, they will act on it. It's very gratifying to find that there are people whose whole approach to politics has been changed by the ideas that we have developed, and come the next election *Time* magazine is going to be surprised to discover that several hundred left-wingers have been elected to local office.

There's something going on. It shows that where you don't have the dead hand of the paralyzed political establishment, people are moving. So I don't think for a minute that the country has turned to the right. There's no evidence of that whatsoever. Sure, the Republicans and right-wingers have gotten smart about raising money and using television, but there is a very deep-seated sense of progressivism in the country. We might end up merging with a labor party—who knows. But we have managed to show that it is possible to create an independent political party on the basis of an integrated set of ideas that are not handed down in some prepackaged political formula. As I told you earlier, I'm absolutely convinced that 1980 will be looked on as the first year of a new political alignment in this country.

NATIONAL UNITY CAMPAIGN

Congressman John B. Anderson of Illinois admits that he was only an asterisk in the polls when he first announced he was running for the Republican nomination for president of the United States in early 1979. Although he had served in the U.S. House of Representatives for almost twenty years, Anderson did not have a major national reputation when he began his presidential bid.

However, he launched an aggressive campaign in the early New England primary states and did very well in both Massachusetts and Vermont, where he ran an extremely close second to Bush and Reagan, respectively. Anderson's bid for the Republican nomination was lost in the March 18 primary in his home state of Illinois, where he placed second to Reagan, followed by the April 1 Wisconsin primary, where he ran third behind both Reagan and Bush.[5]

On April 24, 1980, Anderson decided to run for president as an independent National Unity candidate. He ran as an independent because it was the only way he had any possible chance of getting on the ballot in all fifty states, since many state filing deadlines for third-party candidates had already passed by the time he announced his candidacy.

Anderson did quite well in the public opinion polls in the late spring and early summer, peaking with about 20 percent of the projected popular vote. However, he was mired down in legal battles to get on the state ballots, and he also had to devote major efforts to fund raising, which gave him less time to campaign and, hence, less national publicity. By the time Anderson designated former Wisconsin governor Patrick Lucey as his official vice-presidential running mate in late August, his standing in the polls was already beginning to slip.

In addition to his legal troubles over the ballot access issue, Anderson faced a number of other difficult problems. After the League of Women Voters decided he enjoyed enough potential support to participate in the presidential debates with the major-party candidates, he appeared with Ronald Reagan; Jimmy Carter, however, refused to debate Anderson. The Federal Election Commission also decided that Anderson could qualify for retroactive federal funding, but that this funding would not be available until after the election was over, and even then, only if he received at least 5 percent of the total popular vote. As a result, Anderson was forced to borrow money from his supporters, and he was plagued with financial difficulties throughout his campaign. Finally, Anderson had to wrestle with the perennial issue that faces any third-party candidate, especially a potentially serious contender: the problem of the so-called wasted vote. Although many voters indicated in polls that they preferred Anderson to Carter or Reagan, they also indicated that they didn't want to risk wasting their vote on him because they thought he couldn't win the election.

Anderson was never able to overcome these obstacles. However, he did realize a number of major accomplishments in his campaign. After many legal hassles, he got on the ballot in all fifty states; in the 1980 election he received over 5,720,000 popular votes, the second highest total for any third-party or independent candidate in American history; and his 6.6 percent of the total popular vote qualified him for retroactive federal funding.

I interviewed Anderson at the National Unity Committee office in Washington, D.C., in mid-December 1981. During our interview, he indicated he was keeping his options open for the future, but that he would definitely plan to organize a new third party if he decides to run again for president in 1984.

John B. Anderson

My overarching philosophy was that there had to be a new approach to politics. There had to be a new politics in the sense that people were going to be willing to accept some very straight answers to some very tough questions.

PERSONAL BACKGROUND

Smallwood: I've tried to have all the candidates tell me a little about their own personal background, particularly about how they got interested in politics.

Anderson: Let's start with my first elective office in the 1950s as state's attorney back in my home county in Illinois. I ran for the office when I returned to this country after a tour of duty abroad as a young foreign service officer stationed in West Berlin.

Did your experiences abroad in West Berlin play a major role in leading you into a political career when you returned home?

Well, I suspect all politicians like to assume they got started from the most lofty of motives, but to be completely honest about it, the opportunity to run for office represented more of a vocational opportunity for me than anything else. When I came back to Rockford, I was successful in making an affiliation with a law firm. However, clients were few and far between. Since I had very little practice to preempt my time, I was attracted to the race for state's attorney in Winnebago County, since it is a legal position, one for which I thought I was at least semiqualified.

Did your work as state's attorney heighten your interest in politics?

Yes, it really did. It was only after imbibing the joys of the campaign that I began to appreciate political life. Frankly, up to that time, I hadn't thought a great deal about it. Four years later, in 1960, when I made my first race for the U.S. House seat from the Sixteenth District, I had been pretty well indoctrinated into what it was like to be a practicing politician in that part of Illinois. So running for Congress seemed to be a natural step up the political ladder. Once I was elected to Congress from a predominately and traditionally Republican district, it just sort of took the form of a two-year cycle, repeated ten times until 1980, when I decided that I'd had enough of it. Actually, I had made the decision the preceding year, in 1979. I had served in Congress for almost twenty years, I was the third ranking Republican in the House, and I wanted to do something that would represent the real fruition, the culmination of all my training and efforts in the political sphere by running for the highest office of all, the presidency.

Before we turn to your presidential bid, I'd like to get a better understanding of your own personal political development. If I read the record correctly, you were a very traditional conservative midwestern Republican when you first came to the House in 1960. Is that an accurate assessment?

Yes. I initially followed a pretty straight Republican Party line. I supported Barry Goldwater in 1964, and I took a pretty conservative position on most issues during my first few terms in the House.

You made one particular decision at that time which later appeared to come back and haunt you when you sponsored a resolution for an amendment to the Constitution which declared Jesus Christ to be a source of inspiration for political leadership. I've never gotten a clear picture of what this was all about. Do you have any further thoughts on this?

It was a mistake. During twenty years in Congress I suspect most of us make some mistakes. In the 1980 campaign, my opposition seized on it, and everyone from Tony Lewis to the liberal columnists looked down their noses and asked how could anyone be that stupid. I think you can only really understand it if you look at the kind of background, the intensely evangelical fundamentalistic religious background, which existed in my home town of Rockford when I grew up there. When the resolution was presented to me, I naively assumed it was just one of those harmless expressions which would have a certain appeal for the kind of people who had supported me. As a new congressman, I wasn't really sensitive to the tremendous ethnic, religious, and social diversity that characterizes this nation.

Who actually prepared the resolution?

It was a kindly old man whose name I don't remember. He consulted me on the grounds that Frank Carlson, the U.S. senator from Kansas, and some others had endorsed this. They didn't really expect it to pass. All they wanted to do was to introduce it in the House just to show good faith and belief in God and all the rest. I made a mistake when I went along with it. It was a very foolish thing to do. Liberals particularly, I think, would love to hang you up by the heels on something like that. Robert Strauss latched on to it and was just merciless. It all took place back at the beginning of my congressional career in the early 1960s. Over the course of the next twenty years my views changed to a point where by 1971 I was voting against mandatory prayers in schools. But it was most damaging, it hurt. I got tired of repeating my mea culpas.

It's very obvious that your political views did change between 1960 and 1980. You retained some of your economic conservatism, but you became much more liberal on civil rights and social issues. Was this due to a personal change in your attitudes, or a change in your constituency's attitudes, or a combination of both?

It certainly wasn't a change in my constituency, which is still pretty conservative across the board. It was a change in my own personal attitudes.

What led to this change?

It was a combination of many influences, particularly the civil rights movement and the Vietnam experience in the 1960s and the movement for women's rights and Watergate in the 1970s. I was trying to grapple with the major changes which were taking place throughout our society.

You cast the key vote to get the Open Housing bill of 1968 out of committee, and hence successfully enacted into law, following the assassination of Martin Luther King. Did King's assassination have a major impact in influencing you to change your views on civil rights and other social issues?

I think it marked a watershed in the evolution of my thinking. The boiling over, the rage, on the national scene led to a realization on my part that we had to drastically alter some of our national attitudes or else we were on the verge of being swept under by a tide of divisiveness and hatred. By the late 1960s, the transition in my thinking was very clear. I still retained some of my former, more traditional conservatism on economic issues, but I had become very liberal in my outlook on most of the major areas of social concern.

POLITICAL IDEOLOGY

Let's turn, then, to what you did try to represent in the 1980 campaign. If you were to summarize the major concepts you were trying to get across to the electorate in terms of ideas and ideology, what were the most important points you were emphasizing?

My overarching philosophy was that there had to be a new approach to politics. There had to be a new politics in the sense that people were going to be willing to accept some very straight answers to some very tough questions. We were not going to get by on the cheap. Energy is a problem we are not going to solve without considerable sacrifice. Defense is not simply thinking that we can regain military superiority in a nuclear age and thereby impose our will and a Pax Americana on the world. It requires a much more sophisticated approach to avoid the otherwise real possibility of nuclear war, limited nuclear war, inevitably escalating into a general war. As far as the economy is concerned, we have to accept a rather rigorous discipline, unknown up to this time, in the form of an incomes policy keyed to the Internal Revue code to reward companies that are willing to hold the line on prices and unions that are willing to accept wage increases that are in line with productivity increases. There will have to be some planning, not centralized planning, Soviet style, but some planning of our economic goals in a way that would take into account new forces at work with the domestic and world economy which make the old rules simply inapplicable to what is happening today.

Basically, then, were you talking about discipline, sacrifice, and an avoidance of simple solutions to complex problems?

Yes. It was a kind of tough-minded approach to defense, domestic policy, and international affairs, cautioning against the dangers of unbridled, chauvinistic, semiimperialistic policies to reimpose our will on the world. In the broad area of social issues, I took a very unabashed liberal position, as it was commonly defined, on questions of prayer, abortion, sexual lifestyles, and all the rest. These are matters of individual interpretation, individual determination, where the heavy-handed application of law through state pressure simply doesn't belong. I advocated a relatively conservative approach to the economy because, other than my incomes policy proposals, I set forth programs which would permit people to shelter income from taxes in new and innovative ways by setting aside funds for their children's education, for retirement, and so on. However, I did not endorse the across-the-board tax cut of Ronald Reagan, nor did I endorse a continuation of the old Democratic approach of trying to pump up the economy with huge expenditures for new governmental programs. Instead, I called for a rather toughly hewn and disciplined approach to economic problems that called for some reining in of the normal American impulse that we are going to just automatically come out of our economic distress and do it cheaply. It will only be through making some sacrifices that we can right the forces in the economy that are threatening to sink us. A good example was my fifty-fifty gasoline tax proposal, which was designed to both reduce consumption while also providing badly needed revenues to prop up our ailing social security system.

You've mentioned an incomes policy a couple of times. What exactly do you mean by this?

It's just having government, business, and the labor unions agree in a tripartite arrangement, or a social contract, that government will apply the tax code in the most favorable way to provide incentives to both business and labor to adopt a noninflationary approach to prices and wages. Certain tax benefits will be conferred on both management and labor if they cooperate. The government will then do its share in promoting a healthy economy by maintaining minimum guarantees through income support programs that will keep people from falling through the cracks altogether. So it's a contractual agreement where government, business, and labor each seize a piece of the problem of inflation and agree to work together to tailor policies that will alleviate the problem.

You've expressed concern over our military posturing. What specific policies do you recommend in the area of defense?

I realize that deficiencies exist in our conventional forces, a lack of operational readiness, a neglect of maintenance operations. Therefore, I would counsel some increased expenditures to correct these deficiencies, but not the automatic 3 percent increase of the Carter administration and surely not the much more exaggerated type of increase called for by the Reagan administration in the name of gaining military superiority. I think we ought to proceed on a two-pronged approach to the problem of security by reorganizing an attempt to negotiate a limitation and reduction of nuclear arms, particularly strategic arms, as being just as important as our efforts to increase spending to build up our defenses. I was for a prudent, measured approach, not in any spirit of panic or emergency, to address any deficiencies I found in our military within the limits of our resources, but not to engage in anything approaching a strategic arms competition with the Soviet Union.

What is your position on other aspects of international affairs?

Increasingly toward the end of my campaign, I embraced the Global 2000 and the recommendations of the so-called Brandt Commission report, the warning that we ignore to our peril the growing gap in per capita incomes between the developed nations of the northern hemisphere and the developing nations of the southern hemisphere. The problems of population increases, global pollution, depletion of resources, poverty, and disease are very explosive, and they are leading to growing violence all over the world. We could make a very valid contribution to the security and defense of our own country by increasing dramatically the level of our efforts to stabilize these countries in the developing world, and to help them build a social and economic infrastructure that would support development. Economic relationships of that kind could do a great deal to guarantee peace and to eliminate the kind of local conflicts that tend to suck in the superpowers and engage them in head-to-head confrontation. We can do more in this area more cheaply to eliminate the causes of war than we can through simply exporting arms to these countries, engaging in military assistance programs, or in building up our own nuclear arsenal.

It's been argued that one of the key roles of third-party and independent candidates is to feed new ideas into the political system. Do you agree with this, and if so, do you think your campaign succeeded in doing this in 1980?

I agree that the role of the third party is to be the cutting edge, the leading edge, of the innovations that are needed to help us break out of the encrusted thinking that keeps us from really mounting an effective assault on our problems.

As far as my own campaign went, I never harbored the illusion that I had some brilliantly worked out scenario about precisely where we go to get from point A to point B to point C. Instead, I think the generation of new ideas is an ongoing process that is closely linked to the types of changes that are taking place all around us.

What concerns me most is that there's all too little evidence of any real perception of the kinds of explosive changes that are taking place, and therefore, I think we should put more, rather than less, emphasis on education. To say simply that education is a local function so we'll abolish the Department of Education is wrong. It's the first foundation we have to lay before we can come up with better ideas and better solutions. We have to understand the dynamics of modern society, what changes are taking place, so we can begin to reorient our national goals and priorities to meet these changes.

Can you provide a specific example of the kind of explosive change that concerns you?

Well, it's been pointed out by Peter Drucker and others that we've become a communications society, that the information industry is the biggest industry in the country today. According to the latest figures I've seen, over 50 percent of the working population in the United States is now engaged in information processing, compared to about 30 percent in industrial production and less than 5 percent in agriculture. This kind of employment revolution is based on massive new technological innovations—microprocessors and computers, electronic media, communications satellites, and all the rest. Under these conditions, we're going to have to retrain and re-educate people on an unparalleled scale because it poses tremendous potential dislocations for our existing work force.

Where do you think these dislocations will be felt the most?

What should we do, for example, when robots can replace as many as 65 percent of the auto workers in an assembly plant by 1990? I voted against the Chrysler bailout when I was in Congress, and I still think it was a bad decision. Maybe we're going to have to become prepared to let some of these traditional employment areas go to societies that are not as far down the road in this postindustrial transformation we're going through in America. In other words, we've got to think more in terms of reorganizing the whole economic process to adjust to a new international division of labor. I think this is only dimly perceived by the general public, but the government, if it is in possession of these facts, has to begin to tell people the truth about our changing role in an interdependent world economy.

It strikes me that this poses a very tough political challenge. Aren't most people more interested in their current bread-and-butter economic concerns, in hanging onto what they already have?

Yes, it's a real dilemma because it's much easier to subsidize the status quo than to prepare for change. The unions could deal a very devastating blow to any politician who says that maybe we're not going to be able to continue to manufacture automobiles competitively in the world market because of our high wage rates and high standards of living. So that's a dilemma, because these are potentially vote-losing issues, but they're the kind of issues we've got to face in order to meet the challenge of the future.

THE 1980 CAMPAIGN

O.K., let's turn to the question of votes and elections. You were a very long shot when you first entered the presidential race. Why did you decide to run in the Republican primaries?

I realized the odds were against me, but we had the precedent of 1976 when a political unknown, Jimmy Carter, had literally come out of nowhere. I thought that if Carter could do it in the Democratic primaries, it might be possible to accomplish the same thing in the Republican primaries four years later. I just had a very simple basic strategy. If I could do what Carter did, attract a lot of attention by winning early in New England, which is the liberal heartland—if there is any liberal heartland—of the Republican Party, then the first big industrial state would be Illinois, my home state, where I should have some advantage. Immediately following Illinois was Wisconsin, a crossover state, where a moderate Republican could perhaps recruit enough democratic votes to do well. That was basically my strategy, no more sophisticated than that. I hoped to build up enough of a political head of steam by the time of the Wisconsin primary in early April to go on and win the Republican Party nomination.

Actually, you did very well in the early New England states, especially Massachusetts and Vermont. However, you were hurt in Illinois, particularly in the television debate when you refused to say you would support the Republican candidate if you didn't win the nomination yourself. How did this come about?

The Illinois debate that took place among most of the candidates was kind of a gangup, orchestrated, I later learned, by Phillip Crane, probably the most conservative candidate for the nomination, and I think Bush and his forces. They managed to portray me in the eyes of the audience that watched it as less than a party loyalist. It really hurt me in Illinois, where I got only 37 percent of the vote against 48 percent for Reagan. That proved to be the coup de grace because I had purposely gambled very heavily on defeating Reagan, which would have been a real bombshell. But you have to take some cataclysmic chances to give an unknown like myself the kind of recognition to be a serious contender. Two weeks later, I ran third in Wisconsin, much more poorly than I had anticipated.[6] By then it was clear that the handwriting was on the wall. In scriptural language: "MENE, MENE, TEKEL, UPHARSIN."* The kingdom had been divided, and it was not divided in a way that anything was going to fall to me.

Why didn't you get out of the race at that point? Why did you decide to run as an independent?

On April 24, I made a formal announcement of an exploratory movement to chart a possible independent course. Time was of the essence in order to qualify for many of the state ballots. However, the announcement was exploratory because I wanted to give myself a little window of opportunity to escape if it appeared to be a totally futile gesture. I had been hearing the cries "go independent, go independent" from the sidelines as I made my way through New England, but particularly in Illinois and Wisconsin. The feeling seemed to be building up that this was the year to forget about the two old parties and their candidates that nobody seemed to want. The polls and surveys were very instrumental because they showed a high degree of support for me, based on a widespread dissatisfaction with both Carter and Reagan. So I relied quite heavily on what I thought was this growing sentiment of intense disillusionment with the old politics, the old parties and their candidates.

* Daniel 5.25–8.

Once you decided to run as an independent candidate, you faced a variety of obstacles in terms of finances, state ballot access laws, media coverage and the like. Let's start with campaign finances. You were in Congress when the Federal Election Campaign Act was passed. Is it a fair law?

No, it's not fair. There isn't any question about that, when each of the older parties, the Democrats and Republicans, start out with $29.4 million plus $4.3 million in federal funding for each of their conventions, while the most that an independent or third-party candidate can expect is retroactive funding after the election is over if he gets at least 5 percent of the total popular vote. Obviously, we are at a severe disadvantage. I don't think it should be impossible to work out some formula whereby a candidate would begin to receive matching money during a campaign after passing some reasonable test, such as raising contributions of $5,000 or more in twenty different states. It's vitally important to give third-party and independent candidates some increment of financial support as the campaign progresses. Barring that, the situation is hopeless. The current law crushes the hopes of any third party to overcome the overwhelming financial superiority of the older parties.

Do you think there is any prospect of reform in the law?

The Republicans and Democrats have a viselike grip on the present financing mechanism of the political process in this country, and I think out of pure political selfishness that it would be naive to assume they would sponsor the kind of reform that is needed. Unfortunately, we have ample evidence to prove that process reforms of this kind do not develop large-scale popular support. These are not the kinds of issues that produce a wide-scale public response.

How much did you spend on your own campaign?

About $14 million. A lot of that was used up in legal expenses just to get on the ballot. A huge amount also went to payroll, our paid workers and staff, telephones and travel. It cost us $200,000 just to rent an airplane for the last few weeks of the campaign. We took a trip to Europe in the summer of 1980, which some people thought was a waste of money; that cost a quarter of a million dollars.

Do you think the trip was a waste of money?

We were desperate to get some media attention. The Republican convention was on television, and we were pretty well submerged. We thought at least if we could get on the "Today Show" from time to time that people would know we were still alive. I don't think it was a waste of money or of time. I saw every important leader I wanted to see except Giscard, and even in the case of France, I talked with the prime minister. I thought the trip was all right.

You mentioned the legal snarls in getting on the different state ballots. How much of a problem was this for you?

It was an awesome problem. I think we must have used probably $1.5 million to pay lawyers and to prosecute lawsuits. It's blatantly unfair for a state like Ohio to say that an independent candidate can't be on the ballot in November unless he has filed the required number of signatures by March 20, which was a month and four days before I announced. The Republicans and Democrats can wait until mid-August to nominate their candidates and be on the ballots. We won that case, although it's still under appeal. We won our ballot access cases, but only by dint of losing a lot of momentum in the sense that our attention was distracted and our funds were poured into that effort when they should have been used building the base and structure to carry us into the general election campaign. So it cost us dearly. We had to litigate the restrictive ballot access laws to the teeth in many different states.

Do you have any suggestions on changes in this area?

We have a Commission on Uniform State Laws that has come up with some excellent suggestions in other areas. At the very least, I would like to see the commission, or the bar, formulate some recommendations on reforming the presidential ballot access issue. I would hope this could be done before any new federal laws are passed, because I think it would be premature for the federal government to move into this area until the states have made some attempt at their own reforms.

How about candidate exposure through media coverage and the presidential television debates. Do you think you were treated fairly in this regard?

I've never been terribly critical of the quantitative aspect of media coverage. However, the qualitative aspect leaves me somewhat disenchanted, with the emphasis so overwhelmingly on the contest dimensions of the campaign and little coverage of the really substantive issues. The focus is so heavily on the polls and on shifts in momentum that the issues tend to get buried.

As for the debates, I think they should be institutionalized. I don't think any informal organization, the League of Women Voters or any other, should have the right to determine who takes part in the debates, where they're held, how they're financed, and all the rest. They are too important to be handled on an informal basis. I would suggest that if any candidates meet the requirements for federal funding, along some kind of reasonable lines like I proposed earlier, they should be required to participate in the debates as a condition of accepting this funding. In other words, if taxpayers' dollars are being used to help finance a campaign, no candidate who accepts these dollars should be allowed to hide behind a cloak of anonymity like Jimmy Carter tried to do in the 1980 debates.

Were you satisfied with Governor Lucey's performance as your vice-presidential running mate?

Well, I appreciate the fact that you were willing to serve as my temporary vice-presidential nominee to help me get on the ballot up there in Vermont, but I think Pat Lucey did a very good job. We had to have an important Democrat to give credibility to my argument that I would form a national unity government, a coalition government, which ruled out many of the suggestions that were made, like Ed Brooke and so on.

I was convinced that, if we were going to draw Democratic votes—which we obviously had to get in order to win—it was essential to have a Democrat on the ticket. I liked Pat Lucey. I thought he distinguished himself. He was a creditable candidate, and we got along splendidly during the campaign.

There was some criticism that your chief campaign strategist, David Garth, focused too much attention on a media blitz approach to your campaign. In retrospect, do you think this was the case?

If you talk with David Garth, he would suggest that he was a media master who ended up without any media to master. I think that's true. We simply didn't have the money to launch a really big media campaign, at least in the form of big commercials.

What about the problem of the so-called wasted vote? I ran into this a lot when people told me that they thought you were the best candidate, but they didn't want to waste their vote because they didn't think you could win.

It was a devastating argument, aided and abetted by the Carter-Mondale campaign in the form of commercials that really parroted that line. Even the Republicans had press conferences saying "don't vote for Anderson and waste your vote." We tried to combat it. I remember when we sat around and brainstormed on this. What were some of the sayings we came up with? "Vote Your Conscience; Conscience Is the Overriding Consideration; Your Vote Is Precious, Use It Wisely; Don't Vote Your Fears." But it was tough. It was a very devastating problem for us.

PERSONAL IMPRESSIONS

Now that the election is over, are you optimistic or pessimistic about the national and international situation?

I'm certainly not terribly optimistic about the domestic situation. I think Ronald Reagan is a very kindly, well-intentioned man who doesn't begin to understand the fundamental changes that are taking place with great rapidity in our world and society. He would like to take us back to the Elysian fields of yesteryear, but they aren't there any more. So, for a host of reasons, I'm not optimistic.

On the international scene, I was even more worried about Reagan's early pronouncements and conduct. However, after his speech about the "zero option" on nuclear weapons in Europe, I'm a little more hopeful. I think we have some reason to believe that maybe, despite his really primitive ideas about the nature of the world, there are enough people around him with enough pragmatism to help him draw back from the very dangerous kind of brinkmanship he was following early in his administration. I think he is going to get intense pressure from our Atlantic alliance partners, who will not allow him to simply act like a raging bull in a china shop in the area of foreign policy and leave the wreckage for them to clean up because it's their continent and they're the ones who have to fight a war if it breaks out there.

Overall, however, I think it is going to be very hard for him, with his very doctrinaire philosophy, to show the flexibility to avoid some very real calamities.

At the beginning of our interview, you talked about the "joys of the campaign" when you first ran for office in Illinois. How do you now feel about the 1980 campaign? Was it worth it?

Oh yes, very much so. I don't see how anyone could spend over two decades in politics and not regard it as the greatest experience of one's life, the greatest challenge, even in defeat. It's exhilarating to have a national forum to express your views, to gain, albeit grudgingly, some respect for your willingness to take on what most people would think is a hopeless, uphill battle. So yes, it was very worthwhile. I derived a great deal of satisfaction from running. It brought to a focus what I had been doing, and it gave me an outlet that I simply couldn't have found in any other way.

You received more than the 5 percent figure necessary to qualify for federal funds, and you got over 5.7 million popular votes, the sec-

ond highest total by any third-party or independent candidate in American history. Were you satisfied or disappointed with this result?

Well, I didn't win the election, but I feel pretty good about it. I feel good about it, not from the standpoint of simply going into the *Guinness Book* of world political records, but from the standpoint that the ground that was broken will make it easier for someone, whether it be myself or someone else, to take those hurdles with more ease next time, because I feel sure there will be a next time.

Does this mean you are going to run for president again in 1984, and if so, will you form a new third party instead of mounting another independent campaign?

Quite honestly, I'm keeping my options open at this point, but I most certainly would try to organize a new third party if I do become involved in the 1984 campaign. My problem in this regard in 1980 was lack of time. When I made my announcement at the end of April, there was not enough time left to legally comply with all of the restrictive state ballot access laws dealing with new third parties. It was more feasible for me to get on the ballot with petition drives as an independent candidate than it was to lay the foundation for the formation of a new third party.

If I were to run again, I would organize a third party, but it was really a function of time. Everything in 1980 was a function of time. We were always running short on time. We've made it clear by refiling with the Federal Election Commission that we certainly have not foreclosed the option of proceeding with a third party. I'm not going to do it if it appears to be a vain, quixotic thing that is really not supported by a ground swell of real enthusiasm. However, if I feel that there really is a vacuum in the political arena, that the Democrats are just coming up with old solutions and the Republicans are going to continue the course they've been following, yes, the option is obviously open and there.

III 1980 AND BEYOND

7 THE TWO-PARTY MONOPOLY REVISITED

It was an awesome problem. . . . We had to litigate the restrictive state ballot access laws to the teeth.

—JOHN ANDERSON

The Democratic and Republican Parties are fighting hard to keep the third parties off the ballot. . . . They sure don't want any competition in their own backyards.

—BENJAMIN BUBAR

The state laws are deliberately restrictive. It's very much a rigged system, very carefully rigged.

—DAVID MCREYNOLDS

Despite their ideological diversity, the third-party candidates who ran for the presidency in 1980 shared one common concern. Each candidate raised fundamental questions about the *process* of presidential politics, about the various institutional and procedural obstacles encountered during the course of the campaign. The ballot access issue was only one of the concerns of the third-party candidates. Additional complaints were lodged against the unfair financial advantages they felt the Federal Elections Campaign Act conferred upon the major-party candidates, and against the fact that they were unable to gain any significant coverage in the national media during the course of their 1980 campaigns.*

These are concerns that have plagued third-party activists over the course of many years. An idealistic Walter Lippman left Harvard College in 1910 to begin his first job as the execu-

---

* Some of the candidates from the parties on the left also referred to a previous history of governmental harassment by the FBI and other agencies, but none of them felt it was a major impediment in 1980, compared to past campaigns. Andrew Pulley of the Socialist Workers Party was the most critical of such harassment.

tive secretary to the newly elected socialist mayor of Schenectady, New York. Less than two years had passed before Lippmann wrote back to Hazel Albertson, his friend in Cambridge, Massachusetts, to express his disillusionment with Socialist Party politics.

We are, dear Hazel, a ridiculous spectacle. Between keeping the half-hearted in line, and proving to the country that we're safe and sane . . . I have all the sensations of a man trying to tie a string around a sunbeam."[1]

Trying to tie a string around a sunbeam. Is this an accurate description of the fate that awaits our third-party candidates? If this is the case, what does it imply about the fundamental fairness, or lack of fairness, of free elections in our open, democratic society? Before examining the problems of ballot access, campaign financing, and media coverage, it is important to summarize the key arguments that have been advanced in support of our two-party system, since these arguments are often used to justify the restrictions placed on our third-party candidates.

As was noted in chapter 1, a variety of cultural and institutional factors have enabled the Republican and the Democratic Parties to dominate the American presidency for well over a century. A number of political analysts have used a dual set of arguments to defend the desirability of this two-party monopoly.

The Electoral Argument. One of the key roles of political parties is to recruit and select candidates in order to present the voters with viable alternative choices in election contests. In Clinton Rossiter's words, they act as "immense personnel agencies"[2] that filter out candidates by means of primary elections or other nominating mechanisms. According to those who favor a strong two-party system, this system minimizes the confusion that would result if multi-party candidates flooded the ballot and allows elections to be conducted in an orderly manner that is comprehensible to the voters. This argument provided the basic rationale for many of the restrictive ballot access laws that the states passed following the adoption of the Australian (secret) ballot system at the turn of the century.

The Governance Argument. A second major role of political parties is to help organize and run the government in an accountable fashion. According to this argument, it is desirable to maintain a strong two-party system in order to minimize fragmentation and to promote coherence, stability, and continuity within the government. When only two major parties exist, it is possible to elect a clear-cut majority winner who will be responsible for running the government. In countries where power is widely dispersed among many different political parties it is impossible to form an effective governing majority. As one recent commentary on the 1980 election concluded, "the parties, and the nation, continue to need the stability, continuity and democratic responsibility that exist in a strong two-party system."[3] In short, the second argument is based on the "widely shared assumption that a strong party system is indispensable to a healthy modern democracy."[4]

A major problem arises, however, from the fact that there is no clear-cut consensus on precisely what constitutes a strong party system. While both the electoral and the governance arguments have been used to justify the two-party approach, this view is not unanimously accepted. An alternative set of arguments has been advanced by theorists who favor third-party, or multi-party, systems because of the diversity of choices these parties provide to voters and the innovative contributions they may make to the policy process. Unfortunately, there is no conclusive evidence on the precise relationship between different types of party systems and governmental performance. As G. Bingham Powell, Jr., points out in a recent article in the *American Political Science Review*:

Empirical studies of the relationship between the strength of the party system and a good performance by the democratic political system are rare. . . . One line of thought favors a two-party, or majority producing . . . system. A contrasting line of argument favors non-majority systems with a number of parties representing a variety of views.[5]

Under the circumstances, our courts have attempted to weigh the relative merits of these different sets of arguments in an effort to determine the legal rights of third-party candidates in election contests.

LEGALITIES OF BALLOT ACCESS

In dealing with the issue of third-party access to the ballot, the courts have given relatively little weight to the argument that a strong two-party system is required to maintain govermental stability and continuity. In the 1968 case of *Williams* v. *Rhodes*, the United States Supreme Court rejected various restrictions the state of Ohio had placed on third-party and independent candidates that were based on the state's claim that it had a compelling interest in maintaining a two-party system in order to encourage political stability:

The State asserts that the following interests are served by the restrictions it imposes. It claims that the State may validly promote a two-party system in order to encourage compromise and political stability. The fact is, however, that the Ohio system does not merely favor a "two-party system"; it favors two particular parties—the Republicans and the Democrats—and in effect tends to give them a complete monopoly.

There is, of course, no reason why two parties should retain a permanent monopoly on the right to have people vote for or against them. Competition in ideas and governmental policies is at the core of our electoral process and of the First Amendment freedoms. New parties struggling for their place must have the time and opportunity to organize in order to meet reasonable requirements for ballot position.[6]

Although it appears to be a very clear affirmation of the right of third-party candidates to appear on the ballot, the *Williams* v. *Rhodes* case was only one in a long and complicated series of decisions the courts have rendered on the ballot access issue. The key legal question the courts have attempted to resolve involves the weight that should be given to the constitutional rights of third-party candidates to appear on the ballot versus the weight that should be given to the states' legitimate interest in adopting "reasonable requirements" in order to conduct orderly and comprehensible elections.

Over the course of many years, the Supreme Court has defined a specific set of constitutional guarantees. While such fundamental rights are not absolute, the Court has declared that they are so important that they cannot be limited by the states under the Fourteenth Amendment unless such limitations serve a compelling state interest and are the least restrictive and the least invidious way of achieving this state interest. The courts have recognized three fundamental rights that relate very closely to the issue of access to the ballot: the right to vote, the right to form associations, and the right to associate in political parties.

Almost a century ago, the Supreme Court first declared that the right to vote is "a fundamental political right because it is preservative of all rights."[7] The courts have also "implicitly recognize[d] that the political system envisioned in the Constitution holds as a fundamental value the right of free association between individuals as political equals."[8] In the 1957 case of *Sweezy* v. *New Hampshire*, the Supreme Court ruled that "since the political party is an indispensable instrumentality of democratic government, the right to associate freely with a party of one's choice is equally fundamental."[9] Thus the courts have declared that "the right to vote and the right to form associations to further political ideas . . . are afforded the most stringent constitutional protection."[10]

Because access to the ballot is so closely related to such fundamental rights as voting and free association in political parties the courts have subjected the states to the "compelling interest" test in cases where third-party and independent candidates have charged that the states have placed unreasonable restrictions on their right to appear on the ballot. In a number of cases, the courts have decided in favor of these candidates. During the past decade, for example, the Supreme Court has ruled that a state cannot require a candidate to pay a filing fee as the only way to get on the ballot; that the Constitution requires that access to the electorate be real, not "merely theoretical"; that the state must provide a feasible opportunity for new political organizations to appear on the ballot; and that a state must provide reasonable means for an independent political candidate to have access to the ballot.[11]

Although the courts have moved toward the view that access to the ballot should be afforded stringent constitutional protection, this does not mean that the states cannot place any limitations on third-party or independent candidates, if such limitations serve a compelling state interest. In essence, the courts have attempted to strike "a balance between states' interests and constitutionally protected interests" of third-party and independent candidates.[12] To achieve this balance, the Supreme Court has given considerable weight to the electoral argument that the state has a legitimate interest in making the election process comprehensible to voters. The Court has emphasized this position in a number of different cases:

[The] State has a legitimate interest in regulating the number of candidates on the ballot. . . . In so doing, the State understandably and properly seeks to prevent the clogging of its election machinery, avoid voter confusion, and assure that the winner is the choice of a majority, or at least a strong plurality of those voting without the expense and burden of runoff elections. . . . We are bound to respect the legitimate objective of the State in avoiding overcrowded ballots. Moreover, a State has an interest, if not a duty, to protect the integrity of its political process from frivolous or fraudulent candidacies.

Bullock v. *Carter* (1971)[13]

There is surely an important state interest in requiring some preliminary showing of a significant modicum of support before printing

the name of a political organization's candidate on the ballot—the
interest, if no other, in avoiding voter confusion, deception and even
frustration of the democratic process at the general election.

Jenness v. *Fortson* (1971) [14]

States may, for example, impose on minor political parties the precondition of demonstrating the existence of some reasonable quan-
tum of voter support by requiring such parties to file petitions for a
place on the ballot signed by a percentage of those who voted in a
prior election.

Lubin v. *Panish* (1974) [15]

Thus, in their attempts to reach a balance between the fundamental constitutional rights of third-party candidates and
states' interests in conducting orderly elections, the courts
have actually created an area of considerable confusion. In
some cases, such as *Williams* v. *Rhodes*, the Supreme Court has
leaned toward protecting access to the ballot; in other cases,
such as those just cited, it has protected the states' interests.
One recent legal commentary has taken issue with the Court's
shifting position:

The idea of a republican form of government involves several distinct, but mutually dependent election rights. The right to vote, the
right of free speech, the right to petition government, and the right
to associate for political purposes have all been discussed and identified as such by the courts. However, the courts have not been able to
decide on the logical relationship between these rights. . . .

Even though the Court has separately identified and discussed
these rights, it has also declared them to be inextricably intertwined.
The Court has further complicated matters by saying voting and
association are firmly established as fundamental personal rights
guaranteed by the Constitution while the right to be a candidate is
not. (The Court serves us a Waldorf salad, but insists that we separate
on our plates the apples and walnuts from the celery.) [16]

This is harsh criticism, yet the even harsher reality that faces
third-party and independent presidential candidates is that
they must digest not one Waldorf salad, but fifty-one quite

separate and distinct salads in the form of the different ballot access laws that are generated by the fifty states and the District of Columbia. Since the courts consider these laws only on a case-by-case basis, and only if they have been subjected to specific legal challenge, they have not ruled on the overall complexity of the entire ballot access process. Instead, this is a challenge the individual third-party and independent presidential candidates must meet on their own.

BALLOT ACCESS IN 1980

A voting assistance guide that was issued to local election officers in 1980 notes that "the immense diversity of the American electoral process has one obvious drawback—it breeds enormous complexity." The guide points out that this complexity results from the fact that, under our decentralized system of federalism, "approximately 64,000 jurisdictions are involved in the administration of federal elections."[17]

The key jurisdictions for presidential elections are the fifty state governments, plus the District of Columbia, each of which establishes the different legal requirements that must be met for candidates to appear on the ballot. The state laws that govern ballot access are so diverse that they literally constitute a crazy quilt of criteria. All of the states specify some type of petition signature requirements that must be followed by third-party and independent candidates, but this is the only common denominator in the entire system.

In some states it is easier to get on the ballot as an independent, while in others it is easier to qualify as a third-party candidate. Approximately twenty states set forth a comprehensible minimum number of petition signature requirements for ballot access. The remaining thirty states describe their minimum signature requirements in considerably more varied percentage criteria. These range from 1 to 5 percent of the registered voters in the state to between 1 to 5 percent of the total votes cast in the state's last general election for (a) the president of the United States; or (b) for the governor of the state; or (c) members of Congress from the state; or (d) members of the general assembly in the state; or (e) the secretary of state of the state!

A number of general conclusions can be reached about the difficulties the third-party candidates faced in their attempts to get on the ballots of the various states during the 1980 presidential election. First, it took between 700,000 and 1,000,000 signatures on petitions to qualify for the ballot in all fifty states plus the District of Columbia, depending upon whether one followed the independent or third-party route.* Second, the minimum number of signature requirements varied enormously from a low of 155 in the state of Washington (one petition signature for every 10,000 votes cast within the state in the previous presidential election) to a high of over 100,000 for independent candidates in the state of California (1 percent of the entire number of registered voters of the state).[19] Third, there was a very direct correlation between the severity of the signature requirements in the different states and the number of third-party candidates who appeared on the ballot in the states.

The correlation is clearly illustrated on Table 2. Both Ronald Reagan and Jimmy Carter were on the ballots in all fifty states as major-party nominees. In addition, independent candidate John Anderson and Libertarian Party candidate Ed Clark qualified for the ballot in all of the states. As a result, a minimum of four presidential candidates were listed on all state ballots. The maximum number of candidates, eleven, appeared in New Jersey, a state that requires only 800 petition signatures for ballot access. Maryland, Florida, and Oklahoma, where the petition signature requirements are much more difficult, had the

---

*A *Congressional Quarterly* analysis indicated that an even larger total of approximately 1.2 million signatures was required, since it estimated that a cushion of approximately 30 percent is needed in each state to compensate for invalid signatures that are struck off the petitions because they are illegible, or involve improper residencies, or are not notarized.[18]

TABLE 2. Petition Requirements for the 1980 Presidential Election

State	Electoral Vote	Criteria	Estimated Signatures Required	Candidates on Ballot
GROUP ONE (states requiring 25,000 or more petition signatures)				
California	(45)	1% of Registered Voters	101,000+	7
Georgia	(12)	5% of Eligible Voters	57,000+	4
Maryland	(10)	3% of Registered Voters	55,000+	4
Pennsylvania	(27)	2% Largest Previous Statewide Vote	48,000+	7
Florida	(17)	1% of Registered Voters	42,000+	4
Massachusetts	(14)	2% Previous Governor's Vote	39,000+	5
Oklahoma	(8)	3% Previous Presidential Vote	33,000+	4
Oregon	(6)	3% Previous Presidential Vote	30,000+	5
Michigan	(21)	1% Previous Secretary of State Vote	28,000	6
Illinois	(26)	Specified Minimum Requirement	25,000	8

SUMMARY: Total Number of States: 10
Total Electoral College Votes: 186
Average Signature Requirement: 45,900
Average Candidates on Ballot: 5.4

State	Electoral Vote	Criteria	Estimated Signatures Required	Candidates on Ballot
GROUP TWO (states requiring 1,000 or fewer petition signatures)				
Washington	(9)	1 Signature/10,000 Presidential Votes	155	9
Tennessee	(10)	25 Electors in 10 Congressional Districts	250	10
North Dakota	(3)	Specified Minimum Requirement	300	10
Utah	(4)	Specified Minimum Requirement	500	9
New Jersey	(17)	Specified Minimum Requirement	800	11
Iowa	(8)	Specified Minimum Requirement	1,000	10
New Hampshire	(4)	Specified Minimum Requirement	1,000	8
Vermont	(3)	Specified Minimum Requirement	1,000	8
Rhode Island	(4)	Specified Minimum Requirement	1,000	8
Mississippi	(7)	Specified Minimum Requirement	1,000	6

SUMMARY: Total Number of States: 10
Total Electoral College Votes: 69
Average Signature Requirement: 700
Average Candidates on Ballot: 8.8

SOURCE: Petition requirements calculated on the basis of the regulations summarized in Thomas M. Durbin and Michael V. Seitzinger, *Nomination and Election of the President and Vice-President of the United States* (Washington, D.C.: Government Printing Office, 1980). Statistical data obtained from Scammon and McGillivray, *America Votes 14*, and Census Series P-20, no. 344.

smallest number of candidates on the ballot. The two groups of states with the most difficult, and the least difficult, petition signature requirements are listed on Table 2. The information summarized on Table 2 shows the relationship between signature requirements and third-party candidate access to the ballot. In addition to Reagan, Carter, Anderson, and Clark, the states in the first group, with the most restrictive requirements, averaged only 1.4 more additional third-party candidates on their ballots. Those states in the second group, with the least restrictive requirements, averaged 4.8 additional third-party candidates on their ballots. Three of the largest states—California, Pennsylvania, and Illinois—were above the norm for their group, presumably because the third-party candidates felt these states' electoral college votes were important enough to justify the effort involved in meeting their ballot requirements. Actually, California presents a somewhat misleading picture, since the American Independent and the Peace and Freedom Parties automatically qualified for the ballot, based on their performance in previous state elections, and it is doubtful whether either of these parties will appear again in 1984.

The desirability of having more, or fewer, candidates on the ballot is, of course, a matter of political judgment. Yet, it is important to note that voters in the Group Two states had a wider range of choices, and for those who value political diversity and pluralism, this was advantageous. In addition, there is no evidence to indicate that the voters in these states were confused by a larger number of candidates.

The third-party candidates faced other legal problems in addition to the ballot access issue. A number of states specified extremely early filing dates, which were particularly hard on John Anderson, since he didn't formally begin his independent campaign until late in April. By the time Anderson announced, he was legally disqualified from appearing on the ballot in states where filing deadlines had expired in March or early April. Two of these states were Ohio, where nominating petitions for independent candidates had to be filed with the secretary of state "no later than 4:00 p.m of the seventy-fifth day before the first Tuesday after the first Monday in June"; and Maine, where candidates who seek nominations by petition had to file "a signed declaration of candidacy with the secretary of state by or before 5:00 p.m. on April 1."[20] Since the Democratic and Republican candidates were not even nominated until the summer of 1980, Anderson's lawyers charged that these early filing dates discriminated against independent candidates, and the courts ordered his name to be placed on the ballot in these states.

Anderson was not the only candidate who raised legal challenges. Gus Hall and Angela Davis brought suit to get on the ballot as independent candidates in Michigan, and the Libertarian and Socialist Workers Parties brought suit against a number of restrictive laws in West Virginia, including a filing fee requirement and a law that permitted canvassers to solicit petition signatures only in the magisterial districts in which they resided. The West Virginia court upheld the parties in most, though not all, of these challenges.[21]

The bottom line on the issue of legal access to the ballot does not rest, however, on the unique, and sometimes bizarre, technical restrictions that some states have attempted to place on third-party and independent candidates. The courts have struck down many of these in the past, and additional technicalities will undoubtedly be subjected to further legal challenges in the future.

The most difficult problem lies in the enormous confusion that results from the lack of any real national system at all. Ballot access requirements vary so widely among the different states that it is difficult to obtain even minimal information on important aspects of presidential elections. Eight states, for example, base their petition signature requirements on their total number of registered voters, yet there are no current federal government publications that report updated statistical data on voter registration by states. In March 1982, I enlisted the help of the Dartmouth College library reference staff and the Vermont secretary of state's office in an effort to gather such information, but the only published data we could find was a three-year-old Census Bureau report that estimated the voter registration in 1978 for the twenty-five most populous states.[22] After examining state ballot access barriers in his study of third parties, Daniel Mazmanian concluded that "the only effective means of addressing these many wrongs is through a national election code. Its underlying premises must be fairness and openness, without regard for party size."[23]

Any such code, however, could only be enacted into law with the support of the major political parties, and there is no indication that they have any interest in promoting ballot access reforms that would help the third parties. In addition, Article II, section 1 of the Constitution is quite explicit in granting the state legislatures the authority to appoint presidential electors. Under the circumstances, the most promising practical strategy for third-party candidates is to see if they can persuade groups like the Commission on Uniform State Laws to encourage cooperative state action on a voluntary basis. Short of this, there appears to be little prospect of meaningful relief in this area.

CAMPAIGN FINANCING

While the requirements governing ballot access are decentralized, complex, and unwieldy, the requirements governing campaign finance have become much more rigid and highly structured as a result of the various Federal Election Campaign Acts that were passed in the 1970s. Paradoxically, these new requirements have been fashioned in a manner that makes the previous financial problems of third-party candidates even more difficult.

Complaints over the financing of political campaigns have always been a part of American politics:

In his race for the House of Burgesses in Virginia in 1757, George Washington was accused of campaign irregularities. He was charged with dispensing during his campaign 28 gallons of rum, 50 gallons of rum punch, 34 gallons of wine, 46 gallons of beer and two gallons of cider royal. "Even in those days," noted George Thayer, a historian of American campaign financing, "this was considered a large campaign expenditure, because there were only 391 voters in his district, for an average outlay of more than a quart and a half per person."[24]

The costs of running for political office have increased rapidly since Washington's day. According to a study by Stephen J. Wayne, Abraham Lincoln spent an estimated $100,000 on his presidential campaign in 1860. The first million dollar presidential candidate was James A. Garfield, who spent $1,100,000 in 1880. The first ten million dollar candidate was Richard M. Nixon, who spent $10,128,000 in a losing effort against John Kennedy in 1960. In 1972 over $90,000,000 was spent by the Nixon and McGovern campaigns, with Nixon spending $61,400,000 of this total—this time on a winning effort.[25]

During the 1970s it had become obvious that the cost of political campaigns was escalating rapidly. The catalyst was television. In the 1948 campaign, none of the parties spent money on television, though over $1 million was spent on radio advertising. By the time of the 1968 campaign, the combined television and radio expenses totaled over $18 million.[26] Largely as a result of these spiraling costs, Congress passed the first Federal Election Campaign Act (FECA) in 1971, which set a ceiling on amounts federal candidates could spend on media advertising (it was later repealed) and required disclosure of campaign contributions and expenditures.

Following the Watergate scandal, Congress enacted a second FECA law in 1974. This 1974 legislation set maximum contribution limits of $1,000 per individual for each primary, runoff, and general election, and an aggregate total individual limit of $25,000 per year for all federal candidates. It also imposed maximum limits on total campaign spending, established a new Federal Election Commission (FEC) to monitor disclosure and reporting requirements, and provided federal funding for major-party candidates in presidential elections and proportional retroactive public funding for minor-party candidates if they attained at least 5 percent of the total popular vote.[27]

The 1974 law was immediately challenged in the courts. In January 1976, the U.S. Supreme Court, in *Buckley* v. *Valeo*, upheld the limits on individual contributions, the disclosure and reporting requirements, and the provisions for public financing of presidential elections. However, the Court ruled that the maximum limits on total campaign spending were violations of the First Amendment's guarantee of free expression. The Court also struck down the method of selecting members of the FEC.[28] Congress quickly amended the FECA legislation in 1976 to conform to the Supreme Court's decision, and this amended act serves today as the basic federal law that governs campaign financing.

Criticisms of the new law emerged almost immediately. Shortly after the 1976 election, the Institute of Politics at Harvard University held a conference that involved many of the campaign managers who had worked for both the Democratic and Republican Party candidates in the primaries and the presidential election. Only one of them (Walter Mondale's manager) indicated that he thought the law worked well. The others complained that it gave too much advantage to incumbents, discouraged grass-roots activity, made planning difficult, took too much time to administer, or that the individual contribution limitations were too low.[29] Three years later, in 1979, the Institute of Politics completed a major analysis of the FECA that concluded that individual contribution limits were too low (and should be raised from $1,000 to $3,000) and that overregulation was placing extreme burdens on the candidates. The Harvard study focused exclusively on the impact of the law on the two major parties, however, since it was concerned about a potential weakening of these parties, and it made no attempt to analyze the impact of the law on third parties.[30]

While all of the third-party candidates in the 1980 election expressed concern about financial problems that plagued their campaigns, a number of them singled out the FECA legislation for their most bitter criticism. According to Anderson, "The FECA is not fair. There isn't any question about that. The current law crushes the hopes of any third party to overcome the overwhelming financial superiority of the older parties." More specifically, noted Ed Clark, "The Federal Election Campaign Act directly restricts competition and abets the two-party monopoly. . . . Its actions almost invariably act to entrench incumbents." Finally, in a blanket condemnation of the FECA, John Rarick asserted, "I voted against the FECA. All they were doing was creating more regulations to make the major parties stronger."

This outpouring of criticism resulted from the fact that the third-party and independent candidates were caught in a vicious cross-fire under the FECA legislation. They were required to follow all of the law's restrictive provisions (including the $1,000 maximum contribution limitation on individual donors and the costly and cumbersome reporting regulations), with virtually no real possibility of receiving any federal funds in return for their efforts.

The only third-party or independent candidate who received any federal funding was John Anderson, and this was a close call. Anderson qualified for $4.2 million in retroactive federal funds after he received 5,720,060 popular votes, or 6.6 percent of the total cast in the 1980 presidential election (thus surpassing the required 5 percent). However, Anderson only received these funds after the election was already over, and after he had already raised over $10 million private contributions and loans. None of the other third-party candidates received any federal funds at all.

Each of the candidates was required to report his or her total expenditures to the Federal Election Commission. Anderson led the list by reporting total campaign expenses of $14,979,141. The second largest third-party expenditure of $3,210,763 was reported by the Libertarians, with over $2 million of this coming from the party's vice-presidential nominee, David Koch, a wealthy New York chemical engineer, who was permitted by law to contribute an unlimited amount to his own campaign.[31] The other third-party candidates spent considerably less than either Anderson or Clark; none of them reported expenses of more than $200,000 to finance his or her 1980 presidential campaigns. The complete list of expenditures reported to the FEC by all eleven of the third-party and independent candidates who ran in two or more states in 1980 is as follows:[32]

John Anderson (Independent)	$14,979,141
Ed Clark (Libertarian)	3,210,763
Gus Hall (Communist)	194,775
Andrew Pulley (Socialist Workers)	186,257
Ellen McCormack (Right-to-Life)	81,101
Deirdre Griswold (Workers World)	39,772
David McReynolds (Socialist)	38,180
Barry Commoner (Citizens)	23,411*
John R. Rarick (American Independent)	13,932
Percy Greaves (American)	13,488
Benjamin Bubar (National Statesman)	890
	$18,781,710

The figures above make it obvious that none of these candidates, except Anderson and possibly Clark, had the financial resources necessary to gain the more than 4.3 million popular

---

*As Barry Commoner explained in his interview, the Citizens Party ran a decentralized series of state campaigns. Under the FECA legislation, state political parties can spend unlimited amounts. The $23,411 figure represents national party (central office) expenses, and presumably the Citizens Party spent more than this amount on a state-by-state basis.

votes required to qualify for retroactive federal funds under the 5 percent cutoff threshold. Hence, as was previously noted, they had to comply with all of the restrictions of the FECA legislation with no real hope of gaining any federal funds in return.

The big winners in the big money game were the two major-party candidates. Under the FECA legislation, Jimmy Carter and Ronald Reagan automatically qualified for $29.4 million apiece in federal funds prior to the 1980 election. In addition, both the Democratic and the Republican National Committees were given another $4.6 million in federal funds that they could spend during the campaign.

Since the Supreme Court had struck down any limits on total campaign spending in the *Buckley* v. *Valeo* case, Carter and Reagan were free to spend more than the $34 million they each received from the federal government. State party organizations, which are not covered under the FECA limitations, provide one of the largest sources of additional funds. In addition, though the FECA legislation was supposed to minimize the influence of special interest groups, it permits political action committees (PACs) to contribute $5,000 per candidate per election. There is no limit on how much a candidate can receive in combined PAC donations. The 1976 amendments enabled individual companies or labor unions to establish multiple PACs, thus multiplying the money they could funnel to any single candidate. "In addition, once a PAC contributes to five or more federal candidates, [it] can make unlimited independent expenditures . . . on behalf of candidates or parties (e.g., taking out advertisements in the . . . media supporting a candidate)."[33] The result has been an explosion in the number of PAC's created by corporations, labor unions, and special interest groups from 600 in 1974 to over 1,600 in 1981.[34]

Because of the flood of state party and PAC money, Reagan and Carter were able to obtain large additional amounts to supplement their federal funds. Herbert E. Alexander, a political scientist at the University of Southern California, estimates that the two major-party candidates spent more than $118 million in federal and private funds in the 1980 general election—$62 million for Reagan and $56.1 million for Carter.[35]

What, if anything, can be done—short of repeal—to modify the inequities in this legislation? As a minimum, there appears to be no valid reason to place any restrictions on the amount of contributions that individual donors can make to third-party and independent candidates if these parties agree not to accept any federal funding. The combined total spent by the ten third-party candidates in the 1980 presidential election was less than 3 percent of the approximate total expenditure of $137,000,000 by all of the candidates in this election. Even if Anderson's expenditures are added, the combined total for the eleven third-party and independent candidates was only 13.6 percent of the overall expenditures in the 1980 presidential general election. If the individual contribution limitations were relaxed for third parties, it hardly seems that they would represent a major financial threat to the major parties.

In addition, if the two major-party candidates do accept federal funding, they should also be required to accept the obligations that are inherent in spending public money. If there are future presidential debates, for example, these candidates should be required to participate as a condition of receiving federal funds and not be permitted to engage in the type of hide-and-seek game that Jimmy Carter played in the 1980 election.

These are, of course, only modest proposals that barely scratch the surface of the campaign-financing imbroglio. Politics today is big business. The FECA legislation was supposed to control all of this, but the *Congressional Quarterly* estimates that a total of $900 million was spent on all U.S. political campaigns during the 1980 elections—more than three times the amount spent just twelve years earlier in the 1968 races. Yet, while the Federal Election Campaign Act hasn't succeeded in controlling campaign spending, it certainly has crippled the financial capabilities of the third-party candidates. As Ben Cotton, the general counsel of the Republican National Committee, admitted in 1980, "if the FECA has done nothing else, it has institutionalized the two-party system."[36]

MEDIA EXPOSURE

The final major complaint of the third-party candidates involved the issue of the exposure—or more accurately, the lack of exposure—in the national media. While virtually all of the candidates indicated that they received local coverage from newspapers, radio, and even television stations during the campaign visits to the smaller cities, most were unable to obtain any significant coverage from the large television networks or national newspapers. According to the Rosenstone study, "in 1980 Reagan and Carter received about ten times more coverage in leading newspapers and weekly magazines than did *all the eleven* third party and minor party candidates combined. This disparity existed in network television news coverage as well."[37]

In considering the role of the media in political campaigns, it is important to distinguish between the print media (newspapers, magazines, journals) and the electronic media (television and radio). Under the First Amendment, the print media enjoys a fundamental right to freely interpret and report the news without the threat of governmental encroachment or control. As a result, it would be unconstitutional—and, in my opinion, highly undesirable—to attempt to guarantee a specified amount of newspaper coverage for third-party, or any other, political candidates. As a matter of general principle, the print media should be free to exercise judgment as to what is newsworthy and which aspects of a political campaign deserve coverage.

The situation with respect to the electronic media is quite different, since the government assigns broadcasting frequencies to television and radio, and both of these are regulated industries which are subject to governmental licensing. Two basic problems have arisen with respect to the electronic media. The first involves the so-called equal time concept, and the second grows out of the increasingly significant role that the television debates have played in presidential elections.

Congress first attempted to resolve the equal-time issue with the passage of the Federal Communications Act of 1934. Under this act, Congress established the Federal Communications Commission (FCC) as an independent executive agency and empowered the FCC to grant, revoke, renew and modify radio and television licenses. In addition, section 315(a) of the 1934 Act provided that a broadcast licensee who provided time to a legally qualified candidate for any public office must also afford "equal opportunities" to all other candidates for the same office. This equal-time requirement, which was originally used to protect third-party and independent candidates, explicitly guaranteed candidates equal access to the broadcast media, though it did not guarantee equal exposure to all candidates.

As the costs of radio and, more particularly, television, began to increase dramatically, the broadcasting companies argued that they could not absorb the expense of providing free time to all third-party and independent candidates. However, they repeatedly expressed an interest in providing free time for candidates of the two major parties, which they promised to do in exchange for the repeal of section 315(a).

In 1959, Congress amended the equal-time provision in response to the broadcasters' requests. Candidate time on newscasts, news interviews, and news documentaries was excluded from the section 315(a) requirements, provided the candidate's appearance was "incidental to the presentation of the subject covered" in the news program.[38] As a result of this amendment, the networks were allowed to make their own determination of what was newsworthy in their coverage of the different candidates. In 1960, Congress went even further by temporarily suspending section 315(a) in order to exclude third-party candidates from the first televised presidential debates that were held between John F. Kennedy and Richard Nixon. Since this action was not challenged by any of the other candidates, the courts never ruled on the issue before the temporary suspension expired.

As television took on an increasingly significant political role in presidential elections, there was continuous jockeying between the major-party candidates over the equal-time doctrine. When incumbent presidents requested television time to deliver "newsworthy" announcements during the course of election campaigns, the major-party opposition candidate often demanded equal time to reply on the grounds that these were political broadcasts rather than news broadcasts. A key point of controversy involved what one network spokesman referred to as "the nearness doctrine"—specifically, the nearness of a presidential address, or press conference, to the election.[39]

By 1970, Congress had become frustrated with the concept of equal time. A bill that permanently repealed section 315(a) cleared both houses. However, it was vetoed by President Nixon, presumably because he did not want to be confronted with another debate challenge from his democratic rival during the 1972 campaign, as had been the case in his unsuccessful campaign against John Kennedy in 1960. The only modification involving broadcasters that was enacted into law tightened up requirements on networks to provide time for paid political advertisements. When Congress passed the first Federal Election Campaign Act of 1971, Title 1 of this act authorized the FCC to revoke any broadcasting station license for willful or repeated failure to permit the purchase of reasonable amounts of time by legally qualified candidates.

There the matter rested until the 1976 election, when the equal-time issue was revived after the League of Women Voters had agreed to sponsor a new series of televised presidential debates. Since section 315(a) was still in effect, the Federal

Communications Commission was forced to rule on whether or not third-party and independent candidates should be included in these debates. In a split decision, the FCC determined that the debates were a news event, and hence they would be exempt from the equal-time requirement, but that they had to be sponsored by a neutral and nonpartisan group (such as the League of Women Voters).

When the league and the networks announced that the debates would be limited to the two major-party contenders, President Ford and Jimmy Carter, independent candidate Eugene McCarthy attempted to seek injunctive relief in the U.S. District Court of the District of Columbia. The district court refused to grant such relief and directed McCarthy to take his case through regular channels, including an appeal to the FCC. In his book *The Ultimate Tyranny*, McCarthy argued that he should have been included in the debates for the following reasons:

By any reasonable standard I should be considered a major candidate, unless that term was to be applied only to Democrats and Republicans. . . . At the time we filed our petition for injunctive relief, only three candidates, Carter, Ford and myself, met three basic tests of being on the ballot in twenty or more states, being on the ballot in enough states to win a majority of the electoral college, and receiving more than 5 percent in the polls.[40]

In light of its previous ruling, which exempted the debates from the equal-time requirement, it is hardly surprising that the FCC (once again in a split decision), turned down McCarthy's appeal. Subsequently, the U.S. Court of Appeals for the District of Columbia Circuit also ruled against McCarthy, and the U.S. Supreme Court refused to review the case.

Controversies over network exposure continued during the 1980 presidential campaign. Two of these involved the issue of paid political advertising. As Ed Clark indicated in his interview, the Libertarian Party threatened to bring legal action against NBC when it felt the network was refusing to run its ads, but this question was eventually resolved out of court. Another legal dispute occurred when the Carter-Mondale presidential committee requested each of the three major networks to provide prime time for a thirty-minute paid documentary between December 4 and December 7, 1979, which was to be shown in conjunction with Carter's formal announcement for reelection.

Both ABC and NBC refused the request, arguing that they were not prepared to sell political time for the 1980 presidential election as early as December 1979. CBS also refused to provide thirty minutes of prime time on the grounds of disruption of its regular programming, but it did offer to sell a five-minute segment during both the daytime and late evening. The Carter-Mondale committee filed a complaint with the FCC charging that the networks had violated their obligations to provide reasonable access for paid political advertising under the Title 1 provisions of the Federal Election Campaign Act of 1971. The FCC ruled that the networks had violated the law, and in July 1981, the U.S. Supreme Court upheld this ruling.[41] Thus, in its most recent decision, the Court has held that the networks do have some obligation to provide access to political candidates, though the case was limited to paid political advertising and involved an incumbent president rather than any of the third-party contenders.

The third, and most significant, controversy over access to television in the 1980 campaign was, once again, centered on the presidential debates. As had been the case in 1976, the League of Women Voters agreed to sponsor the debates, and during the summer of 1980, the league developed guidelines for determining if any of the third-party or independent candidates were serious enough contenders to participate in the debates with the two major-party nominees. In early September, the league announced that John Anderson met its standard for inclusion in the debates—a 15 percent standing in the polls. As soon as the league announced its decision, one of the major-party nominees, Jimmy Carter, refused to participate in the debates at all, while Ronald Reagan agreed to appear with Anderson. The final result was one early debate between Reagan and Anderson and one hastily arranged final debate between Reagan and Carter.

Since television has become such a powerful force in American politics, and since televised debates played an important role in both of our past two presidential campaigns, the controversies that surrounded the 1976 and the 1980 debates highlight a number of serious questions. First, is the League of Women Voters an appropriate group to sponsor such debates? Second, should major-party candidates such as Carter be permitted to opt out of the debates at their own convenience? Third, is standing in the polls the appropriate criterion to use in determining which candidates should be allowed to participate in the debates?

In considering the first issue, a number of the 1980 candidates, such as John Anderson and David McReynolds, questioned whether it was appropriate for an informal, voluntary organization such as the League of Women Voters to manage the debates. Yet, there isn't any clear-cut alternative. Unless some truly impartial and nonpartisan public agency can be established to take on this task, it appears that a voluntary organization such as the league can play a responsible role in this area.

This organization's task would be made considerably more creditable, however, if firm criteria were established well in advance of election campaigns to deal with the second and third questions—namely, the major party candidates' availability and the third-party candidates' eligibility to participate in the debates. Can some formula—short of abolishing the debates entirely or inviting all of the candidates to participate in all of the debates—be devised that would be fair and would also provide an opportunity for a manageable exchange of views?

It seems that this is one area where all of the problems analyzed in this chapter may actually converge. As was pointed out in the discussion of the ballot access issue, third-party candidates face a series of stiff hurdles in many states because the courts have attempted to strike a balance between their constitutional rights to gain access to the ballot and the states' interest in conducting orderly elections. The major-party candidates receive large amounts of federal financial assistance during campaigns, while the third-party and independent candidates do not receive any funds at all, except on a possible *ex post facto* basis after their campaigns are already completed. The evaluation of the equal-time provisions governing access to the broadcast media has indicated that these provisions have provided increasingly less protection to the third-party candidates with the passage of time. It would appear that the presidential debates represent a golden opportunity to help remedy some of these deficiencies.

The key is to be found in that most venerated of all governmental incentives—the power of the purse. If any candidate who accepts federal funds to help finance a campaign had to agree to appear in the debates as a precondition for receiving such funds, candidates would remain free to refuse to participate in the debates—as Carter did in 1980—but only at the price of forfeiting their federal financial support. In addition, if the federal government set aside a portion of the funds it now allocates to the two major-party candidates ($68 million in the 1980 election), it could purchase prime time on all of the major television (and radio) networks for a minimum of four separate presidential debates of one and one half hours' duration each.

These four presidential debates could be organized as follows. One debate would be between the two major-party candidates. A second debate would involve the two major-party candidates, plus any of the other candidates who have qualified for the ballot in all fifty of the states. A third debate would include any of the third-party and/or independent candidates who have secured a position on the ballot in states with a total electoral college vote of at least 270. A fourth debate would be between any of the third-party and/or independent candidates not covered by the above criteria who have qualified for the ballot in five or more states.

If such criteria had been used in the 1980 presidential election, it would have produced the following results:

FIRST DEBATE	Carter and Reagan
SECOND DEBATE	Anderson, Carter, Clark, and Reagan
THIRD DEBATE	Anderson, Clark, Commoner, and Hall*
FOURTH DEBATE	All six other third-party candidates with the exception of McCormack, who was only on the ballot in three states

By dividing the debates between different groups of candidates, it would be possible to accomplish a number of objectives. First, it would continue to permit the two major-party candidates to engage in at least one face-to-face confrontation. Second, it could stimulate at least a minimal degree of interest in the other third-party and independent candidates and presumably lead to some follow-up newspaper coverage of these candidates. Third, it would limit each of the debates to a manageable number of participants. Finally, it would provide an added incentive to third-party and independent candidates to qualify for the ballot position in as many states as possible in order to enhance their opportunities to participate in the debates.

If some type of proposal along these lines were adopted, various details regarding the timing and the actual format of the different debates would still have to be worked out by the appropriate sponsoring agency. As more experience was gained with the new criteria, appropriate modifications could be made, though any changes would have to be announced well in advance so that candidates would know what conditions would govern their potential participation in future debates.

Some might argue that these types of revisions would give

---

*The Socialist Workers Party was on the ballot in states with a total of 315 electoral college votes, but this party split its ticket among three different candidates.

too much exposure to the third-party and independent candidates. Yet today these candidates are completely excluded from the presidential debates unless they have reached some arbitrary standing in the polls. Any such standing is largely dependent on the degree of exposure these candidates receive. Thus they are trapped in a no-win situation.

If we really believe in the concept of open elections in the United States, any revised procedure along the lines proposed would certainly be more fair than the present system. In addition, voters might actually learn something from the third-party candidates that would help them make more meaningful choices when they cast their future ballots in presidential elections.

SUMMARY

A review of the ballot access, the campaign finance, and the media issues reveals that the third-party and independent candidates face an extremely difficult series of institutional and procedural obstacles. During recent years these obstacles have increased in severity with the passage of such legislation as the FECA financing provisions and the erosion of equal-time access to broadcast media.[42]

Despite the homage that is paid in American politics to the concepts of free enterprise and free competition, the two major parties are intent on doing everything possible to kill off their third-party rivals. As Rosenstone and his colleagues at Yale point out, "the FECA is a major party protection act," and "the major parties are not content to merely try legislating other parties out of existence, they are actively engaged in a fight to keep them from qualifying for ballot positions."[43]

Under the circumstances, if any reforms are to be made in this area, these reforms will have to come from the American public. Voters will have to decide what kind of political system they want, according to their values. By attempting to accommodate the widest possible constituency, the two major parties help to simplify the electoral process, and they also tend to provide stability and continuity by making it more possible to elect majority leaders who have the power to govern.

The third parties, on the other hand, place a much higher premium on diversity and pluralism, on issue argumentation, and on providing more direct access to the policy process by different segments of the public, especially concerned minorities. Third parties have challenged the status quo and fed ideas into the political system. As the Supreme Court stated in the *Williams* v. *Rhodes* case, "competition of ideas and government policies is at the core of our electoral process."[44] Yet the third parties received very little attention during the 1980 presidential campaign, and most books that have appeared on the election devoted only minimal coverage to these parties.[45]

The long-range consequences of this type of neglect raise serious questions about the future role of third parties in American politics. As one recent commentary noted, "so long as the two-party system remains entrenched, minor parties and independent candidates generally have only a slight chance of electoral success. Nonetheless, they perform important functions in the political process. . . . Without this alternative, dissatisfied voters who find themselves repeatedly confronted with unattractive policies and candidates may come to doubt the legitimacy of the entire electoral process."[46] If this proves to be the case, we will have lost much of the vitality and diversity that has helped to shape our political development over the course of many years.

8 THE FUTURE OF THIRD PARTIES

Although the two major parties have attempted to fortify their positions of legal, financial, and media superiority, the 1980 presidential election results show a higher than average level of voter support for independent and third-party candidates.

In 1980, the independent and third-party nominees collected 8.2 percent of the popular vote, with John Anderson accounting for 6.6 percent of this total. This is the second strongest percentage showing by such candidates in well over half a century. As Table 3 indicates, the 1980 independent and third-party vote was surpassed only once during the post-World War II period, when George C. Wallace received almost 14 percent of the popular votes cast in the 1968 election.

At the conclusion of the preceding chapter, reference was made to the fact that a number of studies have appeared on the 1980 election. These studies indicate that political analysts disagree significantly on the long-range meaning of this election. Some scholars, such as Professor Carey McWilliams of Rutgers, conclude:

> It didn't mean much. The election of 1980 did not try our souls; it tried our patience. . . . Carter was a humorless bungler and Reagan was an amiable simpleton. . . . Even the enthusiasm for John Anderson was negative, deriving from distaste for the major-party nominees. . . . Americans stopped believing in progress in 1980 . . . That is the central meaning of the election.[1]

Other observers, such as Norman Podhoretz, the editor of *Commentary*, believe that 1980 represented one of those rare critical elections that result in a major realignment in American politics. According to Podhoretz, "The landslide of 1980 has given the Republicans a new majority to build as they try to reverse the decline of American power."[2]

TABLE 3. Third Party and Independent Vote

Presidential Election	Total Popular Votes Cast	Third-Party and Independent Vote	Percentage of Total Popular Vote
1980	86,515,221	7,127,185	8.2
1976	81,555,889	1,577,333	1.9
1972	77,718,554	1,378,260	1.8
1968	73,211,875	10,121,229	13.8
1964	70,644,592	336,838	0.5
1960	68,838,219	503,331	0.7
1956	62,026,908	413,684	0.7
1952	61,550,918	299,692	0.5
1948	48,793,826	2,623,190	5.4

SOURCE: Compiled from presidential election results reported in Scammon and McGillivray, *America Votes 14*, pp. 2–20.

According to classification schemes developed by political scientists such as V. O. Key, Angus Campbell and his colleagues at the University of Michigan Survey Research Center, and Walter Dean Burnham, presidential elections can fall into one of the following categories.

Maintaining elections occur when the prevailing voting patterns persist, and the majority party wins the election. Historically, this has been the most prevalent type of election; note, for example, Roosevelt's victories in 1936, 1940, and 1944.

Deviating elections take place when the prevailing voting patterns persist, but the minority party wins the election as a result of the influence of short-term forces. This was the case in the 1952 and 1956 elections when the force of Eisenhower's personal popularity overcame the prevailing Democratic Party majority.

Critical (or *realigning*) *elections* involve a long-term shift in the electorate when a new party balance is created. Such shifts have been quite infrequent, but one occurred in 1896 that led to a long period of Republican Party dominance, and another in 1928–32 that led to a long period of Democratic Party dominance.[3]

These three classifications are based on shifts, or lack of

shifts, in voter support for one of the two major parties. A number of political analysts have expressed growing doubt as to whether any of the three classifications accurately portrays current trends in American presidential politics, since support for both of the major parties appears to be eroding. These analysts argue that the current pattern is one of political *dealignment*. As Everett C. Ladd explains, "a realignment involves the movement of large numbers of voters across party lines, establishing a new majority coalition or at least the radical transformation of the makeup of the old party coalitions. In dealignment, voters move away from parties altogether; loyalties to the parties, and to the parties' candidates and programs, weaken, and more and more of the electorate become 'up for grabs' each election."[4]

The significance of the unusually high third-party and independent vote in 1980 depends on how one interprets the nature of this election. Was this higher third-party vote a result of the fact that 1980 was a "deviating election" in which short-term distaste for both the major-party nominees increased the vote for Anderson along the lines suggested by McWilliams? Or, was the 1980 third-party and independent vote a result of the fallout that accompanied a major realignment toward the Republicans as suggested by Podhoretz? Or, did this vote signify a genuine shift away from both of the major parties and thereby provide evidence for the type of dealignment politics described by Ladd?

As was pointed out at the beginning of this book, three factors have played an important role in determining past levels of strong voter support for third-party and independent candidates: conditions of political crisis; high levels of public dissatisfaction with the two major parties; and the prominence and visibility of third-party nominees. There is considerable evidence which indicates that the second of the above conditions—dissatisfaction with the two major parties—has increased quite dramatically during the past few decades, and that this is leading to the type of dealignment pattern described by Ladd.

One indication of this is the fact that the overall percentage of the voting age population that has actually bothered to cast ballots in presidential elections has dropped from a high of 62.8 percent in the 1960 election to a much more modest 53.2 percent in the 1980 election, a decline of almost 10 percentage points in the past two decades.[5]

At the same time the percentage of those who actually vote in presidential elections has eroded, the percentage of adult voters who identify with either of the two major parties has also declined. According to the Gallup surveys of trends in political affiliation, a total of 77 percent of those surveyed in 1960 identified themselves as Democrats or Republicans; only 23 percent claimed to be independents. In the 1981 Gallup survey, the total of Democrats and Republicans had dropped to 69 percent, while the independents had increased to 31 percent.[6] Even more dramatic results were found in "the 1980 General Social Survey conducted by the National Opinion Research Center (NORC) of the University of Chicago [which] found 38 percent of the public identifying as independents, and [in] a poll taken by Market Opinion Research for the Republican National Committee in September 1980 [which] placed independents at 40 percent—compared with 37 percent Democrats and 24 percent Republicans."[7]

A third indication of widespread disillusionment with our existing political institutions is to be found in surveys that have been conducted to measure public confidence in the levels of honesty and ethical standards in different professions. A 1981 Gallup survey revealed that clergymen enjoyed the highest levels of public confidence (63%), followed by various medical practitioners (pharmacists, dentists, doctors) all of whom were ranked by 50 percent or more of the public as having high or very high ethical standards. Public officials, however, appeared near the bottom of the list—senators at 20 percent; congressmen at 15 percent; and local and state officeholders at 14 and 12 percent respectively.[8] This finding was confirmed in a series of Harris surveys that measured levels of public confidence in major institutions. A 1966 survey indicated that 42 percent of the public had a great deal of confidence in Congress and 41 percent had a great deal of confidence in the executive branch. In the 1981 survey, these totals had dropped to only 16 percent for Congress and 24 percent for the executive branch.[9]

The foregoing survey data reveal widespread public concern and unrest over the course of our national leadership. The cumulative impact of this concern was revealed in a poll the Gallup organization published in the early winter of 1982 that indicated that 67 percent of those surveyed were dissatisfied with "the way things are going in the U.S. at this time."[10] The fact that two-thirds of the respondents were dissatisfied raises the question of whether we are entering an era of political crisis that, historically, has served as a second precondition leading to increased third-party and independent political activity. What are the specific grievances, or sets of grievances, that have led to such a high level of public dissatisfaction?

According to numerous public opinion surveys in the past decade, every major group in the United States (based on sex, age, race, religion, educational levels, politics, and occupation) has identified economic conditions as the most important problem facing the nation. The focus of these economic concerns has varied between too much inflation (that is, high cost of living) and/or too much unemployment. These problems have been listed as the public's foremost concerns in every annual Gallup survey conducted since 1973.[11]

The specific impact of economic conditions on third-party voting is not entirely clear. One group of scholars has indicated that only farmers are directly motivated by economic concerns—especially by long-term farm price changes—while the rest of the electorate is not. According to this proposition, "neither the amount of inflation, deflation, unemployment, or change in income has an effect on the level of third-party voting. . . . As a rule, farmers excepted, economic adversity does not produce more third-party voting."[12]

While this may have been true historically, the prolonged public concern over inflation and unemployment that has dominated public opinion surveys for almost a decade indicates an increasing fear that one of the central tenets of the American economic dream is no longer true. Although many minority groups and women were excluded from the nation's earlier economic prosperity, the bulk of the American work force was nurtured by the belief that a basic social and economic contract exists between the government and the private individual. The essence of this belief is that if one works hard enough and saves enough money, it will be possible to spend the latter years of life in relative dignity and self-respect while one's children go on to greater levels of achievement. In short, the government is expected to manage the economy in a manner that protects and preserves the value of an individual's life earnings.

The persistent growth of inflation during the past fifteen years has badly battered this dream. No governmental administration has been able to devise a solution to the inflation problem, however, without pushing the country into a recession that, in turn, increases unemployment. Once unemployment starts to rise significantly, the public identifies high unemployment as the nation's most important problem. This shift can be seen clearly in the Reagan administration's first year. In January 1981, the month Reagan was inaugurated, 73 percent of the respondents in a Gallup survey identified inflation as the most important problem facing the country; only 8 percent identified unemployment as the most important problem. Fifteen months later, in April 1982, the totals were reversed: 44 percent felt unemployment was the most important problem, compared to only 24 percent who named inflation.[13]

The political crisis that has grown out of these long-standing concerns is not confined to the problems of economics. The deeper crisis involves the public's disillusionment with the ability of either of the two major parties to deal with these issues effectively. In the most recent edition of his book, *Where Have All the Voters Gone?*, Everett Ladd points out that

the majority of Americans, including those who continue to think of themselves as Democrats or Republicans, no longer . . . believe that it makes a substantial difference which party wins. . . . One of the most dramatic illustrations of the weakening of ties to the parties comes from a survey conducted by the University of Connecticut's Institute for Social Inquiry near the height of the presidential campaign, in September 1980. Respondents were asked, "Which party, the Republicans or the Democrats, does the better job (handling a specified set of problems) or don't you think there is much difference?" Depending on the problem area, between 52 and 70 percent indicated that they really did not see much of a difference.[14]

Ladd uses this type of analysis to reinforce his argument that "the present era in American electoral politics is one of dealignment and party decay. . . . Both of the major parties are now weak. While the Democrats were doing more groaning and groping than the Republicans in the late 1970s and early 1980s, neither party commands anything approaching a secure majority. . . . Thus partisan and electoral drift continues."[15]

Other analysts, such as Podhoretz, challenge Ladd's assessment, but Ladd advances a number of arguments to support his thesis. He argues that there are three explanations for our electoral dealignment. The sociological explanation is that "an affluent, leisured, highly educated public no longer perceives the need for political parties as intermediary institutions"; the institutional explanation points to the deterioration of political party organizations as the national communications media and the welfare state have assumed the traditional roles the parties once performed; the psychological explanation is that the American people, themselves, have become ambivalent, undecided, and even contradictory in their demands—they want government to do a lot in many different areas, but they view the state as "clumsy, inefficient, and wasteful."[16]

It is still unclear whether either the Republican or the Democratic Party will be able to deal effectively with inflation, unemployment, and the other critical issues the nation faces as it moves ahead into the 1980s. It is already apparent, however, that one of the preconditions for increased third-party voter support already exists in the form of public disillusionment with both of the two major parties. If economic conditions worsen, reinforcing this sense of disillusionment, it is likely that support for third parties in the years ahead will increase.

The caliber of the candidates the parties nominate for the presidency will be the final significant factor to influence the future level of voter support for the third parties. It seems logical to assume that political candidates enter election contests in the hope of winning public office. However, the interviews with the 1980 third-party nominees indicated that the majority of them had no expectation of actually winning the presidency. Instead, the largest group of candidates indicated that they were primarily interested in performing an educational and recruitment role during the election campaign. They hoped to communicate their parties' positions and, in so doing, to enlist volunteers to support their causes.

This educational-recruitment function was particularly important to the doctrinal parties. As Simon Gerson of the Communist Party put it, "We're interested in spreading our message and building up our party base." According to Deirdre Griswold of the Workers World Party, running for president was "primarily an educational objective to get our program across." While David McReynolds of the Socialist Party noted, "I was doing the job of explaining a political position that can't be done in any other way," Andrew Pulley of the Socialist Workers argued, "Just to begin to break down the effect of the propaganda of the ruling class is very important." In addition, a number of the candidates, such as Ellen McCormack, Percy Greaves, and John Rarick—indicated that they were trying to pressure the two major parties to deal with certain key issues, specifically, abortion, economic policy, and excessive governmental intervention in private affairs.

Only three of the 1980 candidates emphasized the electoral challenge of winning the presidency. John Anderson decided to enter the campaign as an independent candidate, initially expecting that he could win the election in 1980. Ed Clark of the Libertarian Party and Barry Commoner of the Citizens Party both took a more long-range view. They regarded the presidential campaign as an organizational task: they were engaged in party building to lay the groundwork in 1980 for future victories.

Whereas the candidates who focused their major efforts on education, recruitment, and pressure politics each received less than 50,000 votes, the final totals for Anderson, Clark, and Commoner, shown in Table 4, were significantly higher.

When these popular vote totals are broken down among the different states, a number of interesting patterns emerge: (1) Anderson received over 10 percent of the popular vote in nine states, including all six of the New England states; (2) Clark received over 10 percent of the popular vote in one state, Alaska; and (3) when the Anderson, Clark, and Commoner votes are combined, these three candidates received 10 percent or more of the popular vote in sixteen different states, and the District of Columbia. The states with the highest combined popular vote percentage for these three candidates are shown below.[17]

Alaska*	18.7%	Hawaii	12.1%
Vermont	16.7	Maine	12.0
Massachusetts	16.1	California	11.1
Rhode Island*	15.0	Arizona	11.0
New Hampshire	13.8	District of Columbia	11.0
Colorado	13.7	Montana*	10.7
Connecticut	13.3	Minnesota	10.5
Oregon	12.8	Iowa	10.0
Washington	12.8		

These states cast a total of 142 electoral college votes in the 1980 election—not enough to elect a president but certainly enough to have a dramatic impact on the course of any future presidential elections. In addition to all of the New England states, the group includes the key west coast states, plus other trend-setting states such as Arizona, Colorado, and Minnesota.

*Commoner was not officially on the ballot in Alaska, Řhode Island, or Montana, but he did receive a small number of write-in votes in Rhode Island.

TABLE 4. 1980 Election Results

Candidate	Popular Vote	Percentage of Total Popular Vote
Anderson	5,720,060	6.61
Clark	921,299	1.06
Commoner	234,294	0.27
Total	6,875,653	7.94

SOURCE: Scammon and McGillivray, *America Votes 14*, p. 20.

Finally, the total number of states involved—seventeen—is by far the highest third-party showing in the entire post-World War II era, with the sole exception of 1968 when American Independent Party candidate George Wallace was able to gain more than 10 percent of the popular vote in twenty-three different states.

What does all of this mean with respect to the impact of the third-party candidates on the 1984 presidential election and in the years beyond? As was noted at the conclusion of the previous chapter, few political analysts have bothered to pay much attention to the 1980 third-party and independent candidates. Among the exceptions, Professor Gerald Pomper of Rutgers University makes the following observations on Anderson's constituency in *The Election of 1980*:

The Anderson campaign failed in its ostensible objective: presidential victory. . . . The independent candidate never developed a strong electoral base. His appeal remained largely restricted to the "young, liberal, well-educated, white and affluent" voters and extended little into the broader ranks of the middle and working classes. Moreover, Anderson's support was inherently soft, concentrated among younger persons, who vote infrequently, and among persons who were least certain of their preferences. Most importantly, there was no distinctive ideological character to this vote. Anderson ran as a middle-of-the-road candidate in a race in which his opponents also claimed the same place on the political highway.[18]

A second analyst who devotes considerable attention to the 1980 third party vote is the syndicated columnist and political commentator Kevin P. Phillips. In the introduction to his latest book, *Post-Conservative America*, Phillips foresees "the clear possibility of a new party in 1984 based on John Anderson's 1980 splinter electorate of students, affluent professionals, old Yankee progressives, Midwest Scandinavians and Pacific avant-gardists."[19] Later in the book, however, Phillips becomes much more circumspect. While indicating that polls show 30 to 40 percent public support for a new center party, he concludes that "the issue of a strong third party is probably academic. Even though the public supports the idea, current federal election law is . . . stacked against the emergence of successful new parties." Phillips agrees with Ladd, however, that we are in a period of major-party dealignment, and that the erosion of the two major parties will continue. He speculates that dealignment will lead to short-term political coalitions, a multiplicity of parties, and more use of advanced communications technologies to conduct plebiscitary politics (namely, more televised presidential communications; increased initiatives and referenda; mass computerized direct mailings; and the like).[20]

If Ladd and Phillips are correct in their assertions that we are experiencing a period of major-party dealignment—and there is certainly a great deal of evidence to back up their claims—the types of voters who supported the Anderson, the Libertarian, and the Citizens Party candidacies in 1980 could play a critical role in future presidential elections. While Pomper is correct in asserting that this type of younger, well-educated, affluent constituency may be soft in a more traditional presidential election, they possess the high technology skills and expertise, and the financial resources, to exercise a significant electoral impact during a volatile period of major-party dealignment. As Phillips notes in his book, Anderson, Clark, and Commoner were strongest in states that have "disproportionate numbers of universities, environmentalists, resort areas, and high-tech concentrations." He points out that these states "with heavy ratios of post-industrial voters," are also the states that futurists usually look to as the American trend setters. Finally, Phillips sees the same "high-tech" lifestyle patterns in the major counties that supported Anderson, Clark, and Commoner. These three candidates received over 15 percent of the popular vote in such areas as Chittenden County, Vermont (Burlington), Marin County, California (San Francisco suburbs); Santa Clara, California (Silicon Valley); Denver County, Colorado; and King County, Washington (Seattle).[21]

In a recent analysis in the journal of the American Political Science Association, William Schneider of the American Enterprise Institute observes that during periods of dealignment "mass marketing contributes to greater volatility in the electorate . . . as peripheral voters are buffeted this way and that by the skillful application of the new campaign technologies."[22] Two factors will determine whether or not the third parties will be able to exploit these technologies effectively in 1984 and beyond.

The first factor is how successfully Ronald Reagan deals with the economic problems currently facing the nation. There is no question that Reagan is a remarkably effective communicator. He conveys the image of a decisive leader. John Rarick may be too effusive when he asserts "he's the only President we've ever had who talks like an American," but there is little doubt that it has been a long time since the country has had a president who speaks as effectively as Reagan. The key question, however, is whether Reagan can translate rhetoric into reality. If Reagan can do a reasonable job turning around the growing unemployment crisis, and if he avoids a major calamity abroad, he is going to be a strong candidate, assuming he decides to run again in 1984.

The possibility of a third-party coalition is a second key factor that can influence the 1984 election. The three groups to watch here are the Anderson supporters, the Libertarians, and the Citizens Party.

Anderson is the most well known of the third-party candidates, and he demonstrated the broadest base of appeal in the

1980 election. As was noted in chapter 6, Anderson may qualify for over $4 million in federal funding if he decides to run again in 1984 because he received over 5 percent of the popular vote in 1980.

The Libertarian Party spent most of its energies during the 1970s building up its organizational base at the state and local levels. As a result, the party increased its presidential vote from 3,600 in 1972, to 173,000 in 1976, to 920,000 in 1980. As Ed Clark indicated in his interview, the party plans to run over 1,000 candidates in local, state, and congressional elections in 1982. Hence, the Libertarians are well on their way toward building a strong "grass-roots" party organization.

The future direction of the Citizens Party is more difficult to project. The party initially emphasized an anticorporate stance that was articulated by Barry Commoner in his interview. More recently, however, the party has begun to place more stress on environmental and antinuclear issues, and to call for a nuclear weapons freeze. The latter concern is the type of highly charged issue that could take on increasing political significance in the years ahead.

As has been noted in the preceding analysis, Anderson, Clark, and Commoner all drew upon similar constituency groups in the 1980 election. The question is whether these groups will be interested, or able, to reach any mutual agreement in 1984, or whether their ideological and other political differences are too deep to permit any cooperative effort on their part. At the conclusion of the 1980 election, John Anderson speculated on "an emerging coalition which could have a profound significance for future voting patterns" in the following terms:

I predict a revival of a long-dormant peace movement. . . . I can foresee the emerging of a grand coalition of those left behind in the administration's economic blueprint—youth, more affluent upper-middle and higher income groups disturbed by growing signs of social pathology, and those concerned about our hawkish military and foreign policy.[23]

Hence, the third-party situation is as fluid at this point as the general political dealignment. If Ronald Reagan does not successfully solve the nation's major problems through his "supply side" economic policies, the third parties should do well in 1984 even if they remain divided. If Reagan is unsuccessful, and if John Anderson achieves a coalition effort with the Libertarian and/or Citizens Party, the third-party vote in 1984 could surpass the 13.8 percent of the 1968 election. If this proves to be the case, the third parties will play a decisive role in determining who will occupy the White House unless, or until, such time as the current major-party dealignment comes to an end, and a new majority coalition is forged by either the Republicans or the Democrats that will dominate the presidency once again in the years ahead.

APPENDIX A
NOTE ON INTERVIEW METHODOLOGY

The interviews with the ten third-party candidates and with independent candidate John B. Anderson were conducted between June 1981 and January 1982.

Prior to each interview, I attempted to collect background material on each candidate and on the various political parties they represented. The amount of material available on the different candidates varied greatly.

I was able to obtain biographical materials, party literature, and commentary by political reporters on John Anderson, Ed Clark, Barry Commoner, and Gus Hall. I also read articles and books they had written, such as "Developing a Grand Coalition," by John Anderson, Ed Clark's *A New Beginning*, Barry Commoner's *The Politics of Energy*, and Gus Hall's *Labor Up-Front*. A sizable amount of party literature and 1980 campaign material was available on David McReynolds, Andrew Pulley, Deirdre Griswold, Percy Greaves, and John Rarick. I was also able to obtain some biographical information on Rarick, based on his years in Congress, and on Andrew Pully from his Socialist Workers Party pamphlet, *How I Became a Socialist*. It was more difficult to obtain any information on two of the candidates—Benjamin Bubar and Ellen McCormack—since current party literature and biographical information on these two candidates was very scarce.

I conducted personal interviews with each candidate, except for Gus Hall, who arranged to have his campaign manager, Simon Gerson, speak as his surrogate. During the interviews, which lasted from one to two hours, I attempted to cover a common set of general topics—personal background, political ideology, the 1980 campaign, and personal impressions. I also attempted to press all of the candidates with follow-up questions about their ideological positions, but each of the interviews was conducted in an informal and nonconfrontational manner in an effort to encourage the candidates to convey their own thoughts in the most open fashion possible.

I advised the candidates in advance that I wanted to tape record the interviews, and they all agreed to this procedure. After the rough tapes were transcribed, I edited the transcripts to eliminate redundancies and to condense the interviews. I then sent the edited transcripts to each of the candidates to make sure they conveyed an accurate record of our conversation.

Seven of the candidates returned the edited transcripts, and none of them made any major alterations. Two of the seven (Anderson and Pulley) suggested only very minor changes, correcting misspellings of names and the like. The remaining five who returned the transcripts (Clark, Commoner, Gerson, Greaves, and Rarick) suggested occasional editorial revisions to clarify their positions. Four of the candidates (Bubar, Griswold, McCormack, and McReynolds) did not return the transcripts.

Since the interviews were designed to record the candidates' own impressions and perceptions, I did not attempt to alter or to correct their observations when I edited the taped transcripts. Thus, there are some factual misstatements as a result of lapses in the candidates' recollections of the precise amounts of their campaign expenditures or the different state ballot access requirements, to give two examples.

In addition, there are some discrepancies in the candidates' perceptions of each other. Simon Gerson, for example, states that the Communist Party in the United States is "completely autonomous" from the Soviet Union, while Andrew Pulley comments that the Communists tend "to follow any line, any twists or turns, that comes from Moscow," and David McReynolds indicates that "although they no longer have formal ties with the international communist movement, they defend most Soviet actions." The book presents these discrepancies as they were recorded on the tapes and does not attempt to pass judgment on them.

I am grateful to all of the candidates for taking the time to meet with me. They were a remarkably open and cooperative group, and I hope the book conveys a fair and accurate account of their positions as they explained them to me during the course of our conversations.

APPENDIX B
THIRD-PARTY ADDRESSES*

AMERICAN PARTY
Box 20466
Salt Lake City, Utah 84120
or
P.O. Box 606
Bedford, Virginia 24523

AMERICAN INDEPENDENT
PARTY
8158 Palm Street
Lemon Grove, California 92045

CITIZENS PARTY
1623 Connecticut Avenue, N.W.
Washington, D.C. 20009

COMMUNIST PARTY USA
235 West 23rd Street
New York, New York 10011

LIBERTARIAN PARTY
2300 Wisconsin Avenue, N.W.
Washington, D.C. 20007

NATIONAL UNITY CAMPAIGN
FOR JOHN ANDERSON
2720 35th Place, N.W.
Washington, D.C. 20007

PROHIBITION PARTY
P.O. Box 2635
Denver, Colorado 80201

RIGHT-TO-LIFE PARTY
Long Island Committee
1123 Little Neck Avenue
North Bellmore, Long Island,
    New York 11710

SOCIALIST PARTY USA
1011 North Third Street
Milwaukee, Wisconsin 53203

SOCIALIST WORKERS PARTY
14 Charles Lane
New York, New York 10014

WORKERS WORLD PARTY
46 West 21st Street
New York, New York 10010

*These were the latest party addresses as of December 1981. More current addresses may be obtained in the *Encyclopedia of Associations* (Detroit, Mich.: Gale Research Co.).

APPENDIX C

OTHER VOTE: 1980

State	Total Other Vote	Independent	Libertarian	Citizens	All Other
Alabama	51,007	16,481	13,318	517	20,691
Alaska	30,491	11,155	18,479		857
Arizona	97,414	76,952	18,784	551*	1,127
Arkansas	36,377	22,468	8,970	2,345	2,594
California	978,544	739,833	148,434	61,063	29,214
Colorado	164,178	130,633	25,744	5,614	2,187
Connecticut	187,343	171,807	8,570	6,130	836
Delaware	18,894	16,288	1,974	103*	529
Florida	220,504	189,692	30,524		288
Georgia	51,794	36,055	15,627	104*	8
Hawaii	37,296	32,021	3,269	1,548	458
Idaho	36,540	27,058	8,425		1,057
Illinois	410,259	346,754	38,939	10,692	13,874
Indiana	142,180	111,639	19,627	4,852	6,062
Iowa	132,963	115,633	13,123	2,273	1,934
Kansas	86,833	68,231	14,470		4,132
Kentucky	42,936	31,127	5,531	1,304	4,974
Louisiana	47,285	26,345	8,240	1,584	11,116
Maine	63,515	53,327	5,119	4,394	675
Maryland	133,729	119,537	14,192		
Massachusetts	412,865	382,539	22,038	2,056*	6,232
Michigan	332,968	275,223	41,597	11,930	4,218
Minnesota	224,538	174,990	31,592	8,407	9,549
Mississippi	22,250	12,036	5,465		4,749
Missouri	94,461	77,920	14,422	573*	1,546
Montana	39,106	29,281	9,825		
Nebraska	54,066	44,993	9,073		
Nevada	26,202	17,651	4,358		4,193
New Hampshire	53,421	49,693	2,064	1,320	344
New Jersey	281,763	234,632	20,652	8,203	18,276
New Mexico	38,366	29,459	4,365	2,202	2,340
New York	579,756	467,801	52,648	23,186	36,121
North Carolina	65,180	52,800	9,677	2,287	416
North Dakota	28,661	23,640	3,743	429	849
Ohio	324,644	254,472	49,033	8,564	12,575

State	Total Other Vote	Independent	Libertarian	Citizens	All Other
Oklahoma	52,112	38,284	13,828		
Oregon	153,582	112,389	25,838	13,642	1,713
Pennsylvania	362,089	292,921	33,263	10,430	25,475
Rhode Island	62,937	59,819	2,458	67*	593
South Carolina	21,845	14,153	5,139		2,553
South Dakota	25,505	21,431	3,824		250
Tennessee	46,804	35,991	7,116	1,112	2,585
Texas	149,784	111,613	37,643	453*	75
Utah	40,269	30,284	7,226	1,009	1,750
Vermont	36,719	31,761	1,900	2,316	742
Virginia	124,249	95,418	12,821	14,024	1,986
Washington	226,957	185,073	29,213	9,403	3,268
West Virginia	36,047	31,691	4,356		
Wisconsin	202,792	160,657	29,135	7,767	5,233
Wyoming	16,586	12,072	4,514		
Dist. of Col.	20,579	16,337	1,114	1,840	1,288
United States	7,127,185	5,720,060	921,299	234,294	251,532

*Write-in
SOURCE: Scammon and McGillivray, *America Votes 14*, p. 20.

NOTES

PREFACE

  1. U.S., *Constitution*, Art. II, sec. 1.
  2. "Election Statistics for Presidential Elections, 1789–1968," *If Elected* (Washington, D.C.: Smithsonian Institution Press, 1972), pp. 493–503. Anderson's total vote, from *America Votes 14*, ed. Richard M. Scammon and Alice V. McGillivray (Washington, D.C.: Congressional Quarterly, 1981).
  3. "Election Statistics," pp. 498–503.

1 THE TWO-PARTY MONOPOLY

  1. Norman Thomas, *Socialism Re-examined* (New York: W. W. Norton & Co., 1963), p. 116.
  2. Clinton Rossiter, *Parties and Politics in America* (Ithaca, N.Y.: Cornell University Press, 1960), p. 3.
  3. Daniel A. Mazmanian, *Third Parties in Presidential Elections* (Washington, D.C.: The Brookings Institution, 1974), p. 1.
  4. Louis Hartz, *The Liberal Tradition in America* (New York: Harcourt Brace Jovanovich, 1955).
  5. Rossiter, *Parties and Politics*, p. 11.
  6. James D. Bennett, *Frederick Jackson Turner* (Boston: G. K. Hall & Co., 1975), pp. 47–48.
  7. Ibid., p. 48.
  8. Ray Allen Billington, *America's Frontier Heritage* (New York: Holt, Rinehart, and Winston, 1966), p. 150.
  9. V. O. Key, Jr., *Politics, Parties and Pressure Groups*, 4th ed. (New York: Thomas Y. Crowell Co., 1958), pp. 227–28.
  10. Richard McCormick, *The Second American Party System* (Chapel Hill: University of North Carolina Press, 1966), p. 21.
  11. Michael A. Krasner, Stephen G. Chaberski, and D. Kelly Jones, *American Government Structure and Process* (New York: Macmillan Publishing Co., 1977), pp. 229, 234.
  12. Norman Thomas, *A Socialist's Faith* (New York: W. W. Norton & Co., 1951), p. 93.
  13. Thomas, *Socialism Re-examined*, p. 118.
  14. Key, *Parties and Pressure Groups*, p. 231.
  15. Steven J. Rosenstone, Roy L. Behr, and Edward M. Lazarus, "Third Party Voting in America" (Paper delivered to the American Political Science Association convention, New York City, September 3–6, 1981), pp. 43–44.

2 THE HISTORICAL IMPACT OF THE THIRD PARTIES

  1. Rosenstone, Behr, and Lazarus, "Third Party Voting," p. 4.
  2. Ibid., p. 2.

3. Mazmanian, *Third Parties*, pp. 27-28.

4. Everett C. Ladd, Jr., *American Political Parties* (New York: W. W. Norton & Co., 1970), pp. 2, 57, 109, 180-83.

5. Historical material on the Anti-Mason, Liberty, Free-Soil, and American Know-Nothing Parties from Mazmanian, *Third Parties*, pp. 4-43; Alexander Johnston, *American Political History*, vol. 2 (New York: G. P. Putnam's Sons, 1905), pp. 230-32, 258-65; William B. Hesseltine, *Third Party Movements in the United States* (New York: D. Van Nostrand Co., 1962), pp. 7-46; and Howard P. Nash, Jr., *Third Parties in American Politics* (Washington, D.C.: Public Affairs Press, 1959), pp. 1-54.

6. Rossiter, *Parties and Politics*, p. 73.

7. Key, *Politics and Pressure Groups*, pp. 281, 296-301.

8. Philip S. Foner, *History of the Labor Movement in the United States*, vol. 1 (New York: International Publishers Co., 1978), p. 127.

9. Thomas, *Socialism Re-examined*, p. 114.

10. Historical material on the Greenback, Populist, Socialist Labor, Socialist, and Progressive Parties from Mazmanian, *Third Parties*, pp. 47-64; Hesseltine, *Third Party Movements*, pp. 46-89; Nash, *American Politics*, pp. 146-288; Key, *Politics and Pressure Groups*, pp. 296-301; Foner, *Labor Movement*, pp. 493-99; Arnold Petersen, *Proletarian Democracy vs. Dictatorships and Despotism*, 4th ed. (New York: Labor News Co., 1937); and Thomas, *A Socialist's Faith*, pp. 86-101; and *Socialism Re-examined*, pp. 113-30.

11. Historical material on State's Rights (Dixiecrat) and American Independent Parties from Mazmanian, *Third Parties*, pp. 1-26; and Rhodes Cook and Elizabeth Wehr, *Profiles of American Political Parties* (Washington, D.C.: Congressional Quarterly, 1975), pp. 177-86.

12. Mazmanian, *Third Parties*, p. 77.

13. Rosenstone, Behr, and Lazarus, "Third Party Voting," pp. 191, 201.

14. Mazmanian, *Third Parties*, p. 148.

15. William B. Hesseltine, *The Rise and Fall of Third Parties* (Washington, D.C.: Public Affairs Press, 1948), pp. 9-10.

3 A VOICE FROM THE PAST

1. Roger C. Storms, *Partisan Prophets: A History of the Prohibition Party* (Denver, Colo.: National Prohibition Foundation, 1972), pp. 23-30.

2. Ibid., Foreword.

4 VOICES FROM THE LEFT

1. W. Pickles, "Left and Right (Current Meanings)," in *A Dictionary of the Social Sciences*, ed. Julius Gould and William L. Kolb (New York: Free Press, 1964), pp. 382-83.

2. John T. Zadrozny, *Dictionary of Social Sciences* (Washington, D.C.: Public Affairs Press, 1959), pp. 311-12.

3. David L. Sills, ed., *International Encyclopedia of the Social Sciences*, vol. 14 (New York: Macmillan Co. and Free Press, 1969), p. 506.

4. Zadrozny, *Dictionary of Social Sciences*, p. 57.

5. Karl Marx and Friedrich Engels, *Manifesto of the Communist Party* (1848), in *Marx and Engels: Basic Writings on Politics and Philosophy*, ed. Lewis S. Feuer (Garden City, N.Y.: Anchor Books, Doubleday & Co., 1959), p. 7. Marx was heavily influenced by the dialectic theory of the German philosopher Hegel (1770–1831) that any one idea (thesis) inevitably generates its opposite idea (antithesis), and the interaction of these two ideas leads to a new synthesis. Marx reinterpreted this dialectic process by substituting material forces for ideas. He then went on to interpret the meaning of history according to a theory of dialectical materialism in which the struggle between the propertied classes (thesis) and the nonpropertied classes (antithesis) would eventually result in the creation of a new social order of communism (synthesis).

6. Friedrich Engels, "Socialism: Utopian and Scientific" in Feuer, *Marx and Engels*, p. 106. Lenin later elaborated on Engels's writings and predicted the "withering away of the state" (see n. 10).

7. Feuer, *Marx and Engels*, p. 41.

8. The Fabian Society, founded in England in 1884, was led by such figures as Sidney and Beatrice Webb, George Bernard Shaw and Sir Ebenezer Howard. They concerned themselves with such practical problems as tax reform, women's rights, the eight-hour day and educational reforms. Howard was more visionary and advocated garden cities or "New Towns" to house the workers. Eduard Bernstein set forth similar revisionist ideas in the German Social Democratic Party, arguing that moral ideas, not the "laws" of economic necessity, should be the guide of the future. After the party officially censured him, he presented his case in a book that became one of the classics of democratic socialism. See Eduard Bernstein, *Evolutionary Socialism* (1899; reprint ed., New York: Schocken Books, 1963).

9. V. I. Lenin, *What Is To Be Done? The Burning Questions of Our Time* (1902; reprint ed., New York: International Publishers Co., 1969), p. 132. In this book Lenin referred to these professional revolutionaries as "the Dictatorship of the Proletariat," a small, secret, tightly organized group that would serve as "the vanguard of all the revolutionary forces in the fight for freedom" (p. 82). In justifying this type of group, Lenin used the famous argument that "it is far more difficult to catch ten wise men than a hundred fools."

10. V. I. Lenin, *State and Revolution* (1917; reprint ed., New York: International Publishers Co., 1932), p. 20. Lenin argued that since the bourgeois state used force and violence to maintain its position, it was necessary to overcome this state through violent revolution. Once the bourgeoisie was replaced by the proletariat, the state would enter into an intermediary stage of socialism before eventually "withering away" into pure communism and a classless society based on the principle "from each according to his ability, to each according to his needs." According to Lenin's analysis, "the abolition of the proletarian state, i.e., of all states, is only possible through 'withering away'" (p. 20).

11. Albert Fried and Ronald Sanders, eds., *Socialist Thought: A Documen-*

tary History (Garden City, N.Y.: Anchor Books, Doubleday & Co., 1964), 489–91. Irving Howe, *Trotsky* (Glasgow: Fontana/Collins, William Collins Sons & Co., 1978), pp. 30–36; Ernest Mandel, *Trotsky: A Study in the Dynamic of His Thought* (London: NLB, 1979), pp. 32–42; George H. Sabine, *A History of Political Theory*, 2d ed. (New York: Henry Holt & Co., 1954), pp. 826–33.

12. See Norman Thomas, *A Socialist's Faith* (New York: W. W. Norton, 1951) and *Socialism Re-examined* (New York: W. W. Norton, 1963).

13. Philip Bart, ed., *Highlights of a Fighting History* (New York: International Publishers Co., 1979), pp. 3–52.

14. Nathan Glazer, *The Social Basis of American Communism* (New York: Harcourt Brace and World, 1961), p. 92.

15. Bernard and Jewel Bellush, "A Radical Response to the Roosevelt Presidency: The Communist Party (1933–1945)," *Presidential Studies Quarterly*, vol. 10, no. 4 (Fall 1980), p. 645.

16. Harvey Klehr, *Communist Cadre* (Stanford, Calif.: Hoover Institution Press, 1978), p. 2.

17. Isaac Deutscher, *The Prophet Outcast, Trotsky: 1929–1940*, vol. 3 (New York: Vintage Books, Random House, 1965), p. 424.

18. Ibid., p. 430. For an eyewitness account of the early history of Trotskyism in the United States, see James P. Cannon, *The History of American Trotskyism: Report of a Participant* (New York: Pioneer Publishers, 1944).

19. I was not able to locate outside material on the Workers World Party. As a result, I relied heavily on the party's own literature, including its statement of party purpose in *Workers World*, the party's weekly newspaper.

5 VOICES FROM THE RIGHT AND THE LIBERTARIANS

1. J. C. Rees, "Conservatism," in *Dictionary*, p. 129.

2. Peter Viereck, *Conservatism* (New York: D. Van Nostrand Co., 1956), p. 11. See also Peter Viereck, *Conservatism Revisited* (New York: Charles Scribner's Sons, 1949).

3. Michael Oakeshott, *Rationalism in Politics* (New York: Basic Books Publishing Co., 1962), pp. 168–69.

4. Viereck, *Conservatism*, p. 15. For a more detailed summary description of "six canons of conservative thought" in British and American thinkers, see Russell Kirk, *The Conservative Mind*, 5th ed. (Chicago: H. Regnay Co., 1972), pp. 7–8.

5. Ibid., p. 15.

6. Roger Scruton, *The Meaning of Conservatism* (New York: Penguin Books, 1980), p. 15.

7. Nigel Ashford, "The Failure of Government: The Neo-Conservative Analysis" (Paper delivered to the Political Studies Association annual conference, Hull, England, April 6–8, 1981), pp. 2–13.

8. James A. Gould and Willis H. Truitt, *Political Ideologies* (New York: Macmillan Publishing Co., 1973), p. 169.

9. Michael Barone, Grant Ujifusa, and Douglas Matthews, *The Almanac of American Politics, 1976* (New York: E. P. Dutton & Co., 1977), p. 338.

10. Murray N. Rothbard, *For a New Liberty* (New York: Macmillan Co., 1973), p. 8.

11. See: *The Cato Journal*, published by the Cato Institute, 747 Front Street, San Francisco, California.

12. *Dollar Politics*, p. 101.

13. Ed Clark, *A New Beginning* (Aurora, Ill.: Caroline House Publishers, 1980).

14. Edward E. Clark, "The Libertarian Agenda and the Reagan Administration," *The Commonwealth*, vol. 75, no. 6 (February 1981), p. 35.

6 NEW VOICES OF 1980

1. Rhodes Cook, "Alternate Party Candidates May Have Substantial Impact on 1980 Presidential Election," *Congressional Quarterly*, October 18, 1980, pp. 3143–48. Cook's article sparked my initial interest in third parties by identifying the key candidates in the 1980 race. I was able to obtain the addresses of the political parties of some of these candidates from the *Encyclopedia of Associations*, 15th ed., vol. 1, (Detroit, Mich.: Gale Research Co., 1980). Cook gave me further assistance in locating the other candidates in a telephone conversation in June 1981.

2. Mazmanian, *Third Parties*, pp. 117–18.

3. *New York Election Laws*, sec. 6-128, 6-144.

4. Barry Commoner, *The Politics of Energy*, 1st ed., (New York: Knopf, 1979).

5. The results in the Massachusetts, Vermont, Illinois, and Wisconsin Republican Party primary elections were as follows: Massachusetts (March 4, 1980): Bush 31.1%, Anderson 30.8%, Reagan 28.8%; Vermont (March 4, 1980): Reagan 31.2%, Anderson 30.1%, Bush 22.4% (*Congressional Quarterly*, March 8, 1980, pp. 645–47); Illinois (March 18, 1980): Reagan 48.2%, Anderson 37.0%, Bush 11.0% (*Congressional Quarterly*, March 22, 1980, p. 781); Wisconsin (April 1, 1980): Reagan 40.3%, Bush 30.6%, Anderson 27.5% (*Congressional Quarterly* April 5, 1980, p. 901).

7 THE TWO-PARTY MONOPOLY REVISITED

1. Frances Davis, "Letters to Hazel," *Harvard Magazine*, vol. 84, no. 3 (January–February 1982), p. 33.

2. Clinton Rossiter, "The Functions of American Parties," in *American Government: Cases and Readings*, ed. Peter Woll, 2d ed. (Boston: Little, Brown & Co., 1965), p. 175.

3. Gerald M. Pomper, "The Presidential Election," In *The Election of 1980*, Gerald M. Pomper et al. (Chatham, N.J.: Chatham House Publishers, 1981), p. 94. Pomper supports a strong two-party system but is well aware of the

6. Williams v. Rhodes, 393 U.S. 23, 32 (1968).

7. Yick Wo v. Hopkins, 118 U.S. 356, 370 (1886). The U.S. Supreme Court has reaffirmed this position in many later cases such as Wesberry v. Sanders, 376 U.S. 1 (1964).

8. Gary Aherns and Nancy Hauserman, "Fundamental Election Rights: Association, Voting and Candidacy," *Valparaiso University Law Review* 14 (1980), p. 465.

9. David Fellman, *The Constitutional Right of Association* (Chicago: University of Chicago Press, 1963), p. 38.

10. David Mohler, "Ballot Access: Applying the Constitutional Balance Test to the West Virginia Code," *West Virginia Law Review* 83 (1980), p. 227.

11. Lubin v. Panish, 415 U.S. 709 (1974); American Party of Texas v. White, 415 U.S. 767 (1974); Storer v. Brown, 415 U.S. 724 (1974); McCarthy v. Briscoe, 419 U.S. 1317 (1976, Powell, circuit justice).

12. Mohler, "Ballot Access," p. 233.

13. Bullock v. Carter, 405 U.S. 134, 145 (1971).

14. Jenness v. Fortson, 403 U.S. 431, 442 (1970).

15. Lubin v. Panish, 415 U.S. 709 (1974).

16. Aherns and Hauserman, "Fundamental Election Rights," pp. 465, 470.

17. U.S., Department of Defense, *Voting Assistance Guide for Armed Forces Personnel* (Washington, D.C., 1980), p. 5.

18. Rhodes Cook, "High Hurdles for the Anderson Campaign," *Congressional Quarterly*, vol. 38, no. 20 (May 1980), p. 1315.

19. California, *Elections Code*, sec. 6831.

20. Ohio, *Revised Code*, Title 25, sec. 3513.257; Maine, *Revised Statutes*, Title 21, sec. 494.9.

21. West Virginia Libertarian Party v. Manchin, 270 S.E. 2d (W. Va. 1980). See Mohler, "Ballot Access," pp. 235–43.

22. U.S., Department of Commerce, Bureau of the Census, *Voting and Registration in the Election of November 1978*, Census Series P-20, no. 344, September 1979.

23. Mazmanian, *Third Parties*, pp. 100–101.

24. *Dollar Politics*, p. 3.

25. Stephen J. Wayne, *The Road to the White House* (New York: St. Martin's Press, 1981), pp. 28–29.

26. Ibid., pp. 30–31.

27. *Dollar Politics*, pp. 13, 26.

28. Buckley v. Valeo, 424 U.S. 1 (1976).

29. Jonathan Moore and Janet Fraser, eds., *Campaign for President: The Managers Look at '76* (Cambridge, Mass.: Ballinger Publishing Co., 1977), pp. 151–54.

30. *An Analysis of the Impact of the Federal Election Campaign Act, 1972–78* (Report by the Campaign Finance Study Group to the Committee on House Administration, U.S. House of Representatives, prepared by Institute of Politics, Kennedy School of Government, Harvard University, Cambridge, Massachusetts, 1979).

31. *Dollar Politics*, p. 101. For a commentary on the financial problems of the third-party candidates during the 1980 campaign, see Rhodes Cook, "Money Woes Limit Anderson, Third-Party Presidential Bids," *Congressional Quarterly*, August 16, 1980, pp. 2374–78.

32. The third-party expenditure totals, reported to the FEC by the candidates' principal campaign committees, were obtained from the Public Records Office, Federal Election Commission, 1325 K Street, Washington, D.C., in January 1982. The reports cover expenditures through December 1980.

33. Nelson W. Polsby and Aaron Wildavsky, *Presidential Elections*, 5th ed., (New York: Charles Scribner's Sons, 1980), p. 21.

34. *Dollar Politics*, p. 41.

35. Dom Bonafede, "A $130 Million Spending Tab Is Proof—Presidential Politics Is Big Business," *National Journal*, January 10, 1981, p. 50.

36. *Dollar Politics*, p. 9.

37. Rosenstone, Behr, and Lazarus, "Third Party Voting," p. 62.

38. Mazmanian, *Third Parties*, p. 105.

39. Eugene J. McCarthy, *The Ultimate Tyranny* (New York: Harcourt Brace Jovanovich, 1980), p. 157.

40. Ibid., p. 166.

41. CBS Inc. et al. v. Federal Communications Commission, 60 L. Ed 2d 706 (1981).

42. For an interesting discussion of the current equal-time rule provisions, see the pro and con debate between Gene F. Jankowski, president, CBS Broadcast Group, and Charles D. Ferris, former chairman, Federal Communications Commission, in *U.S. News and World Report*, vol. 93, no. 5 (August 1982), pp. 31–32.

43. Rosenstone, Behr, and Lazarus, "Third Party Voting," pp. 51, 58.

44. Williams v. Rhodes, 393 U.S. 23,32 (1968).

45. See Elizabeth Drew, *Portrait of An Election: The 1980 Presidential Campaign* (New York: Simon & Schuster, 1981); Thomas Ferguson and Joel Rogers, eds., *The Hidden Election* (New York: Pantheon Books, 1981); Everett C. Ladd, Jr., *Where Have All the Voters Gone?*, 2d ed. (New York: W. W. Norton & Co., 1982), pp. 122–23; Austin Ranney, ed., *The American Elections of 1980* (Washington, D.C.: American Enterprise Institute for Public Policy Research, 1981). Two books that include commentaries from Independent John B. Anderson, but not third-party candidates, are Seymour Martin Lipset, ed., *Party Coalitions in the 1980s* (San Francisco: Institute for Contemporary Studies, 1981), and Jonathan Moore, ed., *The Campaign for President: 1980 in Retrospect* (Cambridge, Mass.: Ballinger Publishing Co., 1981).

46. "Developments in the Law-Elections," 88 *Harvard Law Review* (1974–75), p. 1123.

8 THE FUTURE OF THIRD PARTIES

1. Wilson Carey McWilliams, "The Meaning of the Election," in *The Election of 1980*, Gerald Pomper et al., (Chatham, N.J.: Chatham House Publishers, 1980), p. 170.

2. Norman Podhoretz, "The New American Majority," in *Party Coalitions in the 1980s*, ed. Seymour M. Lipset (San Francisco: Institute for Contemporary Studies, 1981), p. 413.

3. See: V. O. Key, Jr., "A Theory of Critical Elections," *The Journal of Politics* 17:3–18; Angus Campbell et al., *Elections and the Political Order* (New York: Wiley, 1966); and Walter Dean Burnham, *Critical Elections and the Mainsprings of American Politics* (New York: W. W. Norton & Co., 1970). Burnham originally developed one of the most persuasive analyses of party decomposition in his 1970 study that served as a basis for the current dealignment thesis.

4. Ladd, *Where Have All the Voters Gone?*, 2d ed. (New York: W. W. Norton & Co., 1982), pp. 76–77.

5. U.S., Department of Commerce, Bureau of the Census, 102d ed., *Statistical Abstract of the United States 1981* (Washington, D.C., 1982), p. 496.

6. Gallup Report, no. 195, December 1981, p. 33.

7. Ladd, *Where Have All the Voters Gone?*, pp. 77–78.

8. Gallup Report, no. 192, September 1981, p. 4.

9. Kevin C. Phillips, *Post-Conservative America* (New York: Random House, 1982), p. 29.

10. Gallup Report, no. 197, February 1982, p. 13.

11. Gallup Report, no. 198, March 1982, p. 27.

12. Rosenstone, Behr, and Lazarus, "Third Party Voting," p. 177.

13. Gallup Report, no. 187, April 1981, p. 25; no. 199, April 1982, p. 10.

14. Ladd, *Where Have All the Voters Gone?*, pp. 78–79.

15. Ibid., pp. 126–27.

16. Ibid., pp. 102–104.

17. Compiled from voting results contained in Scammon and McGillivray, *America Votes 14*, pp. 19–20.

18. Pomper, "The Presidential Election," p. 84.

19. Phillips, *Post-Conservative America*, p. xix.

20. Ibid., p. 214; 224–26.

21. Ibid., p. 99.

22. William Schneider, "Realignment: The Eternal Question," *PS*, vol. 15, no. 3 (Summer 1982):449–57.

23. John B. Anderson, "Developing A Grand Coalition," in *Party Coalitions in the 1980s*, ed. Seymour M. Lipset (San Francisco: Institute for Contemporary Studies, 1981), pp. 377–78.

BIBLIOGRAPHY

Aherns, Gary, and Nancy Hauserman. "Fundamental Election Rights: Association, Voting and Candidacy." *Valparaiso University Law Review* 14 (1980) : 465–95.

American Party of Texas v. White, 415 U.S. 767 (1974).

Anderson, John B. "Developing A Grand Coalition." In *Party Coalitions in the 1980s*, edited by Seymour M. Lipset. San Francisco: Institute for Contemporary Studies, 1981.

Ashford, Nigel. "The Failure of Government: The Neo-Conservative Analysis." Paper delivered to the Political Studies Association annual conference, Hull, England, April 6–8, 1981.

Barone, Michael, Grant Ujifusa, and Douglas Matthews. *The Almanac of American Politics, 1976*. New York: E. P. Dutton & Co., 1977.

Bart, Philip, ed. *Highlights of a Fighting History*. New York: International Publishers Co., 1979.

Bellush, Bernard and Jewel. "A Radical Response to the Roosevelt Presidency: The Communist Party (1933–1945)." *Presidential Studies Quarterly*, vol. 10, no. 4 (Fall 1980) : 645–61.

Bennett, James D. *Frederick Jackson Turner*. Boston: G. K. Hall & Co., 1975.

Bernstein, Eduard. *Evolutionary Socialism*. 1899. Reprint. New York: Schocken Books, 1963.

Billington, Ray Allen. *America's Frontier Heritage*. New York: Holt, Rinehart, & Winston, 1966.

Bonafede, Dom. "A $130 Million Spending Tab is Proof—Presidential Politics is Big Business." *National Journal*, January 10, 1981, pp. 50–52.

Buckley v. Valeo, 424 U.S. 1 (1976).

Bullock v. Carter, 405 U.S. 134 (1971).

Burnham, Walter Dean. *Critical Elections and the Mainsprings of American Politics*. New York: W. W. Norton & Co., 1970.

CBS Inc. et al. v. Federal Communications Commission, 60 L. Ed 2d 706 (1981).

Campaign Finance Study Group Report to the Committee on House Administration, U.S. House of Representatives. *An Analysis of the*

Impact of the Federal Election Campaign Act, 1972–78. Prepared by Institute of Politics, Kennedy School of Government, Harvard University, Cambridge, Massachusetts, 1979.

Campbell, Angus, Philip E. Converse, Warren E. Miller, and Donald E. Stokes. *Elections and the Political Order.* New York: Wiley, 1966.

Cannon, James P. *The History of American Trotskyism: Report of a Participant.* New York: Pioneer Publishers, 1944.

Clark, Edward E. "The Libertarian Agenda and the Reagan Administration." *The Commonwealth,* vol. 75, no. 6 (February 1981): 35–36.

————. *A New Beginning.* Aurora, Ill.: Caroline House Publishers, 1980.

Commoner, Barry. *The Politics of Energy.* 1st ed. New York: Knopf, 1979.

Congressional Quarterly. March 8, 1980; March 22, 1980; April 5, 1980.

Cook, Rhodes. "Alternate Party Candidates May Have Substantial Impact on 1980 Presidential Election." *Congressional Quarterly,* October 18, 1980.

————. "High Hurdles for the Anderson Campaign." *Congressional Quarterly,* May 17, 1980.

————. "Money Woes Limit Anderson, Third-Party Presidential Bids." *Congressional Quarterly,* August 16, 1980.

Cook, Rhodes, and Elizabeth Wehr. *Profiles of American Political Parties.* Washington, D.C.: Congressional Quarterly, 1975.

Davis, Frances. "Letters to Hazel." *Harvard Magazine,* vol. 84, no. 3 (January–February 1982), p. 33.

Deutscher, Isaac. *The Prophet Outcast, Trotsky: 1929–1940.* Vol. 3. New York: Vintage Books, Random House, 1965.

Dollar Politics. Congressional Quarterly. Washington, D.C.: Congressional Quarterly, 1982.

Drew, Elizabeth. *Portrait of An Election: The 1980 Presidential Campaign.* New York: Simon & Schuster, 1981.

Durbin, Thomas M., and Michael V. Seitzinger. *Nomination and Election of the President and Vice President of the United States.* Washington, D.C.: Government Printing Office.

"Election Statistics for Presidential Elections, 1789–1968." *"If Elected."* Washington, D.C.: Smithsonian Institution Press, 1972.

Elections Code, California, sec. 6831.

Encyclopedia of Associations. Vol. 1. 15th ed. Detroit, Mich.: Gale Research Co., 1980.

Engels, Friedrich. "Socialism: Utopian and Scientific." In *Marx and Engels: Basic Writings on Politics and Philosophy*, edited by Lewis S. Feuer. Garden City, N.Y.: Anchor Books, Doubleday & Co., 1959.

Fellman, David. *The Constitutional Right of Association.* Chicago: University of Chicago Press, 1963.

Ferguson, Thomas, and Joel Rogers, eds. *The Hidden Election.* New York: Pantheon Books, 1981.

Foner, Philip S. *History of the Labor Movement in the United States,* vol. 1. New York: International Publishers Co., 1978.

Fried, Albert, and Sanders, Ronald, eds. *Socialist Thought: A Documentary History.* Garden City, N.Y.: Doubleday & Co., 1964.

Gallup Reports, nos. 187–99. Princeton, N.J., 1981–82.

Gerson, Simon. *Pete: The Story of Peter V. Cacchione.* New York: International Publishers Co., 1976.

Glazer, Nathan. *The Social Basis of American Communism.* New York: Harcourt Brace and World, 1961.

Gould, James A., and Willis H. Truitt. *Political Ideologies.* New York: Macmillan Publishing Co., 1973.

Gould, Julius, and William L. Kolb, eds. *A Dictionary of the Social Sciences.* New York: Free Press, 1964.

Hall, Gus. *The Crisis of U.S. Capitalism and the Fight-Back.* New York: International Publishers Co., 1975.

———. *Labor Up-Front.* New York: International Publishers Co., 1979.

Hartz, Louis. *The Liberal Tradition in America.* New York: Harcourt Brace Jovanovich, 1955.

Harvard Law Review, "Developments in The Law-Elections," Vol. 88, 1974–75.

Hesseltine, William B. *The Rise and Fall of Third Parties.* Washington, D.C.: Public Affairs Press, 1948.

———. *Third Party Movements in the United States.* New York: D. Van Nostrand Co., 1962.

Howe, Irving. *Trotsky.* Glasgow: William Collins Sons & Co., 1978.

Jenness v. Fortson, 403 U.S. 431 (1970).

Johnston, Alexander. *American Political History.* Vol. 2. New York: G. P. Putnam's Sons, 1905.

Key, V. O., Jr. *Politics, Parties and Pressure Groups.* 4th ed. New York: Thomas Y. Crowell Co., 1958.

———. "A Theory of Critical Elections." *The Journal of Politics* 17 (February 1955) : 3–18.

Kirk, Russell. *The Conservative Mind.* 5th ed. Chicago: H. Regnay Co., 1972.

Klehr, Harvey. *Communist Cadre.* Stanford, Calif.: Hoover Institution Press, 1978.

Krasner, Michael A., Stephen G. Chaberski, and D. Kelly Jones. *American Government Structure and Process.* New York: Macmillan Co., 1977.

Ladd, Everett C., Jr. *American Political Parties.* New York: W. W. Norton & Co., 1970.

———. 2d ed. *Where Have All the Voters Gone?* New York: W. W. Norton & Co., 1982.

Lenin, V. I. *State and Revolution* (1917). New York: International Publishers Co., 1932.

———. *What Is To Be Done? The Burning Questions of Our Time* (1902). New York: International Publishers Co., 1969.

Lubin v. Panish, 415 U.S. 709 (1974).

Mandel, Ernest. *Trotsky: A Study in the Dynamic of His Thought.* London: NLB, 1979.

Marx, Karl, and Friedrich Engels. *Manifesto of the Communist Party* (1948). In *Marx and Engels: Basic Writings on Politics and Philosophy*, edited by Lewis S. Feuer. Garden City, N.Y.: Anchor Books, Doubleday & Co., 1959.

Mazmanian, Daniel A. *Third Parties in Presidential Elections.* Washington, D.C.: The Brookings Institution, 1974.

McCarthy v. Briscoe, 419 U.S. 1317 (1976, Powell, circuit justice).

McCarthy, Eugene J. *The Ultimate Tyranny.* New York: Harcourt Brace Jovanovich, 1980.

McCormick, Richard. *The Second American Party System.* Chapel Hill: University of North Carolina Press, 1966.

McWilliams, Wilson Carey. "The Meaning of the Election." In *The Election of 1980*, Gerald Pomper et al. Chatham, N.J.: Chatham House Publishers, 1980.

Mohler, David. "Ballot Access: Applying the Constitutional Balance Test to the West Virginia Code." *West Virginia Law Review* 83 (1980), p. 227.

Moore, Jonathan, ed. *The Campaign for President: 1980 in Retrospect.* Cambridge, Mass.: Ballinger Publishing Co., 1981.

Moore, Jonathan, and Janet Fraser, eds. *Campaign for President: The Managers Look at '76.* Cambridge, Mass.: Ballinger Publishing Co., 1977.

Nash, Howard P., Jr. *Third Parties in American Politics.* Washington, D.C.: Public Affairs Press, 1959.

New York Election Laws, sec. 6-128, 6-144.

Oakeshott, Michael. *Rationalism in Politics.* New York: Basic Books Publishing Co., 1962.

Petersen, Arnold. *Proletarian Democracy vs. Dictatorships and Despotism.* 4th ed. New York: Labor News Co., 1937.

Phillips, Kevin C. *Post-Conservative America.* New York: Random House, 1982.

Podhoretz, Norman. "The New American Majority." In *Party Coalitions in the 1980s*, edited by Seymour M. Lipset. San Francisco: Institute for Contemporary Studies, 1981.

Polsby, Nelson W., and Aaron Wildavsky. *Presidential Elections.* 5th ed. New York: Charles Scribner's Sons, 1980.

Pomper, Gerald M. "The Presidential Election." In *The Election of 1980*, Gerald Pomper et al. Chatham, N.J.: Chatham House Publishers, 1981.

Powell, G. Bingham, Jr. "Party Systems and Political System Performance." *American Political Science Review*, vol. 75, no. 4 (December 1981), p. 861.

Ranney, Austin, ed. *The American Elections of 1980.* Washington, D.C.: American Enterprise Institute for Public Policy Research, 1981.

Revised Code, Ohio, Title 25, sec. 3513.257.

Revised Statutes, Maine, Title 21, sec. 494.9.

Rosenstone, Steven J., Roy L. Behr, and Edward M. Lazarus. "Third Party Voting in America." Paper delivered to the American Political Science Association convention, New York City, September 3–6, 1981.

Rossiter, Clinton. "The Functions of American Parties." 2d ed. In *American Government: Cases and Readings*, edited by Peter Woll. Boston: Little, Brown & Co., 1965.

———. *Parties and Politics in America.* Ithaca, N.Y.: Cornell University Press, 1960.

Rothbard, Murray N. *For a New Liberty.* New York: Macmillan Co., 1973.

Sabine, George H. *A History of Political Theory.* 2d ed. New York: Henry Holt & Co., 1954.

Scammon, Richard M., and Alice V. McGillivray, eds. *America Votes 14.* Washington, D.C.: Congressional Quarterly, 1981.

Schattschneider, E. E. *Party Government.* New York: Farrar and Rinehart, 1942.

Schneider, William. "Realignment: The Eternal Question." *PS,* vol. 15, no. 3 (Summer 1982) : 444–57.

Scruton, Roger. *The Meaning of Conservatism.* New York: Penguin Books, 1980.

Storer v. Brown, 415 U.S. 724 (1974).

Storms, Roger C. *Partisan Prophets: A History of the Prohibition Party.* Denver, Colo.: National Prohibition Foundation, 1972.

Thomas, Norman. *Socialism Re-examined.* New York: W. W. Norton & Co., 1963.

———. *A Socialist's Faith.* New York: W. W. Norton & Co., 1951.

U.S., *Constitution,* Art. II, sec. 1.

U.S., Department of Commerce, Bureau of the Census. 102d ed. *Statistical Abstract of the United States 1981.* Washington, D.C., 1982.

U.S., Department of Commerce, Bureau of the Census. *Voting and Registration in the Election of November 1978.* Census Series P-20, no. 344, September 1979.

U.S., Department of Defense. *Voting Assistance Guide for Armed Forces Personnel.* Washington, D.C., 1980.

U.S., Federal Election Commission, *Federal Election Campaign Laws,* Washington, D.C., 1980.

Viereck, Peter. *Conservatism.* New York: D. Van Nostrand Co., 1956.

———. *Conservatism Revisited.* New York: Charles Scribner's Sons, 1949.

Wayne, Stephen J. *The Road to the White House.* New York: St. Martin's Press, 1981.

Wesberry v. Sanders, 376 U.S. 1 (1964).

West Virginia Libertarian Party v. Manchin, 270 S.E. 2d (W. Va. 1980).

Williams v. Rhodes, 393 U.S. 23, 32 (1968).

Yick Wo v. Hopkins, 118 U.S. 356, 370 (1886).

INDEX

FRANK SMALLWOOD, the Orvil E. Dryfoos Professor of Government and Public Affairs at Dartmouth College, has been active in Vermont politics and participated in John Anderson's Independent presidential campaign in 1980. His most recent books include *Free and Independent* (1976), an account of his experiences as a Vermont State Senator; and *The Politics of Policy Implementation* (1980), co-authored with Robert T. Nakamura.